Salt Pork and Dandelion Greens

Growing Up Greenwood

Sandra Martin Morgan

ISBN: 1984371894
ISBN-13: 978-1984371898

CONTENTS

Gratitude   iv

Foreword   v

1   LONG AGO   1

   My World

   The Inquisitive Tomboy

   Grammar School Days

   Growing Up

2   A SYMPHONY OF   141
    SEASONS

   The Long, Cold Wait

   Finally, Spring

   Summer Freedom

   Autumn Glory

   Christmas Cheer

3   LOOKING BEHIND   241

   Family

   Farewell

   Epilogue

GRATITUDE

My thanks to:

My Mom and Dad for being who they were—straight up, no frills parents.

My three brothers, Roland (Tink), Rex, and Curt, for being part of my story.

My beloved Grandparents, Ross and Nellie Martin; Lewis and Iza Libby.

The entire Martin clan that pretty much made up the population of the hamlet.

The people of Greenwood Center, who watched out and cared for the rag-a-muffin kids milling around while their parents worked.

Fast forwarding to my later life, my thanks also to:

My daughter, Debra, encouraging me and supporting me both in this project and in my health issues.

My son, Brian, my son of the earth who supports me and keeps me supplied with the fruits of his labor on his farm in the hills of Maine.

My son, Gary, for taking on this project and bringing it to fruition. He shared his vast knowledge of the publishing world to make this project successful. I shall be forever grateful for his dedication to his profession and to me.

My son, Alan, who has devoted the last few years caregiving to his step-dad and then caring for me with my health issues. There are no words to thank him for his devotion to both of us. Many of these words would not have been written had it not been for him.

Special friends who picked me up on dreary days and always there for me: my BFF Pearl Jordan, Irma Bovair, Lynne Lord, and my special sister-in-law, Martha Martin. You have been my sunshine!

And a big thank you to the readers of my blogs, who suggested they should be published.

FOREWORD

There was something very special about the little hamlet of Greenwood Center, Maine, where I made my February debut in 1938. My eightieth birthday approaches, and my heart is drawn back to those childhood days.

I can smell the rain, seeing it move slowly across Twitchell Pond from Moose Cove to the banks by our house. I can feel the warmth of the big rock by the pond, where I perched with my fish pole daydreaming the hours away.

I close my eyes and feel my Dad's hand on mine, guiding it through a mass of honey bees he is lining for future honey in the fall, and hear his voice. "Muff, they won't hurt you, if you don't hurt them." I believed him, because little girls know their Dads will protect them, always.

When the winter winds blow, I see my Mother standing in front of the wood stove, coaxing the fire and making meals from whatever she had. Her voice echoes through my mind. "Don't you get chilled out there and come down with a cold!"

April breezes sneak in at last, and I feel the warm tar on my bare feet as I spread my arms and run up the narrow road, never fearing for traffic. Marbles in the ditch by the side of the road; cumbersome winter clothes peeled off at last.

I sit in my Grandmother's kitchen listening to the turning of the churn. Her little leaf mold awaits the butter that will soon appear, dew covered and ready to spread.

My memories. I share them with you. I hope you can relate, and that somewhere in this world of today there is a little hamlet for every child, whose memories will last for eight decades.

LONG AGO
My World

War

I've been visiting Grammy Martin and am halfway across the field to home when an airplane's roar fills the sky. Running in terror, I jump the brook, dart inside, and race upstairs to bed, pulling the covers over my ears. I'm terrified of airplanes but don't dare tell my mother and father. I stick my head out of the blankets, and all is quiet, again. The plane is gone. Last week, I was at the pond by Mr. Kenyon's cottage when suddenly a big plane swooped down over the ledge; I thought it was going to drop bombs. I ran for the house and bed, heart pounding so much I knew it was going to pop through my shirt. I wonder if I will ever stop being afraid of airplanes.

All I have ever known is this war. I'm afraid of airplanes, because I can't understand where the bombing is going on. Some days there are lots of planes in the sky, which are practicing for the war, Grammy says. I'm only seven years old but know Dad is worried about his two brothers, Dwight and Glenn. Dwight, an Army Lieutenant, is somewhere in the Pacific, and Glenn serves in the Navy. Dad feels guilty that he could not join the fighting. The sawmill made such a mess of his left hand that he can't even play the guitar the way he used to. But you know my Dad! He just tunes it differently, lays it on his lap, and holds a bar in his left hand.

I don't think Ma and Dad realize that we hear when they talk about the war. Uncle Dwight was wounded several times, and apparently each time it scores a deeper impression on my young mind as the old folks talk about it.

Every night after work, Dad goes across the pasture to see if Grammy has heard any news of his brothers. Their letters are blacked out and holes are punched in them, but they still try to figure out where his brothers are and what they are doing. Sometimes when visiting Grammy on Sunday, I'm asked to sing, "There's a Star Spangled Banner Waving Somewhere." Each time I sing it, I get a quarter. Grammy likes that song, and I know it makes her think of her sons. She has a scrapbook, and every time their names or pictures are in the newspaper, she cuts them out and pastes them in it.

I have the stove going, coffee water hot, and potatoes boiling. Ma and Dad are stopping at the grocery store to get things "on the cuff" until they are paid on Friday. The only meat we ever buy is hamburger and hot dogs.

Dad hates hot dogs so they aren't on the table very often.

Groceries are brought in and Ma empties the few things on the tiny cupboard counter. Ration stamps control almost everything, and sugar is a luxury. There's oleo...white in its little plastic bag with the yellow coloring tablet for one of us to squish with our hands to make sure it is an all-even yellow color and looks like butter. While Ma gets the hamburger all in little patties, I sit and squish, squish until she's satisfied it "will do." There are cans of milk. I'm so tired of canned milk; on the days I can have cereal, it tastes awful. She mixes it one can of water to one can of milk. Ma buys Puffed Wheat for my baby brother, Curt, and if there is enough money, the rest of us can have a box of Shredded Wheat. I call them hay bales, but I like it because between each layer of bales are pictures to color. Most of the time we have fried potatoes and eggs, except for Curt, because Ma says he needs cereal and milk for his bones.

It is a treat when we have a piece of bread with some of the "butter" spread on it and just a tiny sprinkle of sugar on top. Ma says she won't touch molasses as that is all she had when she was growing up, but she makes molasses cakes on weekends and we kids eat it.

It seems everyone in the neighborhood is trying to do their part for the war. Last year, our teacher asked us to pick milkweed for the service men— it had something to do with making parachutes. I picked all one weekend. Ma gave Rex and me some change to buy stamps to put in a little booklet to help the war bond effort. We are saving metal, too. The newspapers have pictures of our villages' soldiers and sailors and always report if they are wounded.

Tonight is different. Dad seems very happy, and Ma exclaims it won't be long before we won't be using ration stamps. Dad says he is going to Grammy's to tell her the good news.

What good news are they talking about, I wonder, *and why is Dad so happy?*

"Muff, the war is over," he tells me. "Your Uncle Dwight will be coming home soon."

Does that mean the airplanes won't come? I ask myself. *Does that mean I don't have to be scared anymore?*

Fast forward many months, until it is almost time for snow to fall again. A tall man comes into the house, and we gather in the kitchen. The Aladdin kerosene lamp casts a glow on the painted sheetrock wall. The man is shaking Dad's hand, and Dad is slapping him on the back. He sits in one of our big chairs by the wall. Dad tells me this is my Uncle Dwight and to come meet him. I cannot remember him, but he is very handsome and smiles. He beckons to me, and I go to him very slowly, because I am shy. He hands me a beautiful fan, saying that he brought it home just for me. I thank him.

This uncle would never let the planes bomb me. I should have known. I sit next to him, holding the fan tightly. I am safe.

Greenwood Center

Greenwood Center, Maine, is where I live. Such a peaceful, quiet, tiny community where very little happens—but if it does, everyone knows! It's a hamlet once again content, with the ending of World War II and our soldiers back home with their families. As a child, if I want to go anywhere, my Dad says to use *Shank's Mare*...his way of saying "walk." That I do, because basically I'm a loner. Satisfied with my own company, I can always find something curious to explore or lose myself in a good book.

Our little house is across from Twitchell Pond, which the Summer People call Twitchell Lake. Maybe that sounds fancier to them, but it's a plain old pond to me. It's where I go swimming and sometimes sit on a rock and "plug fish" for some perch. At the foot of Twitchell Pond is a dam. Many times I go down to the dam and just stand there, as I am today. It's so peaceful in this little nook with nothing but trees hanging down and birds perched on the limbs. The Flint cottage sits above on the rocks.

The road is not tarred yet, so the dirt and pebbles hurt my feet until they have toughened in for the summer. If I know I am coming this far, I usually wear the shoes left over from the school year. On the left now I see only trees; on the right a field that is overgrown with alders and such; on the point is a beautiful cottage owned by the Sullivans.

My Uncle Roy lives about a half-mile down the road from our house on this stretch of road. I heard around the kitchen table that he was married once and divorced...that was way before my time. I've spent many a weekend there visiting my friend, Gladys Bailey, when she comes up from working in South Paris. Uncle Roy is very talented and carves things out of wood and paints on toadstools. He likes working in the woods and logging it with Uncle Louie.

Near his house and across the road stands a tarpapered house where the Tapley family once lived. The children went to school with my oldest brother, Roland, but I think the family moved before I started. On the same side of the road was apparently a logging camp, long overgrown, which Ma calls the "Penley Place." Apparently she and Dad lived there when they first married.

There is also an old mill nearby, which I think Grammy's father,

Ransom Cole, owned. The mill has a long history, and Dad said it once was very active. It has not been running for years, however, and looks as though it won't be standing much longer. Sometimes, my brothers and I sneak in there to look around at the rusty machines. There's one little room full of cobwebs where we think perhaps someone filed the saws and fixed machinery. We're not supposed to go in there because it's dangerous, but sometimes curiosity gets the best of us. Ma would really punish us if she knew, and as she always says...curiosity killed the cat. I never went very far into the mill, as I imagined it was full of snakes, mice, or whatever goes into abandoned buildings. It would be my luck to go through a rotten floor board and stay there forever.

I continue walking back toward home, pausing by the ledge to look the length of the pond and see Rowe's Ledge in the sunlight. Here the road is tarred, making it easier to walk. On the left is a beautiful log home built by Henry and Janet Bowers; it's new in the neighborhood. Continuing on, there's the Prall summer home on the right, and on the left is where my Uncle Dwight and Aunt Tessie live. I remember my Uncle Glen working on their house. Next on the left is Charlie and Grace Day's little bungalow, and how I enjoy visiting them. She makes the best Welsh Rarebit!!!!

My Grammy Martin owns the field on the left, which right now is a garden with rows and rows of potato plants. Passing, I look to my right and there is the Wagner summer camp.

Across from their driveway is my Grammy (Nellie) and Grampa (Rawson) Martin's farm, right next door to our house. We can run over there any time we want. We get all our drinking water from their house because we have no well of our own. We can use the brook water for washing dishes and clothes, but it isn't fit to drink. One night, Ma noticed we were almost out, so she sent Rex to get a jug. On the way home, he dropped it on the tarred road and cut his hand so badly Ma had to rush him to the doctor in Bethel for stitches. His hand hurt for a long time.

A few feet beyond our home is the Jacobs' summer home. It was owned by a Mr. Kenyon when I was much younger. Dad called him Kato and liked him very much.

Uncle Glenn and Norma live on the other (north) side of us, and we have a path to their house as well, right through the woods, so we can play with our cousins. How many plays have I written for my cousins, Louise and Carmen!! The picnic table is our stage and we play by the hour. Uncle Glenn has a huge sign with a bear and the word Taxidermist on it. I don't really knew him, except in quiet admiration. He's such an artist. He mixes his own paints, out of which come breathtaking scenes. Uncle Glenn also collects reeds to soak that are woven into pretty pack baskets.

Across from their house is the path to Gram's beach where we all go swimming!

The next half mile on the road north has no houses at all. We call it the "flat" and play baseball there. A little house stands on the corner on the northern end of the flat. Several people have lived there, including Ma and Dad, I think, about the time my brother Rex was born, because Ma speaks of buying eggs at the Lester Cole farm, which sets back a bit from the road.

How I love to see all the hens and chickens running around at the Lester Cole farm! They have a big dump truck, their own gravel pit, cows, and everything. It seems like they're rich! Well, after all, they have the only telephone nearby in the neighborhood. The line has not been run far enough for Grammy to have a phone. Many a time one of us has run a half mile on hot tar with bare feet to call Dr. Boynton after Grampa "has taken a turn." Lester and Netta are very good about our using it.

On that part of the road, Laura Seames lives in a little white house that Dad says used to be a schoolhouse. What a nice lady she is; she buys the *Grit* from me. Oh, that's right! I didn't tell you that I deliver the *Grit* because my brother Rex started it but decided it took too much time from other money-making plans—like catching frogs and selling them to fishermen who stay at Birch Villa Inn in Bryant Pond. He sells them for three cents each and keeps them in a cage in the cool water of the brook.

Near Mrs. Seames lives my Grammy's brother, my great-uncle Elmer Cole. He's blind because of an accident using dynamite years ago. Sometimes if Ma gets laid off at the mill, she works for him doing housework and helping out in general. He has a little store as you enter his house where he carries all kinds of cough drops and other helpful things like Vicks VapoRub and Cloverine Salve. If I have a nickel, I go to Uncle Elmer's, pull on a long cord, which clangs a bell inside, and he comes to the door. Ma told me to announce loudly that I am Sandra, Ethel's daughter.

7

The minute I say that, he always smiles and says, "Come in, come in."

He knows I always get a box of Smith Brothers black cough drops. I don't tell him that when Ma smells one, she says, "Get away from me! I can't stand that smell!" Well, they are my favorite cough drop and I don't even have a cold.

As always, I thank him and leave, glancing over at the wooden path to his shed...all little flat boards laid out in a path. There's a rope hooked to posts along the way so that he can guide himself. He always seems so cheerful even though he cannot see. I know that Grammy keeps sending away to try and find methods to help him see again. She pastes stories of those who have regained their sight into her scrapbook.

Sitting way back up on the hill is the home of Stan and Flossie Seames, and, if I walk a bit farther, on the right is the beautiful Case summer home. They provide an evening of fun, food, and laughter for the Greenwood Center folk each summer. A stage is built and each person can get up and entertain. Irving Cole always plays the guitar and sings; Lillian and her sister Charlotte Cole sing a duet. Everyone comes away with a full stomach and a good feeling!

There are no more houses until I come to Dan Cole's farm on the left. I have never been in there, but that stately white house sits on what is obviously a working farm. The Cole farm is used as a landmark many times when giving directions. To the right is the road that leads to the Rowe Hill community; off that road, a few feet in, is the road that leads to camps along the backside of Twitchell Pond.

Hollis Cushman lives in his camp on the other side of the pond opposite Uncle Elmer. I see Hollie, as we call him, when I deliver his *Grit*. I have a little ivory jackknife he gave me, which he says is made for ladies. He is always glad to see me and makes me sit to rest. From home, it is a mile to Dan Cole's house, and then I have to walk down the backside of the pond to his camp. Hollie is a friend of the family and a very nice gentleman.

We don't have electricity at our house, so we use kerosene lamps. We have a big Aladdin lamp with a fragile mantle for our kitchen table. Ma is always telling us to be careful not to break it, so we sit and read by the table, trying not to make any big movements.

After working in the mill, Dad's favorite pastime is to retire early to bed

8

and read western paperbacks by the kerosene lamp by the bed. He used to smoke in bed, too, until one night he set the mattress on fire and it had to be dragged quickly out the front door. Ma, who was still in the kitchen, heard a yell and ran. Thankfully, the lights were out at my grandparents' farm as the two of them dragged the mattress through the house and out on the lawn. That was a real scene and we four kids stayed right out of the way. Finally it looked safe to drag back inside. Ma really sputtered, and, I must say, he never did smoke again in bed!

With no running water, you can imagine we use an outhouse at the edge of the woods. That's no fun at all, especially in the winter, but Ma says you do what you have to do…and she is right. Even Grammy has an outhouse, but hers is in a corner of the barn with pretty pictures from magazines all glued on the walls. Ours is just a roof and four bare walls, but we are glad for that much!

Well, this is a picture of the place I call home. My world is a very small world, stretching a mile in either direction of our little house. I love seeing the water every day with the sun sparkling on it. Sometimes, we hear the train going up the grade on the other side of Rowe's Ledge and that means the air is right for rain. Ma always tells us when she smells rain in the air. Dad says that's the Abnaki in her, and she admits he could be right. Like clockwork after her announcement, we soon see the rain hit the pond way over by Moose Cove, and watch it come across the pond in our direction.

I guess Greenwood Center is just about perfect for me.

Boundaries

Imagine six people in three tiny rooms and an attic. We think nothing of our little house, having learned to find our way around elbows and outstretched feet. Dad and probably one of his brothers built the house—my very first memories are of my Uncle Glenn working on the inside of our house and me arguing with him over the word "the." God knows, Dad's no carpenter. Our house is a square box, evenly divided down the middle with stairs to the attic for the marking point!

On the first floor is my parents' bedroom, another small room, and a kitchen with rough wooden floors. The kitchen table is round, covered with oil cloth, and, before electricity, an Aladdin lamp sat at the very back. My father lays claim to "his" chair. When we are not eating, one finds him sitting sideways in the chair, legs crossed, cup of coffee within reach. His shirt sleeves are rolled above his elbows or nearly so, hat slung on the back of his head as his mind goes a mile a minute.

The attic is open and unfinished. Sweltering during the summer and frigid during the winter months, it nonetheless is a large enough bedroom for us four kids. My private domain is one side of the attic, partitioned with a sheet hung across clothesline rope. My three brothers and I never question that we should have more room. Many other families are in the same situation. That's the way it is; accept it. We do.

Because the house is small, I'm one to go outside and not return for most of the day. My parents aren't worried because they have taught us boundaries. In my mind, those boundaries are very important and must never be crossed. I can walk "down" the road as far as the ledge on the tarred road and then, with bared feet, mince my way over the gravel section to my Uncle Roy's house. I am never to go down past his house. Never!

If I walk "up" the road, I can go as far as Dan Cole's farm because I deliver the Grit newspaper, but never should I go to the Lester Cole farm and bother them unless I see Danny or Elwin and am invited. Never!

I am taught that to bother a neighbor is probably one of the worse things a kid could do. It reflects on our family, so unless invited, I never go to a house and rap on the door. Of course, in my mind, that does not include my cousins' house. I often hop and skip through the woods on the path between our houses, pausing to smell the trilliums and red Stinkin' Benjamins, skipping past the ledge, hopping the brook, speeding around the corner, and there's their house! Visiting them is not off limits as long as I do not overstay my welcome. Of all things, if a family is getting ready to eat, you do not stay…leave immediately!!

I love Sunday afternoons, because my Grampa and Grammy Martin usually have visitors. If my Aunt Cecile and Myron Winslow come to visit, Dad always goes across the field to visit Myron and always comes home laughing at some joke they shared.

I overstepped my boundary one Sunday when I was at Grammy Martin's. There were some people visiting whom I did not know; I thought about going home. Frank and Leah Waterhouse asked if Beryl and Ethel were my parents, and I said yes. Well, one thing led to another and I stayed a few minutes longer. Oh, boy, when I got home, Ma asked if she had seen a car drive up Gram's driveway. I had to tell her that yes, they had company. Although I admitted what happened, that did not spare me the half hour I was forced to sit in the kitchen chair until she told me I could get up.

There doesn't seem to be any boundaries when we get in the car with Dad. Other than the many trips we take to East B Hill, his favorite of all places, he likes to take us to Greenwood City. That's always fun, with Curt at one side of the backseat of the car and I at the other window. When we see a bottle on the side of the road, we yell, and Dad stops the car. One of us jumps out to retrieve it, tossing the prize on the floor, and we drive on. Down past the Ames turn, by Tracey's Flat, and down Falls Hills we go. Every time we go down Falls Hills, I think of Ma having to walk home in the dark and cold because our car would not get up that darn curvy hill in the winter after she had worked all day at Penley's Mill! Dad always points out the cattle pound, and eventually we make it to Yates filling station, right near the road to Patch Mountain. Dad and Wilbur swap tales and the latest news while Curt and I cash in our bottles and pick out penny candy, which Mr. Yates puts in two little brown bags for us.

Dad jokes on the way home and calls him Wheelbarrow Yates to get us laughing. He has an awful sense of humor, but Ma shushes him a lot and tells him to behave himself in front of us kids. One day, we were at Yates' filling station, getting into the car for the ride home, when I saw someone walking down from Patch Mountain. He looked kind of scary. "Dad, who's that?" I asked, jumping in as quickly as I could.

Dad scoffed and said, "Oh, he's harmless. That's Benny Wells. He lives by himself up on the mountain." I had heard about him, and there were rumblings in the air that he ate rats. I told Dad to hurry up and get out of there. Curt was too busy digging in his candy bag to notice. Dad laughed all the way home, because I was scared and had heard that he ate rats.

Every year, he suddenly gets it into his head to drive us down to the Martin Road and then up a backroad to an abandoned farm where there are lots of apple trees. He knows where all the old farms and roads are as we motor along, and he tells us some of their history. I think we went down to the road that leads to Irving Martin's house, then made a left turn right away. I wonder if that's the road that eventually goes to Rowe Hill or Sheepskin Bog. (I can't keep backroads straight.) Up in there is a farm, and no one lives on it, though there are lilac bushes there. I always notice lilacs remaining where someone once lived and probably raised a family. I try to imagine little kids running in the yard and sounds of laughter coming from what was once a happy home. Wild grape vines are also growing nearby. Dad tells us that he thinks the grapes are pretty sour.

But those apple trees—limbs so heavy with the largest apples I've ever seen that they bow to the ground. Dad says they are Wolf River apples...I don't know...that is how it sounds when he says it...though it sounds more like *wuffriver* when he says it. I just know they are huge and seem like they are three times as big as any other apple I have ever seen. Last year we took bags and boxes and filled all of them, having the best time ever.

Dad is calling now. He loves to look for Indian artifacts while we attack the apple trees. When he calls, we scurry.

Boundaries and respect. I can't think of anything more important that is drilled into our heads, even when dealing with outsiders. We might not like when summer people occupy our fishing and swimming holes, but we are told to keep quiet and find another.

*

That was a long time ago. I can still feel the hardness of that kitchen chair when I did not adhere to the boundaries. Somehow it stuck long enough so that I tried to instill the same theme to my own four children...boundaries and respect...and the look on my Ma's face if I forgot!!

Grammy

Another summer day, and I want to visit Grammy Martin. While Curt is playing with his trucks in the dirt, I hop the rocks across the brook and run the path across the field to my grandparents' farm. Gram is always glad to see me and smiles. She's the sweetest person and makes the best raisin-filled cookies I've ever tasted. On the way to gather eggs, she tells me she needs help. I know she doesn't, but that's the way Grammy is. We stop, and she pulls some straight green narrow stalks from her garden. She hands me one and keeps one for herself to nibble on. It tastes like onions. Cautioning me about the rooster, she unlatches the hen house and tells me not to pick up the china eggs in the nests. Gram then giggles because she tells me that every time! She scoots the rooster to the side of the coop and quickly gathers all the eggs in her basket. Out the door we go before the rooster changes his mind.

I love the little blue sneakers she always wears, which she wipes over and over before we go into the kitchen. I make sure I do the same. She has a wood box with a cover that can be used for a seat. Up on the shelf over the wood box is a little log cabin that smells like pine if you light it. And oh, the cute little Dutch boy and girl who tell what the weather is going to be! I love this kitchen—so warm and cozy and the water coming out of the pipe running into the sink holding tank is so neat. This is where we get all of our drinking water. There is a huge hole at the top of the tank where lightning hit once. Uncle Louie, who lives with Grammy, says it almost blew him across the kitchen. I guess it followed the pipe down from the spring in the pasture hill. He says that was sure a close call.

Grammy has a sewing machine on her porch; sometimes I sit out there with her while she sews on her quilts. We don't have to say anything. She sews, and I look out over the pond, watching the boats and fishermen going by. I know she knits, too, because every Christmas she makes us hats and mittens and they are really warm!

The porch is always the gathering place for Sunday visitors. Grammy has so many of her family off fighting the war that I know she enjoys company. Frank and Leah Waterhouse come and visit, and once in a while a man named Fred Davis stops by and brings his banjo. I love to hear him

play. I run over the path and into Gram's kitchen to see if Fred has his banjo out and plunking a melody. Nine times out of ten, he has it on his lap and playing a tune or two. I'll sit on the wood box lid, listening to the grownups talk, Fred plunk, and just keep quiet. Kids are made to be seen and not heard, Ma always tells us, so we remember that when we are visiting anywhere!

Grampa Martin doesn't say much. He uses a cane, covered with Black Jack Gum, and sometimes two canes. I think he has arthritis, but no one ever has said. He doesn't seem to like kids that much, although he has eight of his own. He has a large potato patch that Rex and I help him with. Carrying a quart jar filled with kerosene, we walk the rows in the hot summer sun. A flick of a finger and another potato bug goes to bug heaven. As the sun rises higher, our faces turn to a sea of sweat, but we trudge onward until the jar is filled.

Getting paid is always interesting. Grampa is a stern-looking man and demands perfection. If, and only if, the jar is completely filled, then we will be compensated in nickels. Rex and I always approach him with great trepidation and only dance for joy with our newly found riches after we turn the corner from where he sits.

Sometimes Grampa's in the barn and Gram will call to us after she's just taken some filled cookies out the oven. Oh, they are so good! She cooks the raisin filling on the stove, puts a little bit in the cookies, and then pricks the top so they are as pretty as they are good. We make sure to thank her every time.

Sometimes I help Uncle Louie, who lives there also, sharpen his axe. His sapphire eyes shining, he'll pour water into the half-cut tire while I turn the crank. "How ya doing, Bridget, you still ok?" he asks every five minutes, holding his axe to the grindstone. I loved being with my Uncle Louie.

Grammy doesn't come to visit us very often, even though we are right next door. I think between waiting on Grampa, making butter, and all the farm chores, she doesn't have time. When Ma sees her coming up the driveway, she says, "Oh, no!" even though she likes Grammy. Ma knows our house is not as nice or neat and clean as it should be, or maybe that's just the way she thinks. I think it's fine; Grammy always comes in and makes herself at home. She doesn't stay long because she is so busy.

If I could choose to be like anyone, I would want to be like my Gram. She always smiles and never has a bad thing to say about anyone. When I told Ma that, she told me I have a lot of practicing to do. I guess she's right!

Are We Poor, Ma?

Lately I've been noticing all the things some other kids have, especially listening to them talk about it at school. How they go places and do things, and their mothers and fathers buy them this and that.

This morning, Ma is trying to bake. She takes out her big tin of flour, opens it, and there're mice in it! She tears out of the kitchen and runs with the big tin, mice and all, into the front yard, yelling like crazy. I don't know if she's screaming because she's afraid of the mice or mad because she has to throw away the flour. When she finally returns to the house, flour is everywhere. She clangs the tin and cover, fills the tin with boiling hot water, and proceeds to scrub. I'm so stunned, I sit, wide-eyed. After a few minutes of scrubbing, she dries the tin, sets it upside down on the counter, comes to the table, sits down, and says flatly, "There'll be no biscuits tonight."

It's probably not the best time to ask her, but sometimes my mind thinks of things and right out my mouth they come.

I blurt out, "Are we poor, Ma?"

Well, there she sits, now looking at me. "Only if you think you are," she replies, simply.

All my life, I figure we have as much as everyone else in Greenwood Center. Well, there are those people who have bigger houses and better cars, but still we get along.

We don't have to go places to have fun. Rex and I play ball in our front yard. We pretend we are at Fenway, and Rex is second baseman Bobby Doerr. We use the big rock by the driveway as second base, and third base is a little rock by a tiny flower garden off to one side. Home plate and first base are whatever we get our hands on. I remember one day when we were playing ball, Rex decided it was his turn to bat. See, we made up our own rules as there were just the two of us playing. I decided he'd batted many more times than he'd a right and declared it my turn. He retorted that he was not going to play if I had to bat all the time.

He went into the house, and then I showed him. I took the bat, put it over Dad's sawhorse, took his bucksaw, and sawed it into two pieces. That took care of the problem. (Ma says I have a very short fuse, which I think means it does not take much for me to get stomping mad—I guess this proves it.) Rex said he didn't care if he ever played ball with me again. In a few days, however, we were back at it, having found something to use for a bat.

We're always united in cheering for the Red Sox. The Philco radio stands in the kitchen corner, its wires running out the window and grounded to the side of the house. We have to be careful not to run down the battery as Dad likes two things: boxing matches and an occasional newscast. We sit on the front steps, cheering on Ted Williams, Johnny Pesky, and Bobby Doerr.

Sometimes we have to wear mittens that don't match in the winter, but at least our hands are warm, no matter what the colors are. Gram Martin always knits us Christmas hats, so our ears are warm. Sometimes I am a little embarrassed if I have to wear the boys' flannel shirts to school, but no one mentions it to me. (Maybe they know about my short fuse?) Not to mention the loose buckles on our rubber overshoes clanging as we walk into school!

We always have food on the table, so we don't go hungry like most poor folks. Sometimes Wilmer Bryant sends us over a gallon of milk by our mailman, Johnny Howe. That's surely appreciated as Dad uses it with crackers and milk, he says, for his ulcers. Dad is always hunting and fishing, and he makes sure there is game for us to eat. I don't mind rabbit stew, but one time he brought home a bear, which was plain awful. It isn't like we don't have meat from the store—Ma brings home fish sticks, hot dogs, and hamburger. As long as a person isn't fussy and eats what's on the table, Ma says no one will ever go hungry. We always tease Ma if we have a frosted cake, telling her we know she burned it and that's why we have frosting on it. She laughs, because that old oven is propped up with a stick and so terrible that she never knows what her baking will turn out to be.

One night, we were all eating, when suddenly my father put his fork down and looked at us. This was so out of character that forks were poised halfway in mid-air, and all eyes turned his way.

"Which one of you kids told that I shot a deer?" Talk about a thundering silence. Yes, he had shot a deer out of season, but it was because we needed the meat. (My father did have one fast rule that no matter how much meat was needed, he would never shoot a doe at the time of year of births.) We said nothing and told no one, because it meant food on the table.

I knew I hadn't. My younger brother probably had no idea when deer season was legal at that point. It was my oldest brother, Tink! I remember staring at him. He was the last person on earth who would say a word! But he owned it. He admitted he had told his best friend. Of course, the best friend was sworn to secrecy but told his father, who went the mill and teased my father about it.

"I didn't think he would tell," and with that Tink quietly left the table. It was a searing hurt that his best friend betrayed him, and he had, in turn, betrayed our father's trust.

We may not have much, but we have music in our house. Ever since I can remember, Dad has played the guitar. I can't remember him playing it like other folks, because the accident at the saw mill crippled the fingers on his left hand. He lays it on his lap and plays it with either a round green bar or a flat silver one. He taught me how to play "Iwo Jima Isle" and a couple other songs on it. Tink has his Gene Autry guitar hanging from a nail on the stairway. Rex can play some, too, and we all can sing. So I guess we don't have to go anywhere for entertainment!

We don't have electricity yet like some folks. Ma puts a lot of value on the kerosene lamps. Once Rex and I were fighting in the little room off the kitchen. I had a broom and tried to hit him with it but instead broke the chimney of a lamp sitting there. Ma was sure mad that time! She sent me packing off to all the neighbors to see if I could borrow a lamp chimney 'til she could get to town. I tried to explain that it was Rex's fault to begin with, but she wouldn't hear a word of it. I did hear something about my short fuse when I went out the door.

I guess, when it all boils down, you're only poor if you think you're poor. The way I see it, we have just about everything that anyone else has but maybe not quite as grand.

Salt Pork and Dandelion Greens

Dandelions! Ma is bending over on the side grass (I say grass as we did not have a lawn in the Center). Setting a big, dented, silver-colored pot to one side, she grasps a little pair of snippers. Bent in the shape of an upside-down letter "U," she moves from one green plant to another. Soon, she crosses the brook carefully, balancing on the two rocks and planks, which affords us access to the path to my grandparents' farm. Apparently, my Grandfather Ross does not mind her digging there, and soon the pot is full.

Even though the kitchen is hot, Ma takes two sticks of wood and lifts the lid to make sure the stove is warm enough for the meal for which she's been waiting. I watch as she pours water over and over into her silver pot. With a resounding "THERE," she covers the treasure with water, and on the stove it goes. We're in for the season's treat of dandelion greens! She cuts a piece of salt pork and sticks it on top the greens, remarking that they will boil down so there will probably be just enough for a "taste" for everyone. I know a couple in our household who will pass on their taste to someone else.

The greens bubble, and the kitchen begins to reveal that dandelion smell. Reaching for her frying pan, Ma cuts up slivers of salt pork, which soon are crisping and snapping along with the bubbling of the greens. A symphony of music coming from the old wood stove!! Next, out comes the salt pork and into the grease goes the slicing of the leftover potato from last night's meal. Soon, it's golden brown on both sides. The table is set, glasses of water at each plate, and we all sit down to our potato, salt pork, and dandelion greens (with vinegar on top, of course) supper.

*

As I stare at the yellow dandelions in the yard so many years later, I wonder about the nutritional value of that meal. There was no such thing as a food pyramid in our house. We ate what was on the table if we liked it, and, if we didn't, we waited for the next meal to come or plain picked at it and hoped Keno, the husky, was under the table waiting for anything a stealthy hand could get to her.

Looking back, it is hard to believe how much we lived and ate off the land. Dad was a voracious fisherman and hunter. We ate smelts in the spring, yellow perch (but not in

August because they were wormy), white perch (if he was trolling and ran into a school of them), and brown trout. Dad shot partridge, rabbits, and the Lord only knows what else that Ma put on the table at one time or another. We had deer each year in the frigid fall, with the hind quarter nailed to the side of the house. It was high enough so the neighbor's dog could not get it but low enough so Dad could cut off slabs with his hunting knife and hand to Ma, who dumped them into the hot fat in the frying pan.

We seldom had dessert, unless it was a holiday, and certainly no candy unless we found bottles to turn in and bought some two-for-a-penny sweets. We ate plain food. Sometimes there was plenty; other times not, but somehow, someway, Ma always found enough to feed her four kids. If anyone could make something out of nothing, it was Ma.

When I read about school lunches and students protesting about the food; parents up in arms because this or that has been taken from the menu, I wonder how we survived. Each of us carried our own little brown bag and usually there was a biscuit with peanut butter, sometimes jam on it, and maybe a marshmallow cookie if Ma thought she should pay the extra at Vallee's store for the treat. Our drink was water from the school fountain in the hallway.

I look out again at the yellow and know there are chemicals that can kill the dandelions. Not on my lawn. There are too many chemicals and too many preservatives in the world as I see it today. Perhaps had I not survived so many decades of living, I would not see such a difference in the way we were and the way we are this day.

I would give anything for one more day in the old kitchen with Ma bustling around the old wood stove, stirring up the greens and making sure we knew before they went on the table that they "were good for us."

Dandelions…good for so many things. When I was grown, my friend Charlotte Cole introduced me to dandelion wine. But therein lies another story.

Flipping the Switch

Well, it's hard to believe. I am so excited because at last—at last!—we actually have electricity!!!! The power company had to set the pole right up in our front yard but enough out of the way so Ma won't hit it when she's backing up the car. She doesn't drive too well in that direction and once scraped the side of the porch (she then asked me who had moved the porch). The meter box is on the side of the house. Dad looks at it, watching it go round, and seems pretty fascinated. His friend, an electrician, has wired our house.

Ma is proud that she now has a bona fide electric clock on the wall, with its cord running down to an outlet over the kitchen table, and a round fluorescent light right in the middle of the ceiling. There's a switch at the bottom of the stairs for a big light at the top so we can see our way better into the attic when we go to bed. Dad has a reading lamp by his bed now and says it is sure better than the old kerosene lamp. It doesn't stink either when he blows it out at night.

Last week, my oldest brother Roland bought Ma a second-hand refrigerator. Now this has to be the best thing ever for her! He told Dad that he still has to keep his beer cold in the brook; Ma gave Dad "the look" so that's just where he keeps it. It seems strange not to see the tall, metal, white cabinet where we always have kept our cereals and canned goods. Ma made provisions for them and says having it is wonderful for keeping her meat cold!

Another great thing happened last week. When I spied Uncle Harold, who is married to Aunt Vi, outside in his garden, he said he had something he bet I would like to see. He invited me to come over to Grammy Martin's a little before eight o'clock that night and to bring anyone who wanted to come.

Rex, Curt, and I went to Grammy Martin's that night and went into her little parlor. There in the corner was a television set...I had only seen them in magazines!! I got so excited. We all sat and watched Dragnet in black and white—it was like having the movies right in your own house! I liked Joe Friday when he said, "Just the facts, ma'am." Uncle Harold just kept grinning all the time. I think we all wanted to stay forever to watch this wonderful invention, but we knew it wouldn't be polite, so we thanked them and went home.

But since then, let me tell you, Grammy, Aunt Vi, and I have discovered a great program. It's only fifteen minutes long but worth the hop and skip across the field. The man is named Liberace and sits at a piano with his candelabra and wears long tails, which he keeps flipping up when he has to move to start playing. Aunt Vi always giggles when he flips them! At the end, he looks right at us and sings, "I'll be seeing you in all the old familiar places." Well, let me tell you, Aunt Vi just giggles and giggles, and Grammy says he's one fine piano player.

Saturday night is the best night for TV, Grammy tells me. On this Saturday, I think Uncle Harold and Aunt Vi are dancing and Ma and Dad are off, so I go over. Grammy does some fiddling with the knobs. After the picture straightens out, what do I see but two men pushing and shoving each other around a ring. They aren't boxing, that's for sure.

Gram exclaims, "You'll like this, Sandra, they wrassle all over the place!" Well, we get so excited and start yelling for the one we like the best. I didn't know Grammy could shout so loud. She never yells that way even when the pig gets out...but oh my, don't those men throw each other around!

The next men to come up are, Grammy tells me, great big men, and I might not like them. They are what are called Sumo wrestlers. Well I don't like them at all, but this is better than sitting at home doing nothing. Grammy yells some more, finally one of them comes out the winner, and his hand is held high for the world to see. I then tell Grammy it's late and I have to go home. She tells me to come back and watch the wrassling any time with her. I know I will.

I haven't told Grammy—and don't think I will—that I have a lot of bad dreams about those Sumo wrestlers. I don't think I want to watch them anymore, but for the others I will yell as loud as she does.

I won't tell Ma and Dad about my going over to watch the wrestling with Grammy. I know they wouldn't mind, but it is kind of my secret time with her and we have a good time. I asked Dad if he had thought about getting a television. He said money doesn't grow on trees, but if he had extra he wouldn't mind having a little DuMont stuck in the corner. In fact, he said he would put his Morris chair right in there and probably watch some westerns.

I think eventually Dad will give in and get one, after he sees that Grammy has one in her parlor. Once you watch a program, it's easy to want one. Ma says the dance crowd has really dropped off at Abner's because everyone is staying home to watch a comedian named George Gobel. He has a round face and crew cut and is supposed to be funny. She and Dad are wondering if this will be the end of the dance halls. I know that Ma sure is hoping that it isn't.

So now we are flipping the switch like everyone else. The Aladdin lamp is stored with the other kerosene lamps for when the power goes out. You know, nothing is perfect, and, for sure, country folks don't take anything for granted.

Dad's New Occupation

Well, now that we have the big electrical pole in our side yard like most everyone in Greenwood Center, it only stands to reason that Dad has been talking about getting a television set. This weekend I notice him sitting in his Morris chair, surrounded by loose papers and booklets. He's usually out fishing on Twitchell Pond or at Indian Pond, but the look on his face tells me he is determined to do something. There's a big black case next to his chair, and I am waiting for him to tell me what is in it.

He sees me standing in the doorway and looks up. "Muff, I'm studying," he explains.

"What are you studying?" I ask, now very curious.

"Well, it looks to me that everyone has a TV now," he says, "and sooner or later something's going to be wrong with them. I'm going to be ready to fix 'em."

"We don't even have a TV, Dad."

"I know, I know," he says, tapping his foot, "and that's going to be remedied this afternoon. I am going to Norway and coming home with a DuMont. They're supposed to be one of the best."

Well, the thought of our having our own TV is almost too much for me, and I go into the kitchen where Ma is sitting at the kitchen table, resting with a cup of tea.

"Are we going to have a TV for real, Ma?"

She shifts her weight around in the old wooden kitchen chair from MacDonald's on Old County Road in Bryant Pond. "Well that's what your father has said. He's been studying for a couple of months, so he can learn how to fix them when they go bad."

Well, I know Dad only went to the eighth grade in a little school here in the Center, but he's really smart, so I have no doubt he can do it. "That should be interesting," I tell Ma, who raises her eyebrows and mutters, "Well, it should be." I think Ma has a couple meanings behind that statement, but I am not going to even question that right now.

It is hard getting up on Sunday morning, but I crawl out. Ma is already at the breakfast table and seems pleased that she watched Lawrence Welk on the new TV! Yup, it's there, and Dad has placed a moose ashtray he won at Waterford Fair right on top for decoration. Dad only lets the Lawrence Welk show go on because he loves polkas and likes Myron Floren with his accordion. Sometimes, he'll go into the backyard and twist the antenna in the right direction to get a news channel he wants.

"I don't know how he will make out fixing other people's sets," Ma says in a very low voice. "I know he can do it, but people are already asking him to come look at theirs. Guess they heard about it at the mill."

The car is gone and Dad is nowhere to be seen. I figured he had gone to Ray Langway's for the Sunday kerosene. "Oh, no," Ma says, "he has gone to look at a TV and took his tube tester and spare tubes." I can tell she's a little worried that maybe he will come up against something he can't fix.

Well, no need to worry. A half hour later in pulls Dad, who jumps out and carries his tube tester into the kitchen. "There, by gar," he exclaims, "that wasn't bad. I put the tester on there, found the bad tube, and replaced it in no time."

I can tell he's really proud of himself. Ma's beaming in relief. "Do you think you can make out all those State forms each quarter?" she asks him.

"No problem. I can handle that with no sweat," so speaks the victorious television repairman.

"Don't give up your mill job," Ma mutters, swinging by with a basket of clothes to hang on the line.

Dad grins and says, "You know, Muff, some of these people should clean behind their sets. This one had cobwebs in and around the tubes, but the worse was trying not to step in the cat leavings on the floor in the corner."

"No!" I gasp, "You are pulling my leg."

He pulls himself up to his full height and says, "No, but you don't say anything, because they are your customers. You just go with it."

I'm really proud of Dad. I never thought he would want to do anything except work in the mill day after day, year after year. He doesn't mind the work, but now he has something else to fall back on. I finally get up the courage to ask him…why?

He looks at me for a long moment. "It will be a lot easier on me fixing television sets than logging if the mill burns again," he admits.

Now there is a smart man.

*

My Dad's birthday was yesterday, March 8th. I will never forget his carrying his tube tester and working into the night after working all day at the mill. Many people never paid him, and he didn't dun them for money, saying they probably had other bills to pay. Others thought of him as a friend and never considered that he had his own business. He never complained about the non-payments, but those people were put on the bottom of the list when he had a lot of repair work to do. He was not only smart but shrewd. I miss him.

Zip-a-dee-doo-dah

It's Sunday afternoon, and the summer sun is warm and lazy in the sky. Curt and I have run out of things to do, or so it seems. He's five years old, and I am nine. We have rolled the old car tires on the road all morning and are just tired of trying to think of other things to take up the day.

Ma looks as though she's weary as well. We have taken the clothes off the line, brought them in, and folded what we don't have to iron. It's too hot to start the wood stove and heat up the iron today. My cousin, Vance, is visiting at Gram Martin's, but I think they have company so don't want to go there and intrude.

"Would you like to go to the movies?"

I cannot believe what Ma just said. Dad is out on Twitchell Pond fishing, and the car is sitting in the yard. We have never been to the movies...not ever. I ask her if Vance can go with us, and she says it is fine if his grandmother says so.

We all pile into the car, and to the movie theater in Bethel we go! Bethel is "our" city." I love riding up Main Street, making the big circle at the end, and coming back down again. I always glance down the street where Gould Academy is and wonder how anyone can go to such a big school! Ma sometimes stops in at the drugstore at the head of the street. Other times, she'll go to Brown's Variety, which is a Magic Land for Curt and me. All sorts of things laid out in neat little rows, other things in small piles but, oh, so neat. There's always someone behind the counter to greet us with a smile! While Ma looks for sewing supplies, threads, and needle for her treadle Singer machine, Curt and I will wander into the "other room" to look at all the treasures. Coloring books, storybooks, and, oh, the wonders of it all! No one worries that we "kids" might put something out of place.

But today, we're going to the theater. Ma says there is a special movie for kids called *Song of the South*, which should be something we like. I am a little scared, because I've never been to the Bethel Theater before and am not sure what to do. Ma says not to worry, and that she will take care of everything. She says she can only afford one container of popcorn, so we have to share.

Curt takes my hand and I know he is scared, too. Vance walks with Ma, and they go up to the ticket window. She buys three children and one adult tickets. There's a big man standing there, and what a wonderful smile he has! Ma tells us later that his name is Freddie Grover. Well, he certainly is very friendly, and I don't feel afraid anymore.

There are rows and rows of red plush velvet seats, and we sit near the back. First comes the black-and-white newsreel, telling us all that's going on in the world. Then there are comics, which the screen announces are "Short Subjects." We laugh and laugh, and the movie has not even begun.

The movie is magic. Uncle Remus sings in it, others sing, and I have never seen anything like it. The time goes so fast that before I know it the movie is over. The magic's gone! Ma gets us all up, we go to the car, and my head is still spinning. I can see she enjoyed it as well. Maybe the movie was for kids but it was a change from her work at home and at the mill.

All the way home, I sing Zip-a-dee-doo-dah, zip-a-dee-ay, or something like that. I couldn't get all the words, but I knew the tune. Ma says if we are good all week and Dad goes fishing again, maybe we can go next Sunday. I guess she enjoyed it more than I thought. She tells us that next week's movie is a musical with Doris Day and Gordon McRae—she likes musicals. So do I!! Curt is not sure he wants to go to that, and Vance says he'll be gone by next Sunday. Well maybe Ma and I will go together. She tells me that she does not like movies with fighting and blood and all; there's enough of that in the news without it being in a movie.

I think she was talking about the time that Dad wanted to treat Uncle Louie and took him to his very first picture show. It was *Sands of Iwo Jima*, starring John Wayne. Dad talked about it for a week, claiming that Uncle Louie almost popped his sapphire eyes right out of his head when he saw the big screen. Ma said she had heard enough about the war without living it all over again. Maybe that is why she decided we would go to a happy movie. I hope we go again. I didn't know the magic in a movie at the Bethel Theater.

I bet I will be singing Zip-a-dee-doo-dah all week when I roll the tire down the tarred road—want to bet?

Trespassers and Tantrums

The phone line's finally been extended down into our branch of the neighborhood. Hurray! Well, perhaps not. It went right by our house and didn't stop in for a visit. That's because of Dad. No way is he having one of those things on his wall ringing day and night, and, as he says many times, you just know it wouldn't be for him but for one of the kids. And so we are still phone-less.

Dad didn't want a phone, but now he's decided suddenly we should have a garden. Now those who are familiar with Dad take this in stride, knowing full well he'll lose interest the minute the vegetables do not grow according to his timetable. He's more at home hunting in the fall, fishing in the summer, and, in between times, sitting on the porch, boots on the railing and a bottle of Old Narragansett in hand.

And so it is with rolling eyes that the rest of us watch as he finds a hoe and proceeds to break the earth with the strength of his back. In his mind, I'm sure he's a pioneer somewhere in the wilds of the Dakotas or perhaps just emerging from his covered wagon heading to California, determined to homestead. Continuing for a couple of days, he finally pronounces it ready for the great seed dropping. Which he does. Every day thereafter, he hops the stones in the brook and walks up and down the three rows of his new garden, looking for shoots.

It's a day of celebration in our house the day Dad comes into the kitchen, hands on hips, and announces to the eye-rolling family that he's a successful gardener. The lettuce is up, the radishes are doing great, and he knows the carrots are not far behind.

"Well, that's good," Ma says simply, continuing on with biscuit making. The rest of us then smile and add appropriate remarks such as "Gee that's great!" I think he knows in our hearts we are still questioning his dedication to being a master gardener. In private conversations, we all try to remember the last time we saw our father eat a vegetable.

One morning the blue skies turn slightly gray when Dad reports he can see animal tracks around the outskirts of his garden. It's becoming personal. He spends most of that Saturday morning making a fence of fishing line around the garden, complete with little stakes and all. There are no

31

questions asked as we watch with fascination the way he snakes the fish line across the brook and leads it to the porch where he attaches a big bell. Hands on hips once more, he boasts that the minute any animal crosses the yard toward his garden, the bell will sound, and he will roll out of bed, dash to the yard, and shoot his gun in the air.

That sounds like a fine and dandy plan, except that it's Saturday night, and Ma goes dancing on Saturday nights. Ma comes home late, hits the line with her foot, bell clangs, and Dad jumps up and meets Ma at the front door, gun in hand. Cursing ensued and we in the attic, with eyes still rolling, turn over and go back to sleep.

Not to be outdone, Dad decides another course of action should take place. Not that he let the Saturday night debacle fade...no, he injects that into the conversation for quite a few days, causing a lot of face turning and hidden grins. The fish line is staying in place. Dad knows for certain that deer will be nibbling before long...the green shoots are growing and his hoe has been doing its job. It's a weedless garden worthy of many a second look.

Again, fish line is dragged across the brook, but this time he warns us all that no one, NO ONE, should be coming across the yard after nine o'clock. The fish line is draped skillfully around the house this time, through the bedroom window right by his head, and again attached to the bell.

Later, we figured it was about midnight or close to it, when the bell starts clanging. Dad jumps out of bed, grabs the rifle, and yells, "Ethel, grab the flashlight!" Ma does not want to go outside with her nightclothes on, so there ensues a short conversation, interspersed with Dad cursing and, we assume from the attic view, practically dragging her along, flashlight in hand. The front door opens, steps are heard across the porch, and louder cursing. There's no animal in sight.

Back into the house they come, followed by mutterings and banging of the front door. Again, we roll over and go back to sleep.

Fast forward to the next morning. Dad went out at day's first light, apparently, because it was six o'clock. We were in the middle of our fried fish and potato breakfast when he bursts through the door, hair standing on end and obviously in a rage. What had been a garden fit for a magazine cover was now nothing but sad, spikey spears here and there, surrounded by deer tracks obliterating his neatly hoed rows.

Sitting down after delivering this news in a much louder voice than usual, he picks up his coffee cup and announced, "That's it. They're smarter than I am, and they can have the blankety blank garden." (Though he didn't say *blankety blank*, that's for sure.) Another sip of coffee and he mutters, "You know, we would have had vegetables this summer if your mother could hold a flashlight right."

Ma says nothing. We're silent. We know he'd rather be fishing, anyway. The local animals have let him off the hook.

The Stranger

Ma tells us to look for strange men we might see walking down the "flat" and to come to the house if we ever see anyone suspicious. We can see a half mile up the "flat" and know everyone who lives in the Center, so if someone different comes wandering down that piece of road, then we will know for sure.

They are called "tramps," and Ma explains that most of them are not bad but just down on their luck. If one comes to Gram Martin's house, she might give them a sandwich or a little bowl of soup, but they have to sit outside to eat it. She never lets them in the house. Well, no one ever comes to our house as it's far back from the road, and probably they can tell we have a hard job feeding ourselves! Ma says if a tramp finds a house that gives food, they will leave a mark for the next one to see, so that he can be fed as well. I spend a good afternoon looking for marks around our house and come up empty handed.

But then it happens! One hot Saturday afternoon, Rex and I are rolling our tires on the narrow tarred road and stop to catch our breath at the mailbox. I look up the road and in the distance, there's a man coming down the road! He's too far off for me to see his face, but he's dressed in dark clothing. Rex and I stare and both agree we don't know who he is...certainly no one who lives near us!

We do just what Ma has told us to do...we take off running for the house and tell her what we have seen—a strange man coming down the road. She tells us to stay right in the kitchen with her, and we'll watch as he passes by.

Time seems to stand still, and, of course, my vivid imagination has him already knocking on our door for a sandwich. After a bit, we see him by our mailbox, and I bet Gram Martin has seen him now! Oh, no!! He's turning in our driveway and coming to our house! This has never happened before.

"Oh, my Lord," Ma breathes. I guess she's praying that she has something to offer him while he sits on our steps.

He walks ever so slowly up our driveway and is soon close enough so we can see his face. Ma suddenly starts laughing, and we think she's hysterical. "That's not a tramp, that's your Uncle Pete!" she chuckles. Well, if we don't let out a sigh of relief.

Rex and I have no way of knowing as Uncle Pete lives and works in Portland. He's come home for the weekend and decided to walk the three miles to see Ma.

We all have a good laugh afterwards, but Ma still insists that we continue to watch out for strangers and to run to the house should we see one.

LONG AGO
The Inquisitive Tomboy

Tomboy

I'm a tomboy growing up in Greenwood Center. I don't care if my hair is combed or cut even, but I definitely want the center of my baseball glove to be pounded down so that when a line drive comes my way, it plops in and stays there. I don't care if my jeans are ragged or my shirt tucked in as long as my alder fish pole leans against the side of the house waiting for me to grab and head for Wagner's Rock. Pole in one hand and a Maxwell House coffee tin in the other—I'm a happy camper. Sometimes I sit on the rock, fishing with the alder fishing pole Tink cut for me, for so long that my oldest brother asks me how many hours I intend to drown the worm.

You can imagine what my poor mother endures with her only daughter. I take no interest in any of the pursuits she offers. I can't sit still long enough to learn how to thread a needle in her treadle machine. She finally tells me to forget about learning to cook since she has no ingredients to waste. In other words, at some point she's given up. Let her only daughter be her fourth son, it doesn't matter anymore!!

Truth is, I take an interest, just not enough to want to learn how to do these things. Joining the local 4-H club (with a little prodding from Ma), I attend two meetings in town. We learn how to set a table correctly. Now this is no use to me. There are six people in our house and six of each utensil—simple. We learn to fold napkins. Very pretty, except we don't use napkins at home. Maybe paper towels and surely my youngest brother uses his shirt sleeve, but cloth napkins? I can see Ma washing them on the scrub board each Saturday and delicately pinning those to the line between the two trees out back. She would be more than pleased to add those to the ever multiplying pile of clothes.

The second meeting is not as pointless, but I have already decided it will be the final one. We are going to make mayonnaise. Sure, I can go to Vallee's store in nearby Locke Mills and buy a jar, but instead I have to learn to mix milk, eggs, and who knows what. See? There's no logic whatsoever. Suffice it to say, my results are a cross between wallpaper paste and pancake batter. I never go back.

Now you're thinking I am incorrigible and just do not want to learn. Not true. I will sit in one of our high back kitchen chairs near the oven and

watch as Ma puts together her *Finnan Haddie*...or at least that's what she calls it. I take it all in: fish, cream sauce, butter, and the aroma. Before it's cooked and ready to eat, I participate in drool. I just love it and know exactly how to make it. The answer? Give me something I like, and I can do it. Don't put me in competition with Hellman's Mayo, because Hellman's is rolling on the floor laughing while I'm busy counting the minutes of wasted time.

I sometimes just didn't know what was expected and how to behave. Take the time that Uncle Louis, who had the first car in the family, consented to taking us all to Locke Mills. It was a cold, wintry day and we kids managed to squish together in the back. Need I tell you what happened next? I put the tip of my tongue on the frosted window. Just the tip. Oh, my goodness...as soon as it hit, I knew it wasn't ice cream, and I DID pull it off. My tongue was sore for a week, and I didn't dare say a word!

Then there's that birthday dinner at Aunt Mary's, which always happened on the birthdays of me and my cousin, Blaine. Yes, poor Blaine was unfortunate enough to be born exactly one year after me. We both were photographed so many times on our birthdays that there could have been a full length movie made of us.

So it came to pass, on that precious day in February, I left my school desk and walked up Bird Hill with cousin Blaine to have a birthday "dinner" (lunch for the rest of us) with him in Locke Mills. Aunt Mary, in all her goodness and kindness of heart, always had the best intentions on that day; I cannot tell you how many years we plodded together up that hill.

I thought their house was fancy. The outhouse was included in the house and there was no long, cold path to it!

I recall the table being covered with food—remember, our own table at home usually held the fare of fish sticks, deer meat, or trout. Before me, a banquet, in my eyes, topped off with a cake the size of the Eiffel Tower. I ate...and ate...and ate. The cake was served, and Blaine and I went out to play until it was time to head back down the hill to school. Suddenly through the open window, I heard, "Does that child ever eat at home? Where does she put it all? I have never seen anyone eat as much at one sitting as she did."

Blaine apparently did not hear this, as he continued playing. I was embarrassed and started feeling guilty. Did I did take too much? I reviewed my munching—so much maybe this, a lot of maybe that. By the time we got back at our desks, my stomach was as taut as a trampoline. I managed to get through 'til the bus took us back home. Without saying a word to the parents, I swore I'd never go back. I was so mortified.

Fast forward to the following year. Yes, my intentions and vow had been roundly defeated; I sat at Aunt Mary's table, again, looking at the towering display of food and carefully taking just enough to cover a small portion of my plate.

Aunt Mary stands behind me. "My goodness, child, you eat like a bird," she says, encouragingly. "You have to have more than that to get you through this afternoon."

Sigh.

Let's get back to those high back kitchen chairs I just mentioned. I remember the day that Ma nagged Dad, saying it was time we had something decent to sit in...the time had come. I cannot remember the vehicle or if all of us piled in, but I would not have missed it for the world. Over Rowe Hill we sped and up Old County Road to a gentleman's house or store for chairs. His last name was McDaniels, which Dad sang all the way, irritating Ma to no end. We piled chairs in the back seat and trunk, tied some on top, and headed for home. (You know, when Ma in her mid-eighties moved out of the house in Greenwood, there was still at least one of those high back chairs sitting in the corner.)

But back to being a tomboy. At grammar school, my favorite game is "Halley Over the Roof." Kids wait on both sides of the school house, and the ball is thrown over. If it is caught, one runs around the building, throws the ball, and tries to hit one of the kids on the other side, all of whom are fleeing.

How I love baseball! The "flat" is the place to be most evenings when folks come from Locke Mills, and we choose up teams. One time I was playing second base, with a runner on first. The batter hit a line drive, I jumped and got it in the webbing of the glove, came down, and threw it to first for the double play. (I have no idea why I remember this particular play, except being the only girl on the field, I must have been exceedingly proud of myself. Maybe I remember because the runner was so angry and humiliated that a "girl" doubled him up. You know, I may be wrong....but an athletic play like that sure lives in the memory a long time after you fail at making mayonnaise or trying to thread a needle.) Another time I was playing second base, I jumped up to catch a line drive, came down, and someone sliding into the base spiked me in my right foot. I think it broke my toe because it is crooked, but after a while it stopped hurting and seemed to be the right size again. Only one person wore spikes then, and there was absolutely no need of him to even wear them in a field, for heaven sakes.

*

My poor Ma lived to see me cook for four hungry kids and keep them nourished to the point where they were seldom sitting in one place for long; she saw me make little flannel shirts for my three sons on my own treadle machine. She knew all I needed was to sit by myself and figure it out.

But I still like the double play on the "flat" a lot better.

Full of Questions

Ma has just dumped out the last pail of wash water at the edge of the woods. It takes a long time to empty the big tub, and her fingers are red from the scrubbing on the washboard. I can't help her with the scrubbing, but I do help carry the water from the well out back in the brook. When the wash is ready to hang, I hand her the clothespins and grab the poles for her to steady the line. We don't want it all to go down to the ground and have to start over. Ma heaves a big sigh as she watches the last sudsy water trickle into the ground.

"There! That job is done," she declares.

I figure now is as good a time to ask as any, though Ma does look pretty tired. I take a deep breath. "How come we have to have a babysitter some times?"

I swear I see Ma's eyes roll way back in her head. "You are just full of questions, young lady, aren't you?"

Today is Saturday, and for once Dad has agreed to go to Abner's dance hall in Albany. Ma loves to dance, and usually she has to go with one of her lady friends, if she gets to go at all. I secretly think her going to a dance is a reward for sitting at a machine all week at the mill, but, whatever the reason, it doesn't matter. She just loves to dance.

"How come Dad is going tonight?" I ask as she bangs the pail down in the corner.

"Because he promised me."

"Who's going to be our babysitter? Tink is old enough to stay with us."

"Tink's going to be out," she replies.

Oh, great, I think. Ma looks at me and says that Helen is coming over.

Helen, oh great, again. Last time, Curt sat at the kitchen table coloring all evening, I played with my paper dolls, and Rex was reading while Helen, the babysitter, was out in the front yard in her boyfriend's car. We didn't say anything, as it was more fun with her outside, anyway. I guess I should be happy that Ma is pleased Dad is going with her.

Babysitters have not had a great record at our house. There was one who really was a wretch. She babysat while Dad and Ma were working, and

we were pretty little. She went up in the attic—on my side, mind you—and got prowling around and fell through the attic floor. Broke her leg. Yup, she broke her leg. She kind of hobbled 'til Dad and Ma came home, and then Dad took her somewhere to have the leg tended to. We never saw her again. I was sorry she broke her leg, but, as Ma said, what on earth was she in the attic for, anyway?

We like it when Winnie Hanscom comes and sleeps over, so Dad and

Ma can go out. Winnie sleeps with me on my side of the attic. One night she decided to get a drink of water. I rolled over and she climbed out of bed. Suddenly, I heard a clunking noise, and Winnie said a word I'd never heard HER say before. Well, come to find out, Winnie stubbed her toe on the side of the chimney and broke her big toe. Made her forget about her thirst, I guess, but we all felt bad because she was our favorite person to come and stay with us. That attic is cursed for babysitters.

Sunday morning arrives, and we have had our night with Helen, again. We had a fine time entertaining ourselves and went to bed when we felt like it. I guess Helen must have come back in the house before Ma and Dad got home. Ma doesn't seem too pleased this morning.

"Did you have a good time last night, Ma?" I ask, a bit cautiously.

"Yes and no," she replies, grimacing. "Yes, because I like to dance, and your father did do a couple polkas with me, though he practically threw me through the wall on the corners. He doesn't take corners well at all." I couldn't comment on that because I have never seen Dad do any dancing except a clog in the middle of the kitchen floor.

"So what about the no, Ma?"

"You're full of questions this morning, aren't you?" She pours herself another cup of coffee. "Well, your father was hungry, so he bought a hotdog, and at intermission we went to the car to eat it. All he did was complain, complain, complain. Said the hotdog was awful and so dry he could hardly swallow it. Well, I turned on the dome light, and your father had eaten most of the napkin with the hotdog. No wonder he thought it was dry, and I told him so. Then he says if I am going to get picky, he isn't going to go dancing again."

Well, I want to laugh but figure better not even crack a grin. I imagine Dad had a bottle of Old Narragansett and even that did not wash down the napkin.

Ma takes a sip of coffee. "By the way, how was Helen last night?"

"She was about the same as always, Ma," I answer carefully. No point in making her Sunday any worse than it is already.

Dreamer

"Young lady, I am surprised your tongue doesn't wear out." Now when Ma calls me "young lady," I know her patience is just about drawn out. "Sit yourself in that chair and don't you get out until I tell you that you can." How many times have I had that bounce off me? I reason that it's not my fault that I want to know so many things. And there should be a reasonable answer for every question I ask.

Every time I walk to our outhouse at the edge of the woods, I wonder why we can't have pretty pictures on the walls. After all, when I am at Grammy Martin's farm and go to the barn to use hers, the walls are a wonderful display of color. She has cut pictures from magazines and decorated every inch of the walls. It's a place where one can sit and stare for hours just to see all the prettiness! Ma always says though that as long as the outhouse serves the purpose, there's no need to sit there and daydream.

Daydream? Guilty as charged. What would I do without imagination? It takes me everywhere. I use the Teeny Weeny family from the cardboard in the Shredded Wheat to fuel my imagination as I play alone. I spent hours in the dirt with my own little family of stick people living in the little stick and rock village. On rainy days, I cut pictures of little girls from the discarded Sears catalogs my Grandmother saves for me. There on my fishing rock, I dream of what I want to be when I grow up; I write poetry in my mind. Many a time, Ma tells me to get my head out of the clouds. I always do, but in a short while, the head's back in the clouds again. I'm a voracious reader, something I get from my Dad, I believe. I find I can travel anywhere with a good book in my hands. I love every book that comes my way and settle into the attic and read for hours. Rain on the roof lulls me to sleep; some leaking through the roof makes me shift my body around until it doesn't hit me.

I can't help but dream. There are comic books in the house given to us; always, either on the back of the cover or within, can be found wonderful, little ads from the Johnson Smith Co. Oh, the things one can buy for just pennies or a handful of change! Now, I do have a few coins in my attic hideaway that I have earned treading hay for Uncle Harold and collecting potato bugs off plants for Grampa Martin, who, begrudgingly but finally, handed to me. (I fully believe it's reasonable that a quart jar of picked bugs should equal a nickel.)

For weeks, I study the ads and finally decide that some things offered are just too gross. I don't want to fool friends with pepper gum or fake dog poop. What I really want to buy is a whoopie cushion. That won't hurt a soul and I know I will only use it on family (well I'll count my father out on that). I propose the idea to my mother one night while we are washing the dishes in the old, black, iron sink.

Need I even tell you her response? Her dish cloth, dripping with suds, seems to hang in mid-air as the verdict arrives in one, quick sentence: "You will do no such thing, young lady." That idea vanishes as quickly as it had materialized. But being the persistent pest that I seem to be, it does not squelch all my dreams.

Back to Johnson Smith Co. and the comic books. AHA! No one can find a reason for my not ordering something that will make all my dreams come true. I now decide I want to be a dancer...in particular, a tap dancer. Look! There for 59 cents are a pair of taps! All I have to do is order, receive, find Dad's hammer, and nail them to a pair of shoes. I vow not to touch the shoes that still look...well, decent.

I don't ask permission to go ahead with the mission, as I can see absolutely nothing wrong with buying a set of taps. The next day I print out the order form, find an envelope, set it in the mailbox with three pennies on top for postage, raise the flag for Johnny to stop, and watch as he grounds to a halt that afternoon and takes my order out into the big world. Soon, I will be known worldwide as a tapper for sure!

Day in and day out, I wait for the two metal taps to arrive and plot which shoes I could nail them to without Ma getting in an uproar. School shoes will not do. We are bought one pair in September to last us 'til the final school bell in June. I decide to use last year's shoes, worn when walking through the woods and mud.

At last Johnny brings the little package. Ma and Dad are working at the mill, so up the stairs I race, hammer in hand. Little tacks are enclosed with the metal taps with explicit instructions to make me the world's best tap dancer. On the toe of one shoe the tap goes. Soon after, I raise the hammer in victory as now I have a pair of tap shoes.

Instruction book propped on a wooden crate and shoes on my feet—but no music. No problem; I will hum and tap dance at the same time. "Syncopated Clock" is the song, and the attic floor rattles as the taps hit.

I knew it will be a tremendous surprise for Mom and Dad to discover that their daughter can tap dance, and I barely manage to get through supper without telling them. For some reason that evening, Dad hits the bed early with his western paperback. Well, Ma will still be able to hear the rhythm, so I go up to the attic, pop on the tap shoes, and start humming and tapping. About a quarter way through the song, Dad gets up and shouts to Ma, "What's that ungodly racket coming from upstairs? If it's a woodpecker, get my gun before he rips the side of the house off!"

At that point, I figure I should reveal my purchase and intent. Dad sighs, shakes his head, and heads back to bed. Ma asks me when I will ever learn not to believe all the ads I read. She then chastises me for ruining my mud shoes and expecting so much for fifty cents. Thus ends that dream of a world tour.

Gram seems to understand that I am a dreamer. Often, she sits on the porch at her treadle machine, quilting, while I sit in a rocking chair looking out over Twitchell Pond, with neither of us saying a word for hours.

My head is not always in the clouds. One morning, I'm just meandering down the tarred road, thinking about fishing or not, when I decide to stop in and visit a neighbor lady. Her bulkhead door is open and I can see her putting laundry into a washing machine. Not wanting to bother her, I turn to go away.

"Oh, Sandra, you can come down. Come ahead," she says, quietly.

I sit on the cement steps as she continues to load the washer. Suddenly she looks up.

"My mother passed away this morning."

Young as I was, I know I should say something because she looks so sad. "I'm sorry" was all I can get out.

"Please stay and keep me company," she replies, eyes pleading. "It's nice to have you here."

How pleased I feel that she wants me there, sitting silently on the cement steps as she goes on with her chores. I'm needed.

My mother sees me as a dreamer, one who wants to know everything

47

and drives her to distraction many a time, all the while loving me. My grandmother knows me so well, just letting me sit quietly as my thoughts soar far away. My neighbor reminds me of the needs of my little community, here. She sees me as a comfort on her very sad day, which makes me feel worthwhile and that I belong.

Greenwood Center is full of good folks. Every house holds out its arms to each child wandering that narrow, tarred road. No one is ever turned away if help and support are needed. Neighbors help each other, each child belonging to everyone, it seems. And sometimes even a child—a dreamer, perhaps—can bring comfort.

*

Dreamers like me were so fortunate to grow up in that time, with those people. Were I not, I would not remember all this like a film strip passing before my eyes. I can still smell the waters lapping at my fishing rock as I sat there for hours. It's a smell of water-logged weeds at the shore and a tinge of something soothing.

We were a neighborhood of people who were there for each other and cared deeply for others. A simple life, a poor life, but we didn't realize we were lacking in material things because we knew nothing else. We rode on wings of imagination and took each storm in stride. I would like to think that somewhere there is such a place still where a little girl can sit and read, sit and fish, sit and think, and never be afraid to dream.

Visiting Neighbors

Another Saturday afternoon and I am anxious to walk down to my Uncle Roy's house, which is about a half hour away. The chores are done. Ma has been using the scrub board all morning with her Fels-Naptha soap. After she wrings the clothes, I help her hang them on the line. Our clothesline goes from tree to tree at the edge of the woods, and she has special forked poles to prop up the line, so we don't lose clothes in the dirt and dead leaves.

I have a special friend I visit every weekend, if I can. I think she's been around for quite a few years, because Ma has pictures of us kids that my friend took when we were quite small. Her name is Gladys Bailey, and she works all week in South Paris or Norway. On Friday night she comes up to Greenwood Center and stays with Uncle Roy. She's his companion. Gladys is very good to me and loves to have me visit.

Ma gives me permission, so I start out on my journey. Grampa Martin is sitting on the porch and yells, "Hi Sandra!" as I go by, and I wave back to him. I don't see Grace or Charlie Day, so they must be grocery shopping this afternoon. My Uncle Dwight's house is beautiful and stands like a mansion overlooking Twitchell Pond. I think it's one of the finest houses I've ever seen!

The Summer People have gone home, and the Pralls cottage is locked up for the winter. Soon I come to the ledge where the tarred road ends, and there is dirt the rest of the way. I don't mind, because when I walk my mind wanders, and I think about poems to write, or I look for birds in the trees. Soon there's the old mill that Great Grandfather Ransom Cole built and the bridge over the brook that leads to Uncle Roy's house.

He always has a smile on his face, and Gladys always hugs me and asks how my week has been. Sometimes she brings me a pin or some little doo-dad she's picked up at J.J. Newberry's in Norway.

My Uncle Roy's hand curved around a carving knife, and his left hand held a chunk of wood out of which would come a marvelous creation. I love to look in his living room, because everywhere there's a treasure he's carved. That Lincoln Memorial he copied from a picture. I don't know what kind of wood he uses but maybe it's pine, since there's a lot around here. I asked him one day about the huge toadstool carving on the wall; he said that's the Burma Road, which had to do with World War II. It is so beautiful that it's a shame he cannot sell some of his carvings. There is one I don't quite understand, but I think it's President Franklin Roosevelt fishing and a bear in front of him with his fish basket. Roosevelt looks like he has a fish in his hand, but, oh, the bear in back has taken the President's flask, has the cork in his left paw, and is drinking! There's something missing from the President's hand; I am not sure if there was a fish pole, oar, or what. But it's a mighty fine piece of carving. Maybe Uncle Roy was making a political statement, but I don't ask him because it would not be like him at all. Maybe he saw a cartoon and carved it. Who knows!! Gladys says he's like the wind, blowing here and there, and you never know where he is or what he's doing.

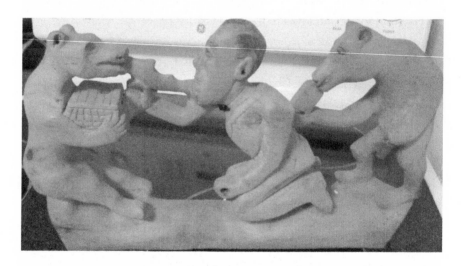

I always look forward to seeing Gladys, because she's so jolly and makes me laugh. I don't think I should ask her about the time Uncle Roy took her fishing for the first time. They stood side by side, and Uncle Roy was trying to show her how to cast the line. I guess she was doing pretty well, so he kind of tended to his own fish pole and let her have at it. But then she made a mighty sweep of the line and the hook caught Uncle Roy right in the nose. Well, he let out a yelp that could be heard in four counties. Gladys spun around and saw the problem. With uncle squirming around, she finally got the hook out of his nose. She took him home and put some antiseptic on it, and he told Dad he was never going fishing with her again. I heard that story when Dad was telling Ma and laughing so hard he almost fell out of his chair.

I know Gladys is tired, and she only has a day and a half before she catches a ride back to South Paris for another week of work. I stay about a half hour and start the walk back home.

I keep thinking as I walk what a nice friend she is to me. The only girls I see are at school since my cousins moved away. I don't use the path through the woods anymore, and it is very lonesome sometimes.

Twitchell Pond is looking a little darker and choppy. It won't be long before we might have a squall, which will take the rest of the leaves off the trees. I can't wait 'til next weekend when I can visit Gladys again.

My stomach has a warm feeling.

Beauty is a Beast

It's Sunday morning and just getting light outside. My little window lets in just enough light for reading before I hear Ma get up and light the fire in the wood stove. I reach for Nancy Drew; I love reading about her detective work. There she is, crouched over with spy glass on the cover. I've taken the nice paper cover off and put it in my little bureau drawer so it won't get torn or dirty. I already know what's going to happen on the next page, because I've read it so many times since last Christmas. I like the Bobbsey Twins books, too. My favorite is *The Bobbsey Twins on Blueberry Island.* I keep all my books and read them over and over.

My oldest brother, Tink, buys the Hardy Boys books. He lets me read each one as soon as he is finished. Frank and Joe, the Hardy boys, and their good friend, Chet, are always on the track of an evil person.

One of my favorite books came in the mail on my seventh birthday. I was so excited! It was a red book entitled *Uncle Arthur's Bedtime Stories* and inside was written that it was from Glenda Waterhouse. I asked Ma and Dad who she was, and they said she was Fred Waterhouse's daughter. I think they must be relatives. I don't know. Now there's a mystery that Nancy Drew can solve for me!

I hear Ma in the kitchen and can smell coffee, so it's time to put daydreaming and the books aside. Dad is up, too, as I can smell his cigarette smoke as he drinks Maxwell House coffee.

I hurry, because some Sundays Dad drives to Locke Mills to Ray Langway's filling station, located on the corner of the Greenwood Road and Route 26, for kerosene. The potato and egg look good that Ma hands me, and Dad says, if I hurry, I can ride with him. We have a little blue container with a spout and cap we keep in the kitchen corner to hold the kerosene for building the fire. Dad says the price has gone up to seven cents a gallon. I like riding up with him, as we talk about fishing and what he plans to do for hunting in the fall. Mr. Langway is always smiling; he and Dad get to talking while I just look around. I glance at the candy counter but mostly linger at the magazines, wishing I have a million dollars to buy all I see. Ray is always so friendly to all and treats me like I am a grown-up. After he and Dad exchange the local goings-on, off we go!

I like Sundays because Ma and Dad are home. Right now Ma says we do not have to go to church or Sunday school because regular school starts soon. As we drive into the yard, I see Uncle Harold picking corn out of his big garden next door. Since he and Aunt Vi moved back with Grammy and Grampa, he has done a lot of outside work. He cleared a path along the edge of the pasture woods, and his cow wanders up and down behind the new fence he built. I like the fence; I don't like that cow.

There's a spot behind Grampa's barn where we dig worms for fishing. Nothing is planted there, but it's a most, rich, dark soil that clings to the shovel and resists leaving until one bangs the shovel on a rock. Just a few shovels of dirt and you have enough worms for the day. Dad, coffee can in hand and shovel in the other, spends many a Friday evening digging his bait there for Saturday morning fishing.

There is one problem for me, now—I have to keep one eye out for the black-and-white cow while also looking for worms on the ground. I've never told Uncle Harold I don't care for cows. In fact, I am downright scared of the creatures. He named this beast of a cow Beauty for no reason, whatsoever. It has a big round face with huge brown eyes. When I look at it chewing cud, the eyes just kind of stare back at me. No sign of intelligence. She's a moving tank on four legs and doesn't even walk like most cows. She strolls or sashays from grass tuft to grass tuft, chewing her cud. She has a swagger to her.

Tonight, my brothers and I are invited to a corn roast. Uncle Harold says the pasture is damp enough, so he wants to burn the brush from clearing the cow's path and at the same time we'll have some fine corn to eat. That sounds like fun, as I love corn.

The stars are out, and a big old moon is shining down on the pasture. The bonfire is going, and my older brothers help pile on the brush. The smell is wonderful as the corn roasts, some of which Uncle Harold will take to Grammy and Grampa when done. I ask Uncle where the cow is, and he says she's down on the path and probably won't come near the fire.

I bite into the ear of corn, so juicy the kernels are swimming. My shirtsleeve catches the juice as it runs down my chin. This is heaven! Hums of satisfaction are coming from my brothers as well. Uncle has a great sense of humor, and we are all laughing and eating at the same time.

What's that I hear?

CRUMP CRUMP CRUMP

The noise of a walking, stalking cow coming in my direction. I eat faster, determined to devour the treat before Beauty comes near.

CRUMP CRUMP CRUMP

I hear twigs breaking. The light from the bonfire reflects one wild, bulging eye, and with a scream in my throat and ear of corn in hand, I run. Not caring if there's a shred of pride left in my body, I vault the wire fence using the fence pole for balance.

CRUMP CRUMP CRUMP

She's running right behind as I make the mad leap. She skids to a halt, and, if cows laugh, she's splitting her sides.

Uncle Harold tries to reassure me that Beauty is no menace, but I thank him and say my stomach is full. I don't tell him it's also fluttering with nerves.

Beauty looks at me, swaggers down her path, and stops to rub her back on an old tree. I swear, she then turns and winks at me.

I do not like cows.

Apples and Donuts

I always love it when my mother is laid off from work at the mill. I know it isn't easy because we need the money, but it seems so good to come home from school and find the house nice and warm. Today was extra special. As soon as we got near the door steps, I smelled something wonderful through the open kitchen door. The door wouldn't be open unless the kitchen was extra hot, so Ma must be baking.

Right in the middle of the kitchen table is a big pile of warm donuts that are draining on brown paper bags. The pot of grease is on the kitchen stove, and Ma warns us to step back as she brings a long fork with two more donuts from the stove to the table. Wiping her forehead, she exclaims, "Thank goodness that's the last of them! Go ahead and have one each. Take from the bottom of the pile or you'll burn your mouth."

Oh, they are so good! It's hard for Ma to do baking or cooking because the counter space is so small. She must have put them together on the table, rolled them out there, and then cut them. These are the best donuts in the whole world—what a treat! I'm surprised she's letting us have one with supper coming in an hour or so.

Rex and I still have to cut up firewood, but with the warm donut in our stomach the chore doesn't seem so hard today. The weather is so much nicer than in the middle of January when we are standing in snow.

Grandfather Martin has an apple tree just across the brook and now full of apples. I asked Ma a couple of days ago if they ever used the apples, because I am dying to take one and see how it tastes. Ma, for some reason, can read my mind and told me never to go near that apple tree unless Grampa says it's all right.

"Grampa is not the friendliest person in the world," I tell her. She scolds me that that was not nice to say.

Still, I want an apple. Today the sun is shining on that tree, the apples are glistening, and I am going to get one. He will never miss one apple off a tree.

The wood box is full and Ma has put the donuts away. This is the right time. Knowing better, I sneak across the brook and just hope that Grampa is not looking. Grammy would not say a word and probably smile, but he might shake his cane at me. I creep up to the tree and there, on a low branch, is one of the biggest apples and as red as can be. I reach for it and out of nowhere a bee stings my lower lip. It really hurts, and I run back to the house. Shall I tell Ma? I'm in really hot water. The apple is still on the tree, so I didn't take it but was trying. My lip is getting bigger and bigger.

Ma is peeling potatoes and looks at me. "Young lady, what have you been into?" she asks. I know I'm in for it. I tell her the whole story, and do you know what she says?

"I told you not to touch those apples, and God decided it was time to teach you a lesson." Whoa! If God decided, I guess the apple will stay on that limb.

Oh, no, Dad is home, and what's he going to say? Ma tells him in twenty-five words or less what happened. He grins. "Oh, is that what happened? I thought you had a fight with Joe Louis."

Ma says, "Is that all you have to say?"

"Not much more I can say," he retorts. "But tell you what, tomorrow we will go on a backroad and get you some apples." Shaking her head, Ma mutters that's like rewarding bad behavior, but we know she is anxious to have apples for pies and apple goodie.

I didn't know Ma had a direct line to God. I'm going to have to be very careful in the future.

The Orange

With a jump across the book that ran by our house, I follow the path across the field to my grandparents' farm. The path winds in and around old apple trees, some still bearing fruit; others left, I think, just because they have always been there since the beginning of time.

This summer day I enter the kitchen to silence. Usually, my Grandmother greets me with a smile and hastens me to the nearest chair. In retrospect, I think she was trying to confine the dirt from my feet to one area.

The linoleum shines from her many rag mop scrubbings and the wood box even has a cover to conceal barks and other residue from the firewood. My eyes focus on the miniature log cabin that burns some sort of pine scent. Where can Grammy be?

Suddenly I notice the bowl in the center of the table. A most beautiful bowl with designs cut into it that I cannot imagine. The sun shines in the sink window and makes a circular rainbow. Mesmerized by colors, I don't notice the contents right away. Bright, shiny, red apples that Grammy must have picked and polished with her apron lay scattered among plump oranges. So fascinated am I by the dancing colors of the bowl and the fruit within, I don't call out.

I want an orange. How I want an orange. One doesn't have oranges sitting around every day. Oranges are special and are only for the toe of your Christmas stocking. But Grammy will never know if one is missing.

I touch the dimpled surface and snatch my hand away as if it's on fire. Stealing is one of the worst things a person can do. Ma preaches over and over: One does not steal; one does not ask for things; one takes what is given to them in life and is satisfied.

But I really want an orange. I wait for Grandmother to appear, hoping against hope that she will offer one. In all honesty, the wait is less than five seconds, and I am out the door, orange secreted beneath shirt.

I run, heart pounding at the enormity of my deed. With legs already stinging from the switch Mother will use, I dash into the woods, jump on a rock with sweat pouring from my face, and sink in a tremble.

I roll the orange over and over in my hands, smelling the aroma as it grows warmer from touch. It's a crime to steal. I can't wait to eat this orange. Your Father will be ashamed. This orange smells so good. And so my conscience battles itself.

Between furtive looks to see if I've been followed, I peel the thick layer to reveal the juicy sections. My hands become sticky as I cram each piece into my mouth, unaware that juice is spurting over my chin and into the air, creating a beautiful, orange-smelling mist. In the same amount of time it took to steal the orange, it's gone. A pile of shredded peel lays by bare feet. I reach out and cover them all with old, dried pine needles.

Guilt locked its tentacles around my entire body, as I lean over the pond to splash away the last of the crime evidence. I have stolen from my wonderful Grandmother. The Grammy who offers me raisin-filled cookies from her jar, eggs from her chicken coop, and buttermilk from her churn. The taste in my mouth turns bitter.

I never steal again. It will be a long time before I can eat another orange. Grammy never told.

Getting Religion

Sunday morning once again and I hate getting out of bed. Ma's bustling about downstairs and the smell of coffee's coming up the stairway into the attic. I crawl reluctantly out and look at the dresses hanging there. I hate wearing dresses but must today and no getting around it. My mother's decided that Curt and I should go to church every Sunday morning.

I finally find a dress that looks good enough, at least to my eyes, and go downstairs to find Curt already eating Puffed Wheat cereal and Dad finishing up his coffee. Curt's wearing a brown shirt with blue pants held up with suspenders. Ma's made sure his face is clean and his hair combed just right.

"Why doesn't Rex go?" I ask Ma, who tells me to never mind and eat my breakfast. I don't think it's fair that Curt and I have to attend, but luckily it's not to the white church in Locke Mills. We're going to the hamlet of Rowe Hill and that's not so bad. Our church is at Colby and Stella Ring's farmhouse, and they are lovely people. We call them Grammy and Grampa because they are just that to our cousins next door.

I hear a car and know it's the minister, Roland Lord, who's coming to pick us up. Thrusting a Bible in my hands, Ma asks if I can remember the Bible verse given me last week. "Yes, I can," I promise. *Well, I sure hope I can.*

Curt and I get into the back seat, and Mr. Lord drives us up the road and over the hill to Grammy and Grampa's house. We are on our best behavior; after all, he's a minister, and I think most ministers are perfect and don't do anything really bad.

We get out and are greeted by Grampa Ring. How I love his bushy mustache! His eyes twinkle as though there were little stars in them when he smiles. We enter the kitchen and, of course, right away I smell their Sunday dinner cooking slowly in Grammy's oven. Oh, the smells! We go to the left into the living room where chairs are lined against the wall in three rows. A few of the neighbors come for the service as well. Grammy smiles at us from her perch on the piano bench in the corner.

Mr. Lord stands up in front of us in the middle of the living room and starts his sermon. He's a very nice man and speaks softly. Curt and I sit in the back row against the wall. Today I have a cold and hope I don't start coughing. I am listening to the sermon but can also see past Mr. Lord and down in the valley to Indian Pond. Wouldn't it be nice to be there right now, watching our fish, Egbert, on the bed swishing her tail in the bog water? Oh well, I had better pay attention. Suddenly I realize I'm chewing gum. Reaching into my pocket for the clean hanky, I slowly get it out of my mouth onto the hanky and back in my pocket. Ma gave me two hankies this morning and told me I probably would need them both. So far, so good.

Mr. Lord stops his sermon and announces a hymn we're going to sing. Grammy starts playing her piano, and we all sing "Bringing in the Sheaves." Curt doesn't know all the words and can't read big words yet, so he thinks it's "Bringing in the Sheep." No one seems to notice.

The song's done, and now Mr. Lord announces it's time for the children to recite the Bible verses Grammy handed out to us last Sunday. A couple of the neighborhood kids recite, and I know I have to wipe my nose. Oh, to get it done before my turn to recite. I grab the hanky from my pocket to wipe, and Curt starts snickering. I turn to quiet him, and he's looking at my nose. Oh no, the gum I snuck out of my mouth is now on my nose. Another hanky out of the pocket; the gum is quickly gone. Curt wants to snicker some more, but I give him what he calls the evil eye. For seven years old, he sometimes gets himself and me into an awful lot of trouble.

My name called, I stand, reciting the verse correctly. I silently thank God for that and the fact I have not coughed. Now, Mr. Lord is making some announcements, but I cannot really focus on what he is saying because Grammy's dinner is beginning to smell more delicious by the minute. I wonder if she has a roast in there. Probably they'll have corn on the cob as well. New potatoes. The whole menu is stuck in my head.

Suddenly, I realize people are leaving their seats, and it is time for us to get our next Bible verse from Grammy and climb into Mr. Lord's car for the ride back to Greenwood. Curt and I walk through the kitchen to leave, and he asks if I know what those good smells are. Shushing him, I tell him we will talk about it later.

Mr. Lord is very good about taking us to his church and bringing us home again. He drives right up to our door, and we thank him properly as he tells us he'll see us next week.

Walking into the kitchen, I give Ma back her Bible, and she asks us if we behaved ourselves—the same question every week. She then tells us to sit ourselves at the table as dinner is ready.

It isn't Grammy Ring's secret oven dinner, but the brown trout all crispy and fried and potatoes sure smell good. Curt and I agree that religion gives us an appetite.

Country Mouse Goes to the City

Ma is hanging the clothes on the line when I run up to tell her the news. One of the Summer People has invited me to return with her and her husband for a week to their home in Massachusetts!!! I'm so excited.

"Can I go, Ma?"

Carefully removing a clothespin from her mouth, she struggles with a towel she's trying to pin. I see a little worry in her eyes.

"Are you sure you want to go?"

Oh, am I sure?? It sounds like an adventure to me and I'm ready to go! I help her pin on the rest of the clothes, and she asks, "What are you going to do for clothes? You don't have too many good clothes, you know."

"Yes, I know, Ma."

She hmms through her teeth. "Well, if you really want to go, I think I will ask Winnie if maybe her niece will let you borrow some clothes."

Well, that was a couple weeks ago and here I am with a borrowed suitcase, borrowed clothes, and ready to see the big city. It's near Boston in a place called Watertown. I can't imagine what it will be like. This is the day, and Mr. and Mrs. J and I get into their beautiful car for the four-hour drive. Wow! This has to be the best car in the world. I sink into the seats and am ready for adventure.

I've never seen so many cars in my life—four lanes of them! Mr. J is driving at top speed; actually I'm a bit afraid as the cars look like they're coming right at me. Back home, I can take four long steps and cross the road, and maybe we have five cars go by in an hour. Well I'll hang on and believe that Mr. J knows what he is doing.

We pull up in front of a huge house that looks like a mansion. Maybe Ma had a right to a bit of worry. I step on to the rug and sink way in. Sink way in, I tell you. I have never been in a house like this in my entire life. I stay very quiet, not sure what to say or do. Mrs. J takes me up a long stairway and shows me my room. MY room, mind you. I have never had a room of my own, and can you imagine? I have my own bathroom right next to my own bedroom. Well, this is like out of a movie!

Mrs. J leaves me to unpack and I look around. There's a glass by the sink in the bathroom and a beautiful bathtub. I wonder if I can figure out the hot and cold water in the bathtub. I don't want to ask because then they will know I have never used one. I will figure it out somehow, and I guess the glass is for me to use.

I will be glad when Ann comes…she's their granddaughter and is flying in for the week, too, so that will be fun. Mr. J has to fly to Philadelphia on business, so Mrs. J and I will be alone for a couple of days.

The night has passed, and I was so tired I fell asleep right away! When I came downstairs, Mr. J had already left, and Mrs. J and I had breakfast. There was half a grapefruit on a little plate and a tiny spoon with a jagged edge sitting next to it. I guess there's a reason for it. I have never eaten grapefruit, so will remember to tell Curt about this and all the other new things. After we clean up from eating, Mrs. J tells me we are going to have a day in downtown Boston. The city boggles my mind. I have never seen traffic, fancy stores, elevators, and escalators before! Secretly, I'm wishing that Mrs. J likes the Red Sox and I can go to Fenway Park, but first we go to a salon. I come out of there with curls you wouldn't believe. Then off to Jordan Marsh for a little shopping and, finally, into Filene's Basement where Mrs. J buys a bathing suit for me.

There's a method to all this, I find the next day. Mrs. J has arranged for me to go to the ocean with some kids from next door. We go, we stay all day, I have no suntan lotion, and come home looking like a red lobster. Mrs. J is not pleased. The kids were not happy to be saddled with a country mouse, but I cannot tell her this. I am just glad that Ann is coming tomorrow!

Ann arrives, and Mrs. J has plans. I like Ann and first thing take a picture of them in front of the big white mansion. I think Mrs. J wants to instill a little culture in us—well, probably me—because we go to the Boston Museum of Fine Arts. I trail along, looking at all the art work and falling in love with Gainsborough's Blue Boy. I want something to show Curt, so ask Mrs. J if I can buy a postcard of it. She shows me where. I tuck it in my purse, and then she whisks us away to the Boston Gardens, or something like that, and takes a picture of me sitting by a little pond.

Well, I figure I have about enough culture for one day. Ann looks a little tired, but we are having fun, and I figure Ma will really like hearing about these adventures. Off to the Isabelle Stuart Gardens we then go for a mid-

afternoon string concert. I don't mind telling you that I am a little bored. It lasts just about long enough…just when I am wishing I was listening to my brother Tink play his guitar, the strings quit, and we go home.

Tonight Mr. J comes home from Philadelphia, and tomorrow we drive to Maine. I think I will be glad to see the little road with no white lines that I can jump across in four big steps. This has been fun but scary, too. I don't think I'll ever like living in a big city. But, oh, the adventures I can tell Ma and Curt. I bet Ma will never believe me when I tell her about soaking in that big tub and learning how to use everything. Country mice aren't dumb, you know!

*

Footnote for my New York friends. Mr. and Mrs. J were the parents of Tom Jacobs, who passed recently and had just been recognized with a beautiful plaque in Glens Falls for his contributions to the community and the Ski World in general. Tom skied in the 1952 Olympics, and his parents sent me a Christmas card with his picture on it. Unfortunately, during my seven moves, I lost the card. I met Tom by accident when I first moved here. My husband and I were shopping for a bike for me and went into the Inside Edge. I saw a man who looked so much like Mr. J that I told my husband the resemblance was uncanny. My husband went over and told the man—yes, it was Tom, Mr. J's son. He was elated to know that I was one of the "Martin" kids who lived across the road from his parents' cottage. My oldest brother and Tom were friends every summer he came to Maine. I hope they both are talking over old times now.

High Finances

Grammy Martin is my best customer when I come up with another money-making scheme. She smiles, reaches for her little snap purse, and digs out the coins for whatever new product I am peddling at the time.

Where to start? Ma and Dad have friends who have a son quite a few years older and who likes comic books. When he's through, he stacks them in a pile, and Ma and Dad are given them to bring home for us. There are all those little ads on the back cover and on a page inside that tell of wonderful prizes one can win if X amount of product is sold.

One product is very attractive to me because of its name. Rosebud Salve. "Now who can resist buying something as wonderful as that even sounds?" I ask Ma.

"Well, if you want to try it," she replies, sighing patiently, "you can, but don't you order more than five tins." I think she was mentally tallying up how many neighbors I could pester to buy one and then added a couple on for herself.

Oh, the day that Johnny Howe, our mailman, puts my order in our mailbox, I'm in heaven. I turn the cap on the tin and the smell of roses just fills the air. BUT, it not only smells wonderful, it has a list of wonderful uses as well...I am sure it has to be like Cloverine Salve but smells like roses!!

I take the box of tins and saunter over the path in the field to Grammy's so I can get her ideas on the salve. Ma won't be home from the mill for a while, and Gram will tell me the truth. I take the pretty little tin out and explain it all to Gram.

"Well, my goodness," she says, smoothing her apron down. "I never smelled anything as good as that, except my own roses." She pokes at her glasses, sits down in the rocking chair on the porch, and reads the list of all the wonderful things this salve can cure or at least help. "I am thinking, Sandra, I should have two of these. I can use one now and have one on hand."

Well, that was easy.

"Why don't you go down and see Grace?" Gram says. "I bet she'll take

66

at least one." At this point, I am getting really excited. Nine-year-old sales people get excited at a big sale right off the bat.

Grace is watering her flowers in the little nook below her house and puts her hands over her eyes to shield from the sun.

"What have you got there, Sandra?"

Well, let me tell you. I go through the same spiel, let her smell the salve, and I'll be darn but she takes my hand and into her house we go. Out comes her black purse with the big snap on top, and she drops enough change for another two tins in my hand. I have sold four out of five of the tins! Ma will be some surprised, for sure.

Making sure I thank her, I head home, peel potatoes, and get everything in order for Ma to come home.

Supper on the table; Dad with his coffee, and Ma with her tea. Timing is everything. I give Ma the big news, and she is some tickled. She smells the tin of salve, goes to the cupboard, and digs out the change for the last tin.

"What's this?" Dad asks, taking another sip. "Maybe I'd like a tin of that salve too. You never know when I might need something to put on my hands. They get mighty dry and sometimes a fish hook snags a finger."

Ma tells him he has better things to do than walk around smelling like a rose bush. I know Dad's kidding because he's tapping his foot, the way he always does when pulling my leg.

Now I can send the money to the company and keep the rest for myself or select a prize. I decide to keep the money and order a guitar from the Sears Roebuck catalog that Gram gave us.

"You don't want that," Ma warns. "That's a toy guitar and not like your brother's guitar. You won't be able to play it." Nothing she says convinces me otherwise, so she makes out the order and away it goes the next day.

Each day I watch for Johnny Howe and wait for my guitar. When it arrives, I realized to my horror that Ma is right. What was I thinking? Ma's always right. The "guitar" is maybe a foot and a half long and the strings are plastic, it's plastic all over, and, oh, there's all my Rosebud salve profit sunk in that thing. Instead of I told you so, Ma suggests hanging it on the attic wall for a decoration. That's what I do…and I think she knows it will remind me to listen to her next time I want to order something sight unseen!

Oh, the way I have earned money through the years. Pitching and treading hay for Uncle Harold, turning the grindstone for my Uncle Louie, mowing Gram's lawn (but I was not allowed to take the dime she offered), picking potato bugs off Grampa's potato plants—and that field of potatoes was BIG—peddling the *Grit*, selling Cloverine salve and Rosebud Salve. I stopped short of selling greeting cards. Ma said enough was enough.

I think she and the neighbors had a secret party the day I started working elsewhere. All but Grammy Martin...she would buy something right this day if I were to go see her with a tin of anything.

I know my Gram.

Traipsing Behind

My mother says I am just like my father. Once in a while she'll say, "You're your father's daughter, that's for sure!" Usually it's when I get in trouble or my sense of humor leads me astray, I should say. She says I'm always "traipsing behind" him and I guess that's true. Sometimes we both get in trouble together.

I think sometimes Dad woke up one morning, realized he had four kids, and didn't know what to do with them. He seems befuddled what to do, so he takes to the outdoors. If one of us wants to join him in what he's doing, well, that's just fine with him.

I can barely remember Ma being off somewhere one day, and Dad had to go to town for kerosene. I was about four years old, and he couldn't leave me alone, so I sat in the front seat looking out pretty proudly as we motored up the little road. All went well until we were back in the door yard, and Dad went to open the door for me…well, you know I thought I was a pretty big person and could open it myself. Somewhere our signals got crossed, and Dad shut the door on my little finger. Well I let out a wail that would put coyotes to shame. Dad had no clue what to do, so he got back in the car. We rode up and down the road to Locke Mills forever, and he kept pointing out ducks and birds and people's houses until I stopped crying. He finally told Ma that night, and she rushed over, looked over my fingers, and exclaimed, "Beryl Martin, that girl will have a crooked finger the rest of her life!"

Well, now I am twelve and Ma was right about that. The finger is crooked but not so you'd notice it unless you point it out, and I'm not about to do that.

One Halloween day Dad asks me to go trout fishing with him on Twitchell Pond. I don't fish but keep Dad company as he runs the little motor on Uncle Louie's boat at a really slow speed. His fish line dangles out, and he is hoping for a brown trout. We go to the back side of the pond where he points out to me Nick's Point, Johnny Howe's camp, and Eichel's camp. It's strange to see the camps up really close when you are used to seeing them from our dooryard on the other side of the pond.

It's peaceful and quiet on the pond. As I sit in front of the boat, I start thinking about how strange it is that I'm the only girl in the whole of Greenwood Center. Since my cousins moved, there have been two girls— but they come and go. Eugenia came for one school year to live with her Aunt Grace and Uncle Charlie. It was so good to have another girl here and we sometimes played ball, passing it between us on their front lawn. One day it rolled in Grace's flower bed, and she was not amused. We were banished from ball tossing the rest of the day! Then Eugenia left. I was alone again! Then another girl named Peggy came to live for a while in the house where my Uncle Elmer had lived. Too soon she too moved. So here I am on this Saturday afternoon, the October sun beating down on the only girl in the Center, afloat in the middle of Twitchell Pond with her Dad.

"Muff? Did you hear what I said?" Well that brings me out of my daydreaming right away. "What do you like best about Rowe's Ledge?"

Well, Dad knows what I always point out! "Pie Rock," I answer. There's this piece of rock on the left of the actual ledge that's shaped just like a piece of pie and I have always called it that.

"How'd you like to go up there?" I can't believe Dad just said that.

Before I can catch my breath, he heads the boat towards Brooks' Beach and we drift in to rest on the sand. "Are we really going up there?" I ask, not quite believing that Dad and I can actually go that far up—it looks really far up.

Dad grins, but says nothing as he secures Uncle Louie's boat to a tree bent over the water. He leads the way, and I follow. The first part is not looking too bad…really kind of flat and I am disappointed. But, before long, the flatness turns to slightly uphill and soon it feels like my feet are higher than my head. Dad hikes ahead, holding back some of the alder bushes so they won't whip me in the face. We climb and climb. What a feeling as the ledge hawks begin screaming at we intruders nearing their nests. Finally he looks back and stops. "Well, here we are."

I'm truly disappointed. "Pie Rock" is not a magical place but a scraggily little pine tree growing out of a giant crack in the rock, some moss here and there, and twigs. I think Dad senses my disappointment, because he then adds quietly, "Look over the pond."

I turn around, and, oh, what a beautiful sight. We are standing on Pie

71

Rock, looking down on the world. It feels like we're at the very top of the world, and way down there is the pond. Our little house looks like a speck in the woods. Grammy and Grampa's farm stands out because the pasture and fields are cleared around it. There are the summer homes on the shore of the pond. It's a beautiful sight to behold. It's like I can see forever, and, yes, that little brown speck is indeed Wagner's camp on the far side of the pond. It's magic after all!!

We sit down for a while to catch our breath. I notice pitch on my pants and shirt and dirt on my arms. Ma will not be too thrilled with that.

"We got to be heading back, Muff." Dad's voice lifts me out of the little wonder world I've entered. So down the mountain we scramble. I and my tired legs call it a mountain; Dad calls it a slope. It's probably a slope to him, since he hunts on Overset, Spruce, Pine, and many other mountains.

I climb into the boat while Dad loosens the rope, and soon we are back on the pond. "Think the trout have gone to bed, so we might as well head home, Muff."

We head across the pond directly home. Ma takes a long look at me. "I never knew Twitchell Pond is so dirty!" she says. I figure I will let Dad tell her about our hike.

Well, I have to say that I've learned a lot from Dad, even though some of it might not be the most useful. He once told me if I caught perch off my rock, I would have to clean them. One day, I come home with a stringer full, and he finds a flat rock and nods. "Go to it, Muff."

I like catching fish but am not too sure about cleaning them. He shows me how to clean the first one, and after that gives me his knife and leaves me to do the rest. The first one is quite a test, but after a while it comes natural and I finish cleaning the perch.

Ma tells me that night it's a nice mess of fish to have for supper. Dad clears his throat to make sure he's heard. "I think she will make a pretty good Maine guide someday."

Giving Dad "the look," Ma informs him he has three sons he can work on for that. Her daughter is not going to be herding men through the woods just because she's traipsing behind him all the time.

Dad grins and taps his foot, takes a sip of coffee, and Ma knows he's got her again.

Bees, Backroads, and Bullets

Sometimes being the only girl in a house full of kids is hard. Ma says I'll never be a girl but a tomboy all my life. I'm twelve and thinking she may be right. I love being outside in the rough and tumble. There's one thing though I do not like—hunting. Lord knows, with six people in this little house and food costing so much, we can use all the meat that's hunted. Just don't ask me to be a part of it. Dad has been hinting that a good age to get used to handling a gun is around twelve, and I think he has glanced at me a couple times, thinking just that. Well, let me tell you, I do not want any part of a gun.

But Dad's insisting that maybe, just maybe, I could become a good hunter. Since we don't talk back to our parents, I just keep quiet and hope he forgets about it. No way.

This Saturday morning, he has taken the .22 off the gun rack and asks me to come outside in the chilly October air. He wants to show me how to hold the gun.

OK, I can do that.

He puts the gun in my arms and shows me the correct way to point it; when not in use, train the barrel at the ground. Then he puts a bullet in it and tells me to aim and pull the trigger.

"No, Dad, I just don't want to do that," I protest.

"Just once," he urges. "Aim at that birch tree."

Oh, Lord, help me. I don't like the sound of a gun, but I will try for his sake. Putting the rifle to my shoulder, I squint one eye, look through what he just pointed out, and squeeze the trigger.

Dad lets out a whoop you would not believe. I've hit the tree! *Well, who couldn't hit something that big a few feet away,* I think. Handing him back the rifle, I tell him that maybe another day, I will try again. I don't think so.

Maybe I can help in some of his other hobbies. Believe me, Dad has a few.

He loves to line honey bees. It's quite an art, actually. He sets up some pans. I don't know then exactly what he does, but the bees come, get his offerings, and off they fly. He times them and watches which direction they fly.

Now my Dad should have been a frontiersman, because he puts his hands right in the middle of the bees. This morning I stood a foot away, and he motioned me to come over. Taking my hand, he put it right square in the middle of the bees.

"See?" he says, reassuringly. "They won't hurt you if you don't crush them." Well, crushing is the last thing on my mind, I can tell you.

I know that after the first frost, Dad will have everything timed right out and know exactly where the bee honey is; then, we'll go and dip some. This year, he's thinking it's up on the Ames Road, just another one of those one-lane dirt backroads around Greenwood that lead to some place remote or nowhere at all. Backroads are meeting points for hunting parties and checkpoints when mapping out an expedition into the woods. They are so much fun to ride on. The car kicks up dirt and, if Dad drives slow enough, we can see different birds on tree branches even. I'm always on the lookout for a coon or hedgehog darting out to cross the backroad. Grass and weeds flourish between the ruts, and Dad keeps an eye out for big rocks that would tear off the oil pan.

The nights are getting colder, and every morning the grass is crisp with white. I know the honey is ready. Dad is ready. I love to get the honeycomb. Ma agrees I can go this year but adds if I get stung, it's my own fault for wanting to follow my father around. He brings a friend, and off we start for the Ames Road.

Armed with flashlights, we leave the car, walk a short distance, and sure enough! Dad shines a light up the tree, and there's a big old bunch of honeycomb and honey just dripping almost. I'm getting chilly, as I really don't have a good warm winter coat, but the excitement is keeping me warm enough. Dad makes me stay in the car so I have no idea what's happening. He and his friend have two pails, and they dip honey and some comb and leave a lot at the site. Putting the pails on the floor in the back seat, Dad tells me it was worth the time he put into lining them, and it would sure taste good.

We drive home and into the driveway. As I start to get out, something crawls under my sock. Oh, no! A sharp sting—I didn't get away free. Ma will have a fit, probably.

Dad and his friend tell Ma about the honey and show her. She's excited, as she likes it in tea and uses it in cooking, too. Suddenly, she looks at me and asks if I'm ok. I have to tell her I have one sting. Ordering me to sit down, she sighs, goes to the cupboard, and takes down the box of baking soda. Pretty soon, she swirls a bit of water into it, makes a paste, and swabs it on the sting. I'm glad Ma knows so much about medicine and pain killers!

I don't like bullets and guns, but I sure do like night adventures with Dad. As for those backroads...I sure wish there were more of them!

LONG AGO
Grammar School Days

First Day

The day has come at last. Whether we want to or not, we have to leave summer behind. My favorite books are piled on one end of my bureau, and there they'll stay until this afternoon. Today I have to pull on a dress and new shoes and get ready for the first day of school.

Ma and Dad left for work around six-thirty. We help myself to the fried eggs and potatoes in the pan, while Curt spoons wheat puffs into his mouth. The dishes are set aside to soak until we return from school.

It's Tink's job to make sure that Curt and I are clean and respectable for the school community. Curt stands in front of the black iron sink, where Tink has taken some hot water from the kettle and cooled it down with brook water. He begins to scrub Curt's neck and ears, and now Curt is doing some sort of a dance and protesting. Tink keeps a good grip on him, and I can see the cloth scrubbing around his ears. Curt whines that Tink is trying to kill him. Tink keeps scrubbing, insisting that Curt isn't going to school carrying summer dirt with him.

Now it's my turn to be inspected. He turns me round and round until I am almost dizzy, and then he takes a comb to my hair. I think it looks fine, but he wants to make sure everything is "all evened out." Rex takes care of himself…I am not sure what would happen if Tink tried to inspect him.

One by one, we go to the kitchen cupboard counter and take a brown bag. I saw Ma making them up last night before we went to bed. I know we'll have a biscuit with peanut butter, jelly, and a cookie. Perhaps there'll be a couple of peanut butter and crackers in there, too. You never know until you open it on the school grounds at noon.

Tink will ride on the bus as far as Locke Mills and then he'll catch a ride to the high school in Bethel. Right now, we're rushing down the driveway because our bus has gone by to pick up Henry Bowers, who lives down below us. As soon as the bus comes back, we need to be right out there and waiting. Our bus driver is "Cass" Howe.

The bus stops. I've seen pictures of big yellow buses, but ours is actually a van. There's a plank on each side of the van where we sit. My knees almost touch the knees of the one sitting across from me. Cass smokes cigars, and I hate the smell of them but am not going to say anything because he looks a little gruff. Maybe he hates mornings as much as the rest of us.

All the four miles past the ponds, I keep thinking about school. I am ten years old and going into the sixth grade, which is in the "big" room where Mrs. Olive Lurvey teaches. We have three rooms in school—the primary, middle, and big rooms. The kids in the big room have always looked so big to me, and now I have a butterfly chorus in my stomach. I have had for teachers Mrs. McAllister, Mrs. Ring, and Mrs. Gunther. I heard that Mrs. Olive Lurvey is a wonderful teacher but also very strict. There are tales of her using a strap on some of the big boys' hands when they get out of line. I thought about that this summer, and I do not intend to misbehave. I have a sense of humor that Ma says will put me in a jail cell some time if I don't straighten out. I don't think I'll land in jail, hopefully, but I must admit that Mrs. Gunther did grab me by the hair last year because something struck me funny and I couldn't stop laughing. She reacted to my smart remark by actually pulling me out of my seat by my hair!! It hurts me to even think of it now. You can bet after that I had my mouth closed when I was sitting near her!!!

Actually, I am no stranger to the new teacher. Mrs. Lurvey came into the middle room to teach writing last year. I sat in the front seat of the row, complete with ink bottle in the little hole and that long, dreaded, pointed, straight pen that had to be dipped every five seconds in ink. I hated that day. I got so tired of making little ovals on a line, and she kept walking up and down the aisle, always pointing out to me that my ovals were not even. Well, of course they weren't even. I couldn't see what ovals and letters had to do with each other; besides that ink dripped everywhere. My writing class always ended the same way—she standing in front of me, looking at my ink-covered hands and wrists, and, with a flourish, pointing in the direction of the hall fountain and basin, all the while shaking her head.

Well, Cass has delivered us to the little schoolhouse. We climb out and walk up the sidewalk. Most of the town kids are here already. We're all dressed for warmth, not for fashion. We're equally working class. Our parents work in the mill across the road from the school; everyone buys groceries "on the cuff" at the local stores and stops by on payday to give what they can toward their bill. No family stands out as "better off" than others; no kid wears designer jeans and fancy clothes.

The smell of the oiled floors hits us as we walk inside. I almost forget to hang my sweater in the big room alcove. To the right is where the middle room kids leave their lunch bags and sweaters; the little room has the whole middle hallway with coat hooks and places to leave lunches. The boys' bathroom is at the end of the hallway on the right, but we girls have to go to the end of the hallway, through a shed, and through another door to our bathroom. It's located more conveniently for the little room kids, though.

Curt goes into the little room while Rex and I look at each other and walk into the big room, choosing desks on the right where the sixth graders sit. We are in the same grade, because Mrs. McAllister got tired of my being bored in sub-primary reading Dick, Jane, and Spot. I had been reading some of Dad's detective stories at home when he was not around. I didn't know all the words in the magazines, but what I did know was enough to make it exciting. Mrs. McAllister first had me trying different arithmetic problems to stave off boredom and to keep my mind off the paper cutter at the rear of the room, which seemed to attract me for some reason. It didn't help. I just stared at the alphabet strung across the top of the blackboard and studied George Washington's portrait by Gilbert Stuart day after day. She finally put me in first grade that same year; when I went back to school the second year, she put me in the second grade with Rex. I wonder if Rex is nervous, but he looks pretty brave. There is only one other girl, Kay, in my class. We always sit near each other and sometimes get in trouble. I'll try not to this year, I promise.

Mrs. Lurvey has just entered the room. She's ready to teach, and the first thing I notice are her long, very red fingernails. I can't see it, but I know lurking somewhere in the shadows must be that strap I've heard so much about. I have a feeling this is going to be a very productive year but a very loooong one.

First Week

Boy, it's been a long week. Even though it's only three days, as we started the Wednesday after Labor Day, it seems like it's lasted forever. I'm just not used to sitting at a desk for hour after hour. However, I do like Friday mornings as this is our day for assembly. All the grades from Primary through the fifth grade file into our room, right after the Pledge of Allegiance. Mrs. Lurvey discusses a few items she has marked down through the week and then the fun begins.

Today the music teacher's here. She travels from school to school, bringing her talent with her. I think this must be a real challenge as the piano is old and some of the keys are chipped. The *American Song Book* is handed to us, and we are allowed to raise our hand and ask for a special song to sing. I don't raise my hand as I like them all. I probably wouldn't anyway since I am not used to Mrs. Lurvey, yet. If I dared, I would request "My Bonnie Lies Over the Ocean" because that's a pretty song, but I will go along with "Old Black Joe" and "Swanee River."

One of the bigger boys always raises his hands and requests "Tavern in the Town." I bet we sound like a bunch of people in a tavern, because the bigger boys not only really sing loud but substitute their own words in the chorus. They hold their books in front of their faces, and when it comes to "do not let our parting grieve thee," well you just know what word they substitute. I look at Mrs. Lurvey to see if she has heard them. Her face looks the same, so I guess she has heard it all and nothing much bothers her as long as everyone is singing.

Sometimes the boys and girls sing separately. The girls sing the part that says, "Rueben, Rueben I've been thinking," and we go through the chorus; then the boys sing back "Rachael, Rachael, I've been thinking," and of course, they sing as loud as they can to make as much noise as possible. The room grows warmer with each rendition; barn smells from the farm boys' overalls mingle with the odor of wet sneakers.

All this time, the music teacher has her back to us and only responds to requests by turning the pages of the song book. I wonder if she enjoys coming to our school, as she says very little and sometimes seems to mouth a prayer. I notice that when the singing is done, she quickly sweeps her songbook into a black bag, gives every teacher a brief smile, and out the door she goes. She's probably thanking God she made it through another session with us.

This is the first time I have been at assembly and stayed here in the big room when it was over. I look at the lower grades, remembering how nervous I used to be when I had to march in here! Last year it seemed so simple. I was a Junior Crossing Guard and wore a white band across my shoulder that came to hook on the white band around my waist. I got out a little earlier at the closing of school to help the town kids cross the busy Route 26, which runs by the school. Last year when school came to a close, we walked single file to Terrill's store along Route 26, each of us getting a Dixie cup with a movie star's picture in the cover to celebrate. I think those days are gone forever.

So here I am in the big room, wishing I were sitting on a rock at Twitchell Pond with a fish pole. But I am not. Looking at Mrs. Lurvey, I know she is not the kind of teacher who forgets how bad and messy I was at penmanship last year. As I said, it may be a very loooong year.

Noon Hour

The clock on the side wall says it's almost noon. That's good because the seat is getting hard, my stomach is growling, and I am ready for some fresh air. Mrs. Lurvey opens the windows at the back of the room, but very little air comes through.

Standing in front, Mrs. Lurvey tells us we are dismissed and to walk single file out of the room. My friend, Kay, goes home for lunch, so I take my brown bag off the shelf and head to the side hill with other kids. This is the first time I've ever eaten lunch there, as this is reserved for kids in the big room. There are no laws written as such, but we just know that's the way it is. I take out a biscuit with the peanut butter and jelly—anything to fill the hole, as Ma says. Before long, the village dog named Sandy comes to us, wagging his tail. I don't know whom he belongs to, but every day we sit outside he makes the rounds and we all give him something to eat. He's such a nice dog, and I am sure he has a good home, but if he has, why does he always look hungry? One day, I leaned close and swore I heard his stomach growl. I worry about such things. Ma has called me a "worry-wart" ever since I can remember.

There are swings on top of the hill for the sixth, seventh, and eighth graders. I haven't used them as they look big and go pretty high. At recess, I have always gone to the other side of the building, which has a "teeter board" and swings for the younger kids. It feel strange to be here. I guess all we have are the swings and a small, flat place where we can play ball.

Now that I am in the big room, we are allowed to go to the two stores in town at noon, but we must tell the teacher. We have been told to walk down the sidewalk, stay on the left, then on to the main street on the sidewalk. We must never take the shortcut across the little brook to Main Street. Mrs. Lister has the post office in her home, and doesn't like us crossing past the post office. She complains to the school when we do; however, if any of the kids are late, isn't it better to run through the shortcut than to go all the way around? Doesn't make sense to me, but I don't want to get in trouble with Mrs. Lurvey.

Today I have a nickel, and Lenona says she'll walk with me to the store. Should we go to Mr. Vallee's store? We walk down the main street, lined

with pretty houses. As always, I look at them and wonder how beautiful they must be inside. Mrs. Marshall at the top of the hill has a big white house that I always admire.

Now, we'll have to cross Route 26 and watch out for the Merrill Transport trucks speeding through town. She grabs my hand, and we run across and up the long cement stairs. To the left are boxes of penny candies. I want to buy enough to share with Kay when she comes back from lunch, but there are so many to choose from. I'll get some of the two-for-a-penny kind. There are little squares called Kix that last forever. I could get a roll of Necco wafers, but that will take my whole nickel. I finally choose the wax bottles with the liquid inside because we can chew the wax after we drink the juice. Mr. Vallee is a very nice man and smiles. He knows Ma and Dad because they get their groceries there. Maybe next time, I will just stay on the sidewalk and go straight up the hill to Cass Howe's store. That way, I won't be scared out of my wits when crossing the street.

I hear the bell ringing, and, sure enough, there's Mrs. Lurvey, bell in hand, swinging it wildly on the little front porch. We run the last few steps into the school, and I plop in the seat. I slip Kay a couple pieces of candy while the teacher is arranging her afternoon schedule.

I'm saving my candy until I get home this afternoon. I don't dare eat it in school but wish I could have had time to at least eat one piece before getting back into this hard seat. I cram the little brown bag into my desk alongside the other books and papers. I don't have a neat desk but know where everything is. Mrs. Gunther is coming in from the middle room to teach hygiene. That's another boring subject but I will try to get through it. I'm very careful to behave when she's around; as I've said, last year she grabbed my hair, and then I went right up straight with her doing the pulling.

Soon we will be getting on the bus again and winding our way down by the four ponds to home. I will start the fire, if Roland isn't home, and peel the potatoes. Rex will go out back and use the bucksaw to get enough wood to keep the fire going for another day. The best part is that it isn't cold, yet, and we don't have to wade in snow to do our chores.

By the time Ma and Dad come from the mill, everything will be ready except for Ma getting out the frying pan and plopping whatever she has in it to go with the potatoes.

I have found the best part of school is making friends and the noon hour. I don't think I'll tell Ma that, though.

The Meal

It's getting colder now and so hard to get out of bed in the morning! Seeing the frost on the nails in the attic roof, I scurry to get dressed and down the stairs to the wood stove. It takes longer to dress now because Ma insists that, come November and snow, I have to wear long, brown, cotton stockings. I hate them. They are fine outside in the cold but seem to suck into my skin the rest of the day at my desk. Rex says I look like a long-legged brown wren. Ha! Well, he says a lot of things. Sometimes I pay attention to his remarks, and we get fighting. That's when Ma steps in and says her Young Lady speech to me: "You, young lady, are going to be the death of me yet!"

Yup, that's what she usually says.

I am putting that out of my mind because today is Friday, and Fridays are a special day come November. All the "bus kids" bring a bowl and spoon to school because we'll have a hot lunch today. We never know what it's going to be, but anything warm this time of year tastes wonderful! We have our bowls and spoons in a bag and are ready for today's treat!!

There are ladies in Locke Mills village who take turns preparing a huge kettle of warm soup or whatever they'd like for us. It is almost as much fun trying to guess what we are going to be eating as the meal itself!

All the way to school on Cass's bus this morning, I am thinking that November is cold, but it is a special month, too. The leaves were pretty in October, but nothing really exciting happened. The kids in town go trick or treating on Halloween, but Ma says that's like begging for food and won't let us do it. Last month, though, Curt asked if he could go out, and I was surprised when Ma said he could—but only if I went with him and only to two houses. We went to Gram Martin's, and she gave us both one of her raisin-filled cookies. I did not say trick or treat but stood back while Curt knocked and recited it to Gram. How she smiled!

"You wait just a minute," she said, soon returning with the two big cookies. We went on to Grace and Charlie Day's house. Grace laughed, too, when Curt announced he was there to trick or treat. She gave us each a big red apple. Curt had a lot of fun and told Ma all about his adventures when we got home. He showed her the apple but had already eaten the cookie!

Here we are now at school...when you get thinking, it doesn't take long to cover four miles. It's kind of scary if the road is slippery, because there are not many posts on the road to keep us from sliding into one of the ponds. Cass is a good driver, though, and takes it pretty slow on the curves.

It's been a long morning. The singing and assembly were fun, but after that were the dreaded classes of arithmetic and writing. I do not like either but try to do the exercises and do them neatly. I notice neatness counts for a lot with Mrs. Lurvey.

She announces it's time for the boys to go to Mrs. Noyes' house on the Knoll to get a kettle of soup for our noon meal. By the time they return, it will be just twelve o'clock. She chooses Rex and three other boys to take the sled for the kettle. They'll take turns hauling the sled while the other three balance and make sure it is secure. Meanwhile, we'll take out our spoons and bowls and wait.

Noon has come and gone; the town kids have left for home to get their lunch. Mrs. Lurvey keeps going to the window and then back to her desk. I admit I'm getting hungry and wish the boys would hurry. I wonder if one of them had a hair-brained idea to stop at a store for candy? No, they wouldn't dare do that knowing Mrs. Lurvey is waiting as are all of us! She goes to the window, again, and this time her hand flies up to her mouth. I wonder what she sees but glue myself to the seat.

The door opens, and there are the boys! Where's the soup? I can't smell anything. Mrs. Lurvey is ushering them back out in the hallway and closing the door. Oh, no, what's happened? Now the boys file in and take their seats. Mrs. Lurvey stands in front and tells us that at the top of the hill, by Cass Howe's store, *somehow* (she says this word very strongly) the sled gained momentum and started down the hill very quickly. Before any of the boys could stop it slipping and sliding, the kettle came loose from the sled, overturned, and our dinner spilled out onto the snow-covered sidewalk. The boys are not looking at her at all as she goes to her desk and begins opening drawers.

I cannot believe what I am seeing. Mrs. Lurvey has a stash of saltine crackers and a jar of peanut butter. She takes a knife out of another drawer and starts making us peanut butter and crackers. She makes two for each of us in the room. After we eat them, we can go to the hall fountain for a drink of water without asking permission, she says.

Well, so much for my dreams of a warm dinner making its way to my stomach. I look at Rex, who is staring off in space. Hmm, I hope I can get the real story of what happened when we get home. I doubt it because those four boys probably made a pact of secrecy after the spill.

All I can say is that Mrs. Lurvey sure knows what to do in an emergency, and, boy, am I glad! Peanut butter and crackers never tasted so good!!

The Note

The days are long now in mid-November. There's enough snow to make walking miserable from our door to the main road. Once the bus comes, we huddle together on the wooden benches and, with the little heat escaping from the front, manage to keep warm. It's not so bad. Most of us live in houses with wood stoves and heat escaping through cracks to the great outdoors, so any warmth is welcome on the way to school.

I hate getting bundled up to go to school. It feels like ten layers as I peel them off in the school hallway. Mrs. Lurvey is seated at her desk, and I can tell she's ready for the day's lessons in all three grades she teaches. Sometimes, if I get my work done, I listen to her teach the other two grades and learn a lot. I figure next year when I go into the seventh grade, I will already know some of the arithmetic, geography, and other subjects she writes on the blackboard.

I sit behind Kay, as I have done for many years, and we are best friends. But, aha, she is also Rex's girlfriend, I think, and has been for a few years now. I don't ask him because he will deny it. She has been writing a note for some time now, and I bet she is going to try pass it to Rex. Well, she knows how strict Mrs. Lurvey is about note passing, but maybe she can time it right.

Rex is passing by handing out papers for us to work on, and Kay slips him a note. I stare straight ahead, but oh no! Mrs. Lurvey has seen her. Now what will happen? I don't want them getting a strap on the hand. I think she has other ideas, because she's now in the corner by her desk, where she hangs her coat and then ties something around her waist. I don't dare stare, but she's calling Kay and Rex to the corner.

I cannot believe it! She has an apron on and has tied one of Rex's hands to one string and Kay's to the other. They are tied to her apron strings, and they have to follow her around as she teaches. How embarrassing is that! Kay seems to be taking it much better than my brother, who is staring down at his shoes and his face is red.

I am very busy, pencil to paper and finishing up arithmetic. I don't want Mrs. Lurvey thinking I have anything to do with the note passing. I have no idea how long it has been because I won't even look at the clock, but my stomach is growling. No one snickers as they follow her around…not even the big boys in the eighth grade. They know they would be the next to be tied or something worse. I hear her announce it's time for lunch, and the town kids are dismissed. Kay is untied and out the door she flies. She'll be back by one o'clock and act as though not a thing has happened. Rex has come out to get his brown bag to take in as we eat at our desks this time of year.

We'll all be so glad when we can go out in the schoolyard and sit in nice, green grass to eat our lunch…what a long time off that seems. Rex stopped coming out to eat about a week after school started. One day after school, I asked him where he was, and he said he ate inside at his desk. Why? One day he had gone in for something, Mrs. Lurvey was playing a record, and he asked her if that was Sammy Kaye. Looking surprised, she said it was and asked if he was one of the Martins that were so musical. Rex told her that yes, he was, and she asked if he would like to listen to some records at noon if she brought them from home. He jumped at the chance, and after that, 'til snow flew, he ate with Mrs. Lurvey while they listened to the big band sounds of Guy Lombardo and Sammy Kaye. He made me promise not to tell the other kids, and they never found out where he was.

So today, I reckon, it's a good thing there's snow on the ground and no promise of big band music. I don't think Rex could look her in the face after looking at her back all morning. It proves to me that Mrs. Lurvey has no favorites. If you're good, she's kind and thoughtful, but you have to obey her rules or else. It doesn't matter if you're musical and love the same music she does, she is the ruler of her classroom. I don't think Rex will forget that right away.

One thing's for sure—we won't be discussing today's happenings at home tonight. Some things are better left unsaid.

Do Men Teach School?

I'm now eleven years old and feel like I've been in school forever. This past summer was way too short, and my bare feet are back in stiff school shoes. My feet always hurt. Ma says my feet never stop growing, just like the rest of me.

Some things have changed, though. Hank Leach has bought the store at the head of the street, and he and his family live in the old Joe Cummings house about a mile and a half north of us. Barbara goes to school with us now, but she's in another room and I don't see her often.

We're now bringing our lunches in pails rather than bags. Ma found buckets in which peanut butter was sold. Oh, that peanut butter was awful, with oil swimming on top…but the pail made it all worthwhile!

We had a very strange start to the school year. Mrs. Lurvey is not teaching anymore in our school, so we arrived to find a very young lady teacher behind the desk. Now, I have to admit we do have some students who like to talk and perhaps not behave as well as they should sometimes. One day I looked up, and our teacher was seated at her desk, crying. I didn't know what to do, so we all kind of looked at each other and pretended we didn't see her.

Monday when we came to school, there was a tall man sitting at the teacher's desk. I have never seen a male teacher before! Do men teach school?? I never knew one to teach school, so my morning was completely confused.

He had a nice smile and said his name was Gail Webber. He wrote Mr. Webber on the board with a flourish. I guess he's going to be with us the rest of the year.

Well, this should be interesting. I wonder if he heard that a couple years ago, some boys set off black powder in the woods behind the school. That was something!! One boy was burned and didn't come to school for a while. The others weren't hurt, but it sure was talked about!! Maybe people think we are such horrible students that they had to search 'til they found a man they thought could handle us. I don't know, but I behaved last year and will this year, too.

My ear is aching again today. My left ear aches sometimes pretty bad.

Dad blows cigarette smoke in it at home and puts a piece of cotton in it after to keep it warm. It seems to help, and it's certainly better than his other idea to help me. My mother turned both thumbs down when Dad announced that some friends had another "cure" for my ear that originated back in the "old country." They used a teaspoon of urine in the ear and that cured all.

This constant earache makes some days at school very long. Ma has a friend who works with her at the mill, and that lady goes home every day at noon. She fills a hot water bottle full and sends it back to school with her son. Her name is Mrs. Corkum, and her son, Carl, gives me the hot water bottle. Mr. Webber does not mind that I put my head on it if he is teaching the other two classes, and it sure helps me get through the afternoon. I tell Carl to be sure and thank his mother for being so kind to me.

The school doctor, Dr. Boynton, looked in my ear and told me to come to my Grandfather's farm next door on Saturday as he comes every other weekend to check on him. He said to tell Ma and Dad that my tonsils should come out and something called adenoids. I told them; they said if I wanted to go, I could. Well, now, if any kid thinks that someone is going to be operating on them sooner or later, are they going to go see the doctor, even next door? Not me, I decided.

Today, however, is a special day as Mr. Webber has us studying something called bartering. He asked us each to bring something from home to barter with someone else. Maybe we have something we do not want that someone else would really want. I found a lined tablet that I had never written in. It turns out that Albert wants the tablet, and he has an autograph book. I think some of the pages are missing, but there are several pages left and I can have my friends sign it. My mother has one from her days at Woodstock High School, where she graduated in 1933, so I know that autograph books have been around for a while! Kay is the first to sign it, and then some others write in it. The boys are goofy and write silly things in it, but that's ok. I will have fun reading it when I get home.

Home! Oh, no, I've spent too much time daydreaming and someone says the bus has left. What am I going to do? I have to have the potatoes cooked, the coffee water hot, and the kitchen warm by the time Ma and Dad come home. I can't wait for the mill to blow its whistle and ride home with them to an empty, cold house. I run to the mill office that is just across the road, being careful not to run in front of the Merrill Transport trucks passing through. My Uncle Dwight works in the office, and maybe he will save my neck.

I'm afraid Ma and Dad will be angry, but I have no choice! I go in the office, and there are women sitting at desks. I see my Uncle Dwight, who gets right up and comes to me. He wears "dress clothes" to work every day. I secretly dream that someday I'll have a typewriter like he uses at his job.

I ask him if he will give me a ride home, and I never even think that he is working at his job and maybe his boss won't like it. He takes my hand and walks me to his car. I am eleven years old, but I feel like I am five right now. How could I miss the bus? I never have in my whole life! Uncle Dwight puts me in the car, and we drive down the Greenwood road, while he tells me not to worry and that he will get me home on time. He pulls into our driveway, and I thank him over and over. He looks at me, smiling, and says, "Anytime you need me, Sandra." He is so nice and handsome. I hope his boss won't be mad that he just walked out of the office.

Sometimes being eleven and having all these chores is a mighty heavy load, I swear.

Another Year, Another Teacher (Sigh)

Sometimes I don't think things will ever change. Every year seems the same, and nothing much happens. I turned twelve years old on my birthday in February. Ma and Dad's friends gave me a pair of green wool slacks and a pretty pullover top to match. Mr. Webber complimented me. Maybe he was as sick of looking at my old clothes as I was. I was really pleased that he wrote in my autograph book: "The youngest in age in the seventh grade but the oldest in the head." Yup, that's what he wrote. Made me feel special for a while.

One day this summer our neighbor, Grace, drove into the yard and brought a big box of clothes into the house. She explained to Ma that a summer resident had a daughter a little older than me who had outgrown the clothes—would she like them for me? Ma hesitated a little but then thanked her. I opened the box later and never saw so many colors in my life. Dresses of all kinds and skirts like the other girls wore. They all looked new to me. When I would get new shoes for school, I would look really nice. It made the new school year something to look forward to for a change!

But this is another Monday morning, and, as usual, I'm tired. Ma lets us stay up a little later on Sunday night as there are radio programs we really like. I like to hear when Henry Aldrich comes on, and his mother yells "Hen-r-r-ry!" It's sponsored by J-E-L-L-O, and I do love that stuff!! We sit in the kitchen chairs against the wall and look at the radio. I wonder if we think that's the only way we can hear it is by looking at it!! Jack Benny, Amos and Andy, Our Miss Brooks, The Great Gildersleeve…those are just some of the programs we really like and look forward to hearing. Dad tries to save the radio battery for the news and for the boxing matches he likes when Joe Louis fights, but he always says it's strong enough for us to hear those programs. That's something my Dad and I share; when Joe Louis fights, he lets me sit up with him and listen. We were so glad when he beat Billy Conn. Ma isn't too thrilled about it, but I think Dad likes company in the kitchen.

Mr. Webber is not teaching us this year. We have another male teacher, who is staying with Norwood and Dora Ford on Bird Hill. The first time I saw him, it was a little scary. We've been going to school for a couple weeks now, and I have yet to see Mr. Meserve smile. Never! He always wears a three-piece suit with a pocket watch and a gold chain that comes down in a loop. He walks around the room with his finger in the loop half the time. He has a gold tooth on each side of his bottom teeth. I noticed that right off and told Ma. She told me to look more at the books and spend less time looking at the teacher's teeth. I guess she has a point, but most subjects are boring as I had already heard them taught when I was in the sixth and seventh grades.

I don't know why, but Mr. Meserve has a favorite saying. Not a day goes by but he bellows, "You're not putting me in a knot hole and putting the plug in behind me!" The first time he said it, I jumped as I've never heard a teacher bellow before. I wonder what he was told about us. We're not a bunch of ruffians. Maybe he's simply warning us not to try anything.

I have to admit that I got in trouble the first week. Kay always sits in front of me, and he caught me talking to her...not once, but twice. So, he made me clean out my desk, sat me in the back seat of the sixth-grade section, and told me if I acted like a sixth grader then I should sit there. That didn't bother me much because right behind me were a few book shelves. When I got my work done, I just reached my hand around and grabbed a book and read. After a couple days, I think he knew what I was doing and back into the eighth-grade section I went.

I don't know why Mr. Meserve is so crabby. Maybe it's because he'is older than most teachers I have had before. Just once I wish he would smile but that doesn't look as though it might happen right away. This is going to be a very long school year.

Thank goodness for the Philco radio and Sunday evenings.

The Contest

There have rumblings around school this morning that there's a contest going on at the store at the top of the hill. Mr. Leach, known as Hank by the town folk, has a huge sign in his window. I didn't know whether to believe it or not but this noon got permission to go to the store and read it myself.

It says that anyone who pays on their bill has a vote for each dollar paid. I guess in a mill town like ours, most everyone picks up what they want and pays on Friday when they get their check. Sometimes there are people who get behind on paying, and, to tell the truth, that's easy to do. I think Mr. Leach would like to catch up on back bills, so he has a contest to elect the most popular girl in the town. I have no idea how he came up with that idea.

Two weeks have gone by, and I decide to climb the hill this noon to see how the contest is going and, honestly, kill some time away from school. Mr. Meserve is not the most pleasant teacher I have ever had, and I still haven't see him smile.

Oh, my goodness—there's my name on the big sign along with the name of my best friend, Kay Dorey. The prizes are a new bicycle and a Kodak camera. Well, I've never ridden a bike in my life but I like to take pictures.

Oh no—I take that back. I did ride a bike once.

I was walking on the "flat," and Elwin Cole came riding down the road and stopped to say hi. I told him I had never ridden a bike; he said I could ride his for just a short way. Well, I was some pleased and hopped right up on the seat and started pedaling. I kept going faster and faster. Elwin began running beside me, hollowing at me to slow down.

"How?" I yelled. By this time my riding was out of control, and I was well ahead of Elwin. I figured to keep upright I had to keep pedaling. It all came to an end when I ran into our mailbox. I thought maybe I would go over the handlebars but instead just tipped over and wasn't hurt—neither was the bike. Elwin finally caught up with me, gasping for breath. Without a word, he just grabbed his bike and rode quickly away in the direction of his house.

Well, he should have told me where the brake was. I told him I had never been on one in my life.

So now there is this splendid blue-and-white girl's bike sitting in the window alongside the Kodak camera. The bike is the first prize and the camera second. Ma and Dad shop at Vallee's down the street, so they won't be buying at the store. I want that camera, so I can take pictures of Keno, our husky, and my brothers.

The month is over and so is the contest. It's Sunday and Dad's going to Langway's filling station for kerosene in the little blue can. He asks if I want to ride along. I usually go and look at the candy and everything while they visit. This morning he stops the car and asks, "Are you going to go up to Leach's and see who won the contest?"

I run up and there in the big store window is my name; I won the bicycle. I race back to the car, and Dad is already waiting for me.

"I won, I won!" I shout, excitedly.

Well, he just grins all over and says, "Good for you, Muff."

Getting the bike home is another matter. It's Monday and I tell Rex and Curt I am not going home on the bus but am going to Leach's to get my bicycle. Mr. Leach is so pleased to see me but cautions that the nuts and bolts or whatever should be tightened before I ride it. I tell him I will ride it straight home, and my brother will tighten whatever needs to be tightened.

"Ok," he says, "but it is four miles."

It's like I'm flying in the wind. My hair swishing behind me, I pedal down past the four ponds. There are no cars on the road as everyone is still working, so I look at the ponds and the birds swooping, go around the bends and down the little hills. This is just heaven. I never dreamed I would have such a beautiful bicycle. I come to our driveway and this time even miss hitting the mailbox.

Rex is ready with the wrench and tightens everything while I hurry in to get the potatoes peeled and afterschool chores done. Not having heard anything from him in quite a while, I go to the door. He's standing there with my bike, which looks a little damp.

"What have you done?" I ask, bewildered.

"I wondered if your bike floated," he shrugs.

If I did not have chores to do, I would chase him to the shores of

Twitchell Pond and make him see if *he* can float.

I'm not sure if he rode it into the pond or not. I like to believe he was washing all the dust off from the Greenwood Road.

Winning that bike is the nicest thing that has happened to me in a long time!

Graduation

It has been coming for some time. I dread it, as I'm not fond of pomp and circumstance and all that goes with it. Mr. Meserve, our "big room" teacher, has stressed to us that we must all act like ladies and gentlemen, which I find not at all to my liking.

For days we have practiced marching up and down the sidewalk in front of Locke Mills Grammar School. John Chase is our Class Marshall, and he walks backwards, leading us on our way, swinging a pole which hopefully will be replaced with something much more attractive. I believe it will be some sort of pole well covered with colored crepe paper and flying paper at each end. We are supposed to be stepping on the left foot when the baton goes down…or is it the right foot? Well, in the end, if all of us can step in unison, I guess it doesn't matter.

We were told the girls must wear white dresses and white shoes. When I asked, my mother flat out refused to let me wear white sneakers. She insisted on buying some white sandals that would make me "look like a lady for one night out of the year."

"I don't want anything on my feet that has a hole in the toe," I retorted. "If they can't put a whole shoe together without leaving gaps, I don't want a pair."

She then informed me that she worked hard for her money and was going to make sure that I wore whatever she chose. I know Ma works hard, so after that I just sighed and heaved my body up the stairs into my side of the attic to think over the whole matter.

We have the afternoon off from classes to decorate the Town Hall, so it will look pretty behind us as we sat in a half circle on stage. There aren't too many of us, and Kay is the only other girl. I am sure she will be wearing a white dress and white shoes as well.

The day has come. We all go to the Hall; the boys are laughing, shouting, running, and just glad to be out of school. John carries the real version of the baton, and we march while the piano pounds out the graduation march. Mr. Meserve has found someone to replace him at school, and he paces back and forth, finger in his watch pocket, swinging as he paces. "Left foot on the down beat, left foot on the down beat," he keeps repeating. Good grief. If I roll my eyes one more time, they'll roll down the aisle in front of all of us. I try just to grin and bear it. I'd think John would get dizzy walking backwards and run into one of those chairs all sitting in a row, but he seems to have it under control.

Well, the night is here. I try not to think that our class will be divided; some will go to Gould Academy and some to Woodstock High School. Ma graduated from there in 1933 so it just stands to reason that we will go to Woodstock. Fine with me. I don't care where I go as long as there are sports to play—but I don't say that out loud.

We line up in a row, and I peek around to see who is in the Hall. Good Lord, it looks like the whole town has turned out for this graduation. There's no one from the lower part of Greenwood this year. Some years there are students from Colista Morgan's school and also from the Tubbs District. I wonder how comfortable those hard wooden folding chairs must be. I'll ask Gram tomorrow. I can see her on the aisle down near the front, her white hair up in a bun and little hat perched on the side of her head. Ma is sitting with her. Dad doesn't come to these things. I guess by now he's in bed reading a western paperback. I wish I were in my attic reading something...anything.

The music starts. John looks nervous. Mr. Meserve raises his hand to let John know when to come down, and he whispers again, "Left on the down beat." We know this! I am getting nervous because I don't like sitting forever on stage with everyone looking at me. Rex looks cool, the way he always handles things like this. Carl and Verne Corkum are brothers, and they look as though they're fine...well here we go.

We sit. Each of us has a little part to get up and recite. Since we have rehearsed this so many times, it's like a bee buzzing in my ear. I get up, say my part as quickly as possible, and scoot back to my chair, hoping I don't fall on my face wearing the sandals. I am amazed I made it down the aisle without tumbling into someone's lap.

It's OVER! Hurray! The piano player starts and we all rise, turn at the same time, and exit the stage. There's a sea of smiling faces as we exit the hall much the same way as we came in...with John walking backwards, swinging the baton. There is only one difference...most of us are heaving a sigh of relief!

I am alone in the attic now, having taken off those dreaded uncomfortable sandals and the lovely white dress Ma bought. I'm remembering my years at Locke Mills Grammar School. I have only been to this school and am not keen on leaving it, to tell the truth. The teacher who quietly gave a pair of mittens to a little girl because her hands were cold and almost deep red in color. Being fingerprinted by the State Police in fourth grade and knowing that I could never commit a crime now because the world had my fingerprints. Being asked to ring the bell to bring in the students; helping to raise the flag outside each morning. The Valentine boxes, the Barter Days, the exchanging of names at Christmas, and all the May baskets hung on me by my friends from the village. I have a feeling that my schooldays are going to change come fall, and I am not sure if life will ever be the same again.

LONG AGO
Growing Up

Jill of All Trades, Master of None

This morning, Gram Martin sees me down by the pond and calls to me. I think she might need some chores done, but she asks me to sit next to her on the big porch. She's heard I won first prize in the poetry department in the Portland Sunday paper. She says she's very proud and then really surprises me!

"How would you like to take over for me and write the local news for the *Advertiser-Democrat?*" she asks.

I draw in my breath sharply. "I can't do that, Grammy. I don't know what to write about." She assures me that she will help me find news. I'll get a free newspaper, and, when through reading it, can pass it on to her.

I love reading and writing but am not confident that I'm old enough to do this. Grammy keeps patting my hand and telling me all I have to remember is to use a pencil and write on the lined copy paper that the paper sends to her free. Going into her bedroom, she returns with a big stack of black lined paper that at the top says Advertiser-Democrat Norway Maine.

Well, Ma's now coming in the yard now from getting some groceries at Vallee's store. I've been feeling pretty important since this morning. I hope she'll agree to me writing for the paper.

"What are you up to, young lady?" is the first thing she asks, again reading my face like a book. I explain, and without a hitch she puts her grocery bag on the cupboard. "Well, that's good practice for you. But don't you start and then get tired of it. Once you start, there is no stopping because your grandmother will not get her paper."

I show her the copy paper and she smiles, so I think she might be a little proud that I'm going to gather the news around Greenwood Center...well, along with Gram's help.

Every year something like this pops up to keep me out of mischief and sometimes earn money for my school clothes. One afternoon, for example, Ma came home with a job offer.

Sitting her lunch pail on the cupboard, she turns to me. "Do you want to babysit Flossie and Stan Seames' two kids while they work in the mill? Pays twelve dollars a week, Floss says."

102

Sure, why not.

Well, here it is, Monday morning, and 6:30 a.m. Dad stops the car, and, eyes half open, I trudge up the little hill to Stan and Flossie's house. It's a small house with a porch and sits up by the woods. I like it already. There's a big rock in front with flowers growing near it. Flossie tells me when the kids have their naps and shows me what to give them for lunch at noon. She then asks if I can make curls like Shirley Temple with Evvie's hair. Evvie is four, so I am not sure how much she will like me fooling with her hair and rat tail comb every morning. Raymond is six, very quiet, and has a cute little grin. Before leaving, Stan asks me if I would mind stirring something in the back room in a tub once in the forenoon and once in the middle of the afternoon. There's a big paddle there to stir with.

Wow, for my first babysitting job, these kids are angels. Evvie sits through her curling job every morning, and Raymond is always busy playing with his toys. Come noon, we all have lunch, and when I tell them it's nap time off they go with no argument. Charlotte Cole lives right next door in a little house, but she works at the mill so we don't see anyone all day.

This summer of 1954 has gone really well, and it's almost time for me to end the babysitting job. I think about a few of the things we've done. One day at noon, we decided to open a can of SpaghettiOs that Flossie had left. Well, I put the old hand can opener to it, and it exploded. Spaghetti everywhere, on me, on the counter, in fact some went up on the ceiling. Raymond and Evvie laughed as hard as I did. I got up in a chair, and Raymond handed me wet cloths so we had everything cleaned up by the time their parents came home.

Let's not forget when the hurricane came through. The kids were napping, and I noticed bottles flying over the porch. Soon Stan and Flossie arrived, followed hurriedly by my parents to take me home. I stood in our living room and watched trees bend almost to the ground.

Another, less exciting, day while they were taking a nap, I decided to surprise Flossie and made a chocolate cake with a recipe that I found. It turned out great; she was pleased and said it helped her so much. And remember, all this time I was stirring Stan's project in the back room twice a day. That was the cause of the only argument between Raymond and Evvie, and I quickly resolved that. They watched as I took the paddle each time and stirred the big tub of liquid around and around…but each time, they both wanted to lick the paddle. Well, neither would give in, so finally I told them that one could lick it in the morning and the other in the afternoon. I guess a lick of home brew never hurt…if it's one lick a day! No more arguing! I am going to miss those kids so much!!

Gram checks in with me with the word of visitors and any other news that comes her way. She makes sure I mail it in time for the paper to get it printed and is really proud of the way I'm writing so nice and clear—the paper has not complained! She says she now has more time to do other things, like care for Grandpa and work on her quilts, knit hats, and mittens for the grandchildren.

Well, it seems like I have had quite the summer. I'm not sure I wrote everything correctly, am not sure I did the babysitting right, but that twelve dollars came in handy when it came to buying my school things!!!

A Day to Remember

I am twelve years old, and this is a Monday...a Monday I have looked forward to for so long. Our class in school can attend a portion of the annual Town Meeting, something I have always wanted to do. This morning, however, Ma asked if I would stay home with Dad, who's not feeling well. She cannot afford to lose time at the mill, and I know she hates to ask me. I don't tell her about missing the Town Meeting. I know I can ask Rex tonight about it and hear about any good arguments.

Everyone has gone. Roland has gone to work at Vallee's store, Ma's off to the mill, and Rex and Curt have climbed on the bus. The house is quiet, and Dad is in bed asleep; at least I think he's asleep.

I have read about everything I can find, from Ma's *True Story* magazine to an old *Police Gazette* Dad left lying around, and it's almost noon. I peek in, and Dad's awake and not hungry but he does feel better. Maybe sleep did him some good. He wants to get up and sit in his Morris chair for a while. I get the stove going and soon there's some water hot for his coffee. Maybe he'll want a cup. Sick or not, he usually drinks it.

There's a pawing at the door, and I know Keno, our husky, wants to come in. She's been outside all morning and probably wants to come in and see what's happening inside. She loves it when it's cold and sometimes burrows in the snow until all you can see is her tail. The snow is all gone now, except for a patch or two here and there, so she's probably bored...if dogs get bored.

I open the door and see Keno's face. My legs go weak as it's full of porcupine quills. She never learns, and this is not the first time it's happened. Usually we have no problem because she sits while Ma pulls out the quills. She won't let Dad near her or anyone but Ma when she gets quills. Ma is at work and won't be home for hours, and now Keno is whining. I don't know what to do. I run to tell Dad where he sits fully dressed now in his chair.

"Show me," he says. I take him to the front door, and Keno is gone. She's fled under the house through a big hole she dug years earlier. In fact, that's where she had her puppies. Dad thinks about it for a while.

"I am going for Louie's rifle," he finally says, shaking his head. I guess

my face looks awful because he adds, "There's nothing we can do, Muff."
Even if there's a veterinarian nearby; we can't afford to pay one.

If he gets Uncle Louie's rifle, he'll shoot Keno. He can't do that. He just
can't. I run into the house and hide my face in some blankets on Curt's bed.

Dad is back, carrying the rifle. "I can't get her out from under the house,
Muff," he tells me. I breathe a sigh of relief. He then says, "You have to
help me."

"No, I won't, Dad." This is the first time I've ever disobeyed my father
but know in the end I'll have to do what he wants. He tells me to get a bowl
of canned milk, go to the hole, call her, and she will come for me.

I feel numb all over. This is not fair. I cannot do this.

"Do you want her to suffer all day?" Dad snaps.

He waits. My shoes scuff the rough floor to the cupboard, and I find the
open can of evaporated milk. The dribble of white splatters the plastic bowl
as I barely tip the can. With a little water, I stir to make it more like real

milk should be.

Dad is still waiting. I can't look at him. With eyes fixed straight ahead, I walk carefully so not a drop be spilled. Kneeling in the dirt by the crawl hole, I call for her, softly. In a few minutes, I see her start to come out. I put down the bowl and run into the house. I crush pillows to both ears but still hear the gunshot. It's not out of place in Greenwood Center. When you live in the woods, that sound's not unfamiliar.

In another minute, Dad is behind me and puts his arm around me. "I had to do it, Muff." He leaves the house, and I go upstairs to my bed.

No you didn't, Dad. Right now I don't like my father at all. My fists pummel the walls, the bed, and blankets piled in the corner. But my fists are really not for Dad. They pound because we are poor, because he had to do such a horrible thing, and because I have lost a friend who gave me an abundance of love. I may understand why he did it but will never forget this day until I die.

Life Is a Mixture

Today I am so excited—I have looked forward to this day for weeks! Every year, the mill where Ma and Dad works has what they call a "Field Day" for all the workers. I always hope that Dad will decide to go, because there are times when he says it's too far.

The field day is held in Bear Pond Park in North Turner, and, yes, it is a long ride. When we get up this morning, Dad's sipping his coffee and glancing out the window. The sky's gray and there are a few drops of rain…a drizzle he calls it. I don't think it's that much of a drizzle, but Curt and I wait and say nothing. Finally he says he doesn't know if we should drive that far and find pouring rain or not. Tossing her apron on the back of the kitchen chair, Ma shrugs and tells him that perhaps it isn't raining in Turner. Holding my breath, I wonder if we're going or not. Even if it rains, it won't be raining in my favorite place at the park. It's so quiet, I can hear the clock ticking on the wall.

Finally, Dad announces, "Ok, let's give it a try, but if it's raining we are turning right around and coming home."

Weeks ago, we were given the usual choice of eating chicken or lobster for the Field Day meal, and all of us always choose chicken. I've never had lobster and Ma says it would be too hard for Curt and me to get into and eat. Well, chicken I know how to gobble up!

We pile into the back seat of the car, drive over to Route 26, and then up over into North Paris. By this time, I am wishing the car could sprout wings and just get us there. It's such a long way through Sumner, West Sumner, and on and on.

"We'll be there before long," Ma turns and says. She doesn't come out and say it, but I can sense that she thinks a day of fun is just what our family needs. She knows Curt and I are getting tired and impatient but won't say a word as Dad wants it quiet when he is driving.

The clouds begin parting, and the sun peeks out just as Bear Pond Park comes in sight. I poke Curt, and we grin at each other. There is my favorite place—the roller rink!!! I cannot wait for it to open, and the music to begin! I have the money to rent skates and will try my darndest not to fall or break a bone.

Dad parks the car and quickly scoots off to find his friends. Giving us each a dollar, Ma goes to hunt up Aunt Norma, as they are going to perform a little skit of songs and jokes sometime during the day on a makeshift stage. Ma has a costume she's sewn, so she'll look like someone coming out of the mountains with a moonshine jug. Charlie Melville put on a dress and is pitching a soft ball game. Such simple fun, but so enjoyed by everyone!

Curt and I cross the road to the Ferris wheel. The roller rink hasn't opened, so we decide to ride. On we get, and around and around we go, looking way over the pond as we rise to the top. Now we've stopped at the top. We are waiting for someone to get on, and I wish they would hurry! I don't like heights, but I feel so much happier than I did a few months ago that I'm not complaining.

I think Ma was glad we could be here today, because it wasn't that long ago when I was very sad. It came during a time when Ma was laid off, so she was home that Friday when I got off the school bus. I came into the kitchen and Ma was at the cupboard rolling out biscuits. She brushed her hands together and the flour flew in the sunlight from the window. I put my lunch bag down as she said, "I want you to sit down, San." Ma looked serious in a sad sort of way.

Well, I thought, *whatever for?* I have chores to do and don't sit in the kitchen chairs, ever, except to eat or be punished.

"I want you to sit down," she repeated it again. I don't know where Rex and Curt had gone. All I remember is how Ma wanted me to sit, and I thought, *now what have I done.*

Ma sat down next to me. "I have some bad news for you." *What is she talking about?* I thought. *Has something happened to Dad? No. The boys would be here, too. Something's wrong. Very wrong.*

"Your friend, Gladys Bailey, has died." I remember her voice sounding as though it was coming from a barrel.

"What do you mean, Ma? She's coming home this weekend and I'm going to see her." Gladys was staying at a new place. One weekend a while ago, I couldn't find her. Uncle Roy told me she was now at a little camp on the back side of Twitchell Pond. With a sigh, I had started up the road and soon found Gladys sitting by herself. She was so happy to see me, and, once again, as if nothing had changed, she produced a treat for me, sat, and listened.

This time, though, she had explained very carefully that Uncle Roy had new friends and had found this place for her to stay on weekends. Young as I was, I thought this change very strange but knew I should not question her... And so our visits had continued in our new meeting place.

But now...

"No, San, you don't understand," Ma went on, patiently. "She was walking across the street in South Paris and was hit by a car. She died. She won't be coming anymore."

The words kind of jumbled up in my brain and were swirling around. I wouldn't be walking down and visiting Gladys any more weekends. She wouldn't be hiding a pen or a pin behind her back and making me guess what she'd brought me for a surprise. How many years had I visited her every weekend? Where did she go when she died?

No! I silently screamed. I remember Ma asking, "Are you all right, San?" as I grabbed my school books, ran up the stairs, and buried my head in my pillow. Life was not fair.

Later, I walked out the house and sat on my favorite rock in the woods by the pond. I didn't cry because Gladys would not have wanted me to cry. I watched the boats go by and after a while just went home. That weekend I stayed by my bed in the attic and just read. I didn't want to think about not visiting her.

Now a few weeks have passed, and the hurt is not as bad. I'm beginning to feel happy again and am at one of my most favorite places in the world. Curt grabs my arm and shouts, "Here we go again!" Round and round we go until it is time for us to get off.

It's also now time for us to line up for our dinners and then dig into the chicken. Suddenly from across the road, the door opens, the music begins, and the roller rink opens. I grab Curt, and we run across the road. Curt will watch while I try to skate around and around. He laughs when one leg goes one way and the other has a mind of its own as I grab the side of the rink. I love the music, so I keep going until my whole body goes in one direction!

Ma and Aunt Norma have everyone in stitches doing their skit over in the field, while others play softball. It's the first good day in a while. Gladys would be proud that I'm finally smiling again.

A New Summer

Graduation is over, and summer is upon us. Uncle Roy's moved and now lives in a house a bit farther down the road. In the front of the house is Duby's store, and he lives in the rooms in back. The shelves are open and built into the walls, holding basic canned goods sold by Joe and Eva, the proprietors. There are two coolers, one which holds soft drinks and the other a variety of beers. Eva has asked if I would like to mind the store when she has to go to Norway to pick up supplies. Ma is not crazy about the idea but says I can do it until another job comes along so I can earn money for school clothes. After all, Rex and I will be attending high school in September and I'd like some nice clothes to wear.

This Sunday, Dad is planning another car trip. I'd like to go along just to get out of the house, but Eva says she needs me at the store. I know that Dad plans to hunt down more old cemeteries. One of his most favorite things in the world is to walk through and find old cemetery stones. Sometimes he jots down the sayings on them. He really likes the markers, some of which might have a history behind them. I don't know how many times he has been to the grave of Metallak, last survivor of the Androscoggin tribe. After such an expedition, that evening he'll talk about what he's found and display stones he dug up alongside the road somewhere. Ma says she never knows when he's going to throw the brakes on and come to a screeching halt to grab more.

I tend the store all day and have a few of the Summer People come in for bread, milk, and odds and ends. One man was pretty disgusted because he wanted beer, and I told him I was too young to sell it. He would have to come back the next day. I don't like that part of this job.

That evening, Ma has a message from Winnie Hanscom. Seems Winnie has always worked for a schoolteacher from Forest Hills, New York, who summers on the Indian Pond road off Rowe Hill. Winnie has other plans and wonders if I would like the chance to work for the teacher. The day would run from 9-4 and I'd be paid $10 a week. If I want to, tomorrow morning I could ride with Ma to Stowell's Mill, where she works, and then walk up to Winnie's and visit until it's time to meet this lady, this Ethel E. Hobbs. She sounds interesting.

On the way to work the next day, Ma tells me that when she was growing up, Miss Hobbs ran a summer camp for girls at the house where she now summers. It was called Camp Sebowisha. From 1925 through 1935, girls came from everywhere to swim, boat, and canoe on Indian Pond. They slept in two separate buildings on the hillside.

Well, this is becoming even more interesting.

After Winnie fills me in on what my duties will be, I begin walking down the dirt road to Miss Hobbs' house. It turns out to be huge, and I begin getting a few butterflies. I rap on the door and quickly step back. The door opens, and there stands a woman, her gray hair twirled up into some sort of "do" like fingers reaching for the sky. One eye looks at me and the other doesn't quite make it to me. In the corner of her mouth hangs a cigarette with an ash threatening to swan dive at any moment. A little dog stands by her legs, not barking, just standing there and also staring at me.

"You must be Sandra," she finally says and, with my nod, goes on. "I am Ethel Hobbs. Come in, come in."

The kitchen is huge, the two living rooms are vast, and I wonder what I have gotten myself into. Still, I am fascinated by it all. Pointing to a kettle shaped like a cauldron, she instructs me put it on a gigantic wood stove. With buckets I fill it; she then tosses a box of 40 Mule Team Borax into the water, followed by her "unmentionables," and tells me that in time the water will boil. I am to go occasionally and stir the "unmentionables" with a big paddle sitting there. Meanwhile, I am given a bucket, nail, and rag and told to follow her. I fill the bucket with hot water and something really smelly, which I think is some sort of disinfectant. She tells me the stairs need a good cleaning and to put the rag over the nail and clean each corner of the stairway. She leaves me alone, which I like. I begin cleaning and dunking the cloth every few minutes.

As I near the top of the stairs, the unmistakable smell of mothballs hits my nose. I hate mothballs. But I will get ten dollars on Friday if I can do the job right. Remembering I haven't stirred her "unmentionables" for a while, I race back down the stairs and give them a couple of turns. Miss Hobbs is in the gigantic "rec room," which still holds signs of the girls' camp from long ago. They must have had such a good time there. I imagine them sitting and having singalongs in the evenings.

Miss Hobbs announces that it is lunchtime. My stomach growls as I realize it's almost one-thirty, a long time since the fried egg this morning at six. She's fixed two china plates with a sandwich, cut corner to corner, and laid a real cloth napkin beside each plate. A tall glass of water stands next to my sandwich. I'm not sure what's between the two pieces of bread, but I spy a piece of tomato sticking out so it can't be all bad.

She asks how the stairs are coming and announces she'll take care of the rest of the boiling laundry. I tell her the corners are cleaned, so she next gives me a wire brush and has me refill the pail with hot, sudsy water to clean the stairs themselves. She says by that time it should be nearly four o'clock and I can leave.

The stairs are done, and Miss Hobbs compliments me on my work, which makes me feel good. I've never been a maid or a cleaning woman before. She says there's plenty of work to be done, including polishing the silver and, when her friends come to lunch, preparing the pretty salads.

Oh, Lord.

I am walking home now and feeling a bit tired, but glad Miss Hobbs liked my work. I pass by the Colby Ring home, Lee Sumner's home, and reach the top of Rowe Hill. Now it's all downhill to Dan Cole's farm. Easier on the legs, for sure, and then just a mile down the tarred road to home.

I can smell beans and hot dogs. Dad doesn't like hot dogs, but he's still talking about visiting Metallak's grave again so Ma probably figured he'll never notice what he's eating. I am almost too tired to eat.

Waking time will come early, and, boy, I am ready to go to bed. Is this what they call the work force?

Working Girl

Well, it's been an interesting summer job, for sure. Each morning when I arrive at Miss Hobbs' home, I have no idea what's going to be in store for me. Lucky, the dog, more or less stays out of my way and follows her around.

Last week was a milestone in my career. Early in the morning, Miss Hobbs announced she had three lady friends coming for lunch, which I would help prepare and serve. Now that was a wakening. The most I'd ever served was a lunch for Curt and me, usually consisting of peanut butter and crackers or a jam sandwich. Well, I would just have to go along with whatever she said to do and say several silent prayers.

We were to have a salad. Not just any salad, mind you, but one with fancy cut baby carrots and cherry tomatoes shaped like tiny roses...mercy. Well, if I succeeded with this, I would have something to tell Ma. Washing the lettuce carefully, I laid it like little cup-shaped fancies first. Miss Hobbs stood over my shoulder, her cigarette smoke wafting down and settling in a cloud under my nose. I prayed again, this time not to sneeze on the salad. My eyes watered. Could I wipe them? No. Hygiene was not only on the top of my boss's priority list, it clung there like cat's claws.

There! Four glass salad plates with little cups of lettuce, two tiny carrots slices to one side, two tomato rose buds. Guess that was to be the first course of this *casual luncheon*, which was how Miss Hobbs described it. Next came cucumber sandwiches. Now I like those but prefer gobs of mayonnaise on mine and stuff it into my mouth ten seconds after it's made. With her instructions and cigarette smoke, I made sandwiches, cut off the crusts, cut them into four tiny decorative pieces, and on and on. I could feel her breath on my neck as I cut the crusts. I know she thought I would do a butcher job on them, but luck was with me. After all, if I can clean a fish and skin it properly, what's so hard about cutting the crust off a piece of bread?

Surprise! Miss Hobbs announced she was doing the dessert, which would consist of some sort of gelatin, coffee, and marshmallows all whipped together. I was so glad I brought my lunch that day and could eat by myself on the other side of the house.

But today is another day! No fancy luncheons to prepare—my least favorite thing to do. Miss Hobbs' mind is fixated on her roses. She has only Jackson Perkins roses and wants them fertilized and watered on a regular basis. They are beautiful, but today her brow is furrowed, and she is absolutely upset over something. She keeps going to the window, peering out at her roses, and mumbling that it has been dry, but the roses have been watered, so why don't they look as striking as usual? Not being a gardener or knowing much about roses, I shake my head and admit I don't know. Suddenly her hand sweeps into the air, and it's as though a light is shining.

"It is the fertilizer," she proclaims. "My Miracle-Gro should have been here last week. No wonder they look drab. Why hasn't it arrived? It should have been at the railroad station in Bryant Pond a week ago. Wait right here, Sandra."

Up the stairs she sweeps, dog Lucky at her heels. She turns for a moment and hollers down, "As soon as I am dressed properly, we are going to the Bryant Pond railroad station."

No, no, no. She said "we," meaning that she will be backing the 1931 Packard out of the garage, and I'll be in the passenger seat. I've heard horror stories from Winnie about Miss Hobbs and her driving.

I stand outside the garage and direct her in backing up. This car is so long, it looks like a bus. I stop her just short of the stone wall, then aid in turning and getting the car headed in the right direction. Climbing into the passenger seat, I have to admit that I've never seen such a luxurious car. The seat is so comfortable that I feel like I'm floating on air. Miss Hobbs assumes an aristocratic pose behind the wheel with her gloves clutching the wheel. Her little tan hat perches on the side of her head, gray and black hair streaming to one side under it, and the ever-present cigarette dangles from the corner of her mouth. With a lurch, we are off and heading up the hill to reach, hopefully, the Rowe Hill road to take us to the village.

We pass by Winnie Hanscom's house whom, I hope, can see that I'm doing duty and risking my life. I want to wave, but it seems Miss Hobbs likes to drive fast and in the middle of the road. Down into Velvet Hollow and up Town Line Hill we go and, at last, to the paved road to the village. I'm not sure if I am happy or not that we are in civilization. I am sure, though, that most people will recognize the big, long vehicle and driver and take appropriate actions. We pull up to the railroad station, and I stay in the car per Miss Hobbs' orders. I do not envy the recipient of her wrath, as surely she will blame the stationmaster for not receiving her Miracle-Gro and informing her it's missing.

Here she comes, marching like a soldier on a mission. This is one of the few times I've seen her without a cigarette. "There, I have solved that one," she declares, settling in the driver's seat. "I cannot abide incompetent people. That man says he hasn't seen any Miracle-Gro, and I informed him that if and when it comes in, I want to be informed that very moment."

I nod my head. (Seems like I nod my head a lot when I'm with her.) She always has a right and wrong way of doing things, but is open to questions. Her classroom demeanor as a teacher just naturally spills over into her summer vacation. Orders are given and to be carried out.

Roaring up the engine and grating the shifting gear, she looks at me and says, "When we get back home, Sandra, I will dictate, and you will write a letter to the company. I shall tell them I am not pleased with their shipping policies."

Oh, boy.

With a lurch, we head on back to Rowe Hill and Indian Pond. I guess writing a letter of protest is a heck of a lot better than making cherry tomato roses. At least in my eyes.

Polishing, Fishing, and Other Stuff

Sigh. It's been one of those days. I think I was tired before even getting to Miss Hobbs' place this morning. She dug out the laundry pan–that's what I call it–and I knew this was the day I would be stirring again her "unmentionables" on the stove until she deemed them ready for a good rinse. She has been talking about an inventory of the "rec" room, where canoes are stored overhead and all sorts of activity things awaited the long-ago campers. (For some reason, she never talks about the days of Camp Sebowisha.) I'll admit, taking inventories is not my favorite task.

But no! Today she has another chore in mind. Goodness! Spread out on her dining room table was more silverware than I have ever seen in my life. At home, there are six people, and we have just enough forks, spoons, and knives to go around and glad of it.

"It will be an all day job, if the job is done right," Miss Hobbs states flatly, another cigarette dangling from the edge of her mouth as the ash readies to jump ship at any moment. The polish is in a wide-mouth jar, and I am given several soft cloths. I polish. I wipe. It IS an all day job, stopping only for a bite of sandwich and glass of water at lunch time. I decide soon enough that this is by far one of my least favorite jobs. I admit though it's satisfying to see the silverware gleaming in the sunlight through her window.

But now, thankfully I'm on the down side of the mountain walking home. My hands feel as though they are still gritty from the polishing, even though I scrubbed them well after the final rinse of Miss Hobbs' "unmentionables." Dan Cole's farm stands out like a beacon, telling me I've only one mile to go.

My mind as always constantly turning and thinking, before I know it I'm walking up the driveway. Dad's sitting on the front steps and gives me a wave.

"Muff, you want to go fishing in a bit?"

Fishing is one of my favorite things to do, and since we aren't playing baseball on the "flat" tonight, it seems like a crackerjack thing to plan. Most nights, some folks come down from Locke Mills and we get together a bunch to play baseball. That's a lot of fun and you never know who's going to show up or what's going to happen.

Apologies, I'm getting distracted, again—tonight, I want to go fishing. Wandering into the kitchen to see what Ma and the rest had for supper long before I got home, I grab a hot dog and big glass of water. The water is always so sweet that comes from Gram's spring way up in her pasture.

Ma looks worn out after her day of work. Finishing with the supper dishes, she flops into a chair. "Are you going fishing with your father?" she asks, tiredly.

"I think so."

"Well don't stay out too late," she warns. "You have work again tomorrow and morning comes quick."

I don't know what she means by staying out too late. Dad has his pole all ready and I see it's his bamboo. He's been over behind Gram's barn digging worms, so I guess we're not trolling for brown trout. It's getting dusky out, and Dad hollers in, "Muff, are you ready? I have a pole for you and plenty of worms." I know now that we are going to one of his favorite fishing places, one he doesn't go to very often.

Into the car we jump and soon are on our way to Greenwood City. We park on the side of the road near Hicks Pond. "Horn pouting we go!" Dad proclaims, placing a pail between us as we get worms on our hooks and toss out lines. I find a nice rock to sit on, and Dad perches in the grass. I'm hoping he will remember that I like to catch horned pout but prefer not to take them off the hook. I've been "stung" too many times. They are mean little critters through and through. Usually we eat perch, trout, or bass, but once in a while Dad likes a good mess of horned pout. I guess this is one of those times.

My alder pole bends over, and Dad says, "You got one, Muff, haul it in." Doesn't take too long for me to flop it up on shore.

Dad looks at me, grinning. "I remember. I'll get it off for you." With a flick of his hand, the fish is off the hook and into the pail.

After a while, we've hauled in five or six good-size fish and are thinking of going home. It's very quiet and peaceful here. Over to the right, we can see lights from farm houses on Patch Mountain. I tell Dad this would not be a bad place to live. He grunts that it's close enough, so we can drive down anytime we want.

It's time for us to load up and go home. An owl hoots off in the forest.

A sudden thought. "Dad, is it true there are lots of snakes around Hicks Pond and Mud Pond?"

"Best not to even think about such a thing, Muff," he replies, a bit quickly. Well, I wouldn't if I were not deathly afraid of them, and it IS dark after all.

We pull into the driveway, and Dad says he will put the pail of fish in the brook water and clean them when he gets home from work tomorrow. They'll stay fresh in the flowing water. He knows I clean perch and such, but will not touch horned pout. He promises me when I get home from Miss Hobbs' tomorrow night, there will be one fried up crisp for me.

Well, I declare, that'll be something to look forward to while I clean the stair corners with my ten-penny nail and rags tomorrow.

State of Confusion

It is a fine summer day with a little breeze coming through the birches behind Miss Hobbs' big house. I am perched on a five-rung step-ladder, washing windows. I don't like the job, but it's providing me the opportunity to get out and breathe in the beautiful, fresh air. After a morning of dragging blankets from the mothballed chest and hanging them on the clothesline, it's like a drink of cool water! I haven't counted how many windows I've washed, but Miss Hobbs said to just go at it and get as many done as I can before it is time for the walk home.

She has a friend visiting from New York City, so the problems of fading roses and other woes have taken a back seat this week. Her gentleman friend is hearing impaired and sometimes his speech is difficult to understand, but once you see him smile that takes second seat. He's an older man and very nice to me. Not long ago, he came wandering by and stopped to chat a minute. When leaving, he handed me a five-dollar bill all folded up and said in a hushed voice, "Take this, you earn it." Stunned, I said thank you and put it in my pocket. He smiled, patted my shoulder, and away he went. I think maybe Miss Hobbs is a bit intimidating to him as well!

One thing good is that I can participate in my favorite pastime—thinking and letting my mind wander as I wash and dry the tiny panes of glass. I am confused whether I am happy to be going to a new school or if I should be a little scared. All I have known is the Locke Mills Grammar School and its three rooms. I am not used to being around a lot of kids, with some much older than me. I am only thirteen and know some of the kids are at least five years older than me in high school.

So many memories with the old grammar school, some good and some not so good. My own cousin, Colby Martin, chased me around that school with a snake in his hands. I was about eight years old, I think, and screamed and screamed because I was and still am terrified of snakes. I ran to the teacher, and she assured me he would not be allowed to put the snake on me.

Again, when I was quite small, I came around the school house one noon, and Leslie Roberts threw a football that hit me square in the nose.

Oh, how the blood gushed. I didn't know he was around the corner, and I am sure he was surprised to see where the football landed. The teacher held my face over the washbasin in the hall and cleaned me up pretty good.

When I was sick with the old fashioned measles, Rex came home from school with the prettiest box. It was decorated with beautiful crepe paper; all the kids had brought something from home to put in it to make me feel better. It was called a "Sunshine Box." Rex and I had frequently taken something from home to contribute to the Sunshine Box when one of the schoolkids was sick for a long time. I was beginning to recover, and in the box were horehound drops. They tasted pretty good, so I kept eating them since my parents were still at work. By the time they got home, I was sick again in good shape. Sputtering to me, Ma took the drops away and told me how wrong it was to eat all those. I know now she was scared because she thought I was almost well, and there I was, retching away.

Now I am going to a school that's so grown up, there won't be Sunshine Boxes, Valentine Boxes, or anything else fun, probably. I don't know if I am going to like it or not.

I remember when the State Police came to the grammar school! I was in the fourth grade, they took our fingerprints, and one great, tall man was taking notes. He noted I had a mole on the side of my face. I wanted to tell him that Grammy Martin says that it's a beauty spot, but I was afraid of him, with that uniform and all. I could see Ma's face if they put those handcuffs on me and dragged me out the front door for being smart mouthed!

And the school doctor! Will the new school have its own doctor? I doubt it. Dr. Boynton comes every once in a while to check up on our health. I was not too keen on standing in line in the hallway for our smallpox vaccination. I think I was about nine years old. Since everyone else in front of me got it and didn't say anything, I figured I could do it. Well, let me tell you, I went home with that little round thing on my upper arm, and I still have the imprint of it to this day. We took little booklets of information home, so our parents could read about how to treat it and how long it would take to heal.

Miss Hobbs has her head out the upstairs window to tell me it's four o'clock and time for me to walk home. How a woman can speak that clearly with a cigarette in the corner of her mouth is beyond me. I wonder how she teaches school all day without it.

Enough thinking for one day. I have washed all the windows downstairs on the backside of the house. I'll grab the step ladder, put it in her "rec" room, and head up the road for the walk home. Bet when I get to the top of the mountain and see that house, I'll start thinking again about the days of Vacation Bible School a few years ago, and how much fun I had staying at Winnie Hanscom's for a week, walking up every day and making new friends. Before I know it, I will be down the other side of the mountain.

It's a good afternoon for walking and especially with a five dollar tip in my pocket!!

Looking Back, Moving Forward

It's been a long summer working for Miss Hobbs, but on the other hand, I've seen how other people live and learned a great deal from her. Although her outward appearance is somewhat deceiving, she must be quite the teacher in Forest Hills, New York, because she's taught for years and is well respected—at least she seems to be, from the correspondence she receives and comments to her friends. During the summer, her friend, Mrs. Goldberg, came to visit for several weeks and was delightful, making the days go so much faster.

Rex is still trapping. He gets up really early and checks his traps every morning. Dad told him if he was going to trap then he had to check them every day; some trappers do not do that and it's not right. If he catches a muskrat, he takes the animal and comes back with the hide stretched out on a board. He has to let it dry before he packs it off to get paid. Of course he hangs them at the head of the stairs. If I'm not careful, I run my face into a muskrat hide early in the morning, certainly no way to come awake. He has a book called *Tips to Trappers* and when he gets teasing me, I tell him to go read his book "Tips to Twappers." That always gets him.

My overnight stays with Winnie and Ray Hanscom will come to an end when I start high school. Curt and I usually go together, and we popcorn while Winnie makes fudge for us. How much am I going to have to give up just to get an education? I'm beginning to wonder!!

I think Rex is a little nervous, too, but he never appears so. We've been going to our little school for so long and had the same friends for years.

Well, anyway, I think I'm just about ready. Ma took me to Norway last weekend, and we went in J.J. Newberry's to buy school supplies. I'm not sure what to take but got some pens, pencils, notebooks, and, to top it off, a pencil box. I don't know if I'm supposed to have one of those or not, or if they're just for grammar school. I don't want to take chances.

We looked all over the place for a new dress and finally found a plaid one with a gold chain that hangs from one collar to the other and looks very fancy. I bought some socks, and Ma bought a pair of penny loafers for me. I have got to put a penny in each one, as I am sure the other girls will do that. Maybe, though, I had better wait and just see.

My whole world is changing, and I am not sure I like it that much. But I love to learn and I guess it's the thing to do. Above all, though, I love to play sports. They have basketball and softball at Woodstock High, so I'm looking forward to that. I am now 5'6" tall and am skinny as a rail (that is what Ma says), so maybe I will get to play on a team.

Today is my last day of work for the summer. Handing me my money, Miss Hobbs says, "Now, Sandra, you are going to high school. If you learn typing, I will rent a typewriter from the *Bethel Citizen* and next year instead of housework, I will have you do all my correspondence and help me prepare next year's lessons." Well, that sure makes me smile...to think she wants me back and to do something I know I will really like to do!

Life keeps changing...from grammar school to high school, from cleaning stairs with a ten-penny nail to tapping a typewriter. I think I can live with that.

Onward and Upward

Well, the day has come. High School. I roll myself out early this morning, drag down the stairs, and dawdle over fried egg and potato until Ma reminds me that if I want to get on the school bus, I have to ride with them. I sit there, with the new dress and penny loafers on, wondering what on earth I am getting myself into. With a big sigh, I gather my things together.

We sit on Hank Leach's steps...we, meaning everyone in Locke Mills attending Woodstock High School this year. The big—and I mean *big*—yellow bus comes up Route 26 and does a big swing toward the Greenwood bridge. This is no Cass Howe van. It's a huge bus, and I am not sure whether I want to get on or not. The driver opens the door, and I have no choice. A girl I have never seen before climbs on the bus, looking a little scared, so I pat the seat next to me and she sits down.

"Hi, my name is Sandra. What's yours?"

"Louise," she replies in a very small voice, looking as scared as me.

So here we are, pulling into the schoolyard after driving over the Gore Road, taking a right through Pinhook, reaching the top of Merryfield Hill, and finally to school. It's certainly not like the crow flies, but I see some country I haven't seen. It's kind of fun watching the kids get on the bus and wondering who they are.

The steps into the school are many and steep. I follow along behind and hope the kids are going where I am supposed to be going. Up the stairs and a long hallway...hmm, now I can go to the left or the right, but so many are going to the left and up the stairs that's where I'll go. Louise is hanging right beside me. I hope she isn't trusting my judgment, as I have no clue what's going on. Up one flight of stairs, turn, and up another flight of stairs to a long hallway with coat hooks. Hmm. Well, off with the jacket, on to the hook, and I guess the lunch bag goes on the floor beneath it, if I am seeing correctly down the hallway.

Someone says "study hall." Like I'm in the midst of a flock of sheep, I follow everyone into a huge room with a gazillion windows. This is not Locke Mills Grammar School. We are freshman and sit down front. Okay

FRESHMAN CLASS

Faront row: Luna Farrington, Louise Lavalley ,Phillip Farrington, William Mason, Rex ford Martin, Andrea Poland, Maynard Cushman, Leona Whitman, Arlene Brown. Secon row: Elizabeth York, Nada Hinkley, Jackie Rich, Benjamin Wilson, Alicia Emery, Alber Cross, Adelaide Emery, Lillian Lavalley, Sandra Martin.

with me. Just give me a seat to sink into…and that's what I do. The first one I come to, I'm in it and Louise is behind me. We change our minds, as she's short and I'm tall, so she switches to the front seat and I sit behind her. Across from me is a gangly, big boy all stretched out reading a western paperback.

The principal, Mr. Douglas Thompson, stands at the head of the room, making announcements. He says we have twenty-one new freshman this year and welcomes us.

I want to be sitting on a rock, fishing, somewhere on the banks of Twitchell Pond. There are too many kids and too many things to think about.

I'm given my list of subjects, including biology and algebra. Those are two subjects we never covered in grammar school. Well…maybe this will be interesting.

At last, it is almost time to go home, after going to classes and meeting teachers. The English teacher is a Miss French, whom I am convinced hates me. I know it the minute I enter the room. The other teacher is Mrs. Crockett. Now she taught Ma, and Ma says she's a very nice person. I like her soft voice and how very seldom she raises her voice. Miss French is a totally different story. Geesh, she should have been married to Mr. Meserve from my 8th grade. This is going to be a long year. I put all these things in little boxes in my mind to mull over once I get to where it is quiet.

I'm just not sure I'm going to like Woodstock High School too well. There are some very nice kids in our class, but I am too shy to look around much. It seems as though I've been looking at the floor all day. I don't like where our bathroom is located…a trip down two flights of stairs, a short hallway, and then down more stairs. On the other hand, one could take one's time going there and coming back and not have to sit in the study hall looking at windows and being quiet. Everyone needs a break now and then.

I know Ma is going to ask us how we liked our first day. She graduated in 1933 and has many stories to tell. I am not sure what Rex will tell her, but I have a feeling he and I are waiting for the same thing…the announcement when sports will begin!

Thirteen years old and thrust into this big school. There must be over fifty kids in this school. I hope I make it through!

Sports Fever

It's the 50's, and I live now for the days we play high school softball and basketball. They are my sole comfort amongst the dull subjects handed to me—biology, algebra, and all the other subjects that bore me to tears.

In softball, I play left field and third base...wherever needed most. I doubt that Rex remembers showing me a little trick I use while batting. I doubt, also, that it's anything anyone uses, but it works for him...and for me. I get up in the batter's box, look out to see where there is an empty hole, and when the pitcher delivers, shift my feet and weight so that I can hit the ball where there is no opposition. I look pretty good using that trick. Rex meanwhile is an outstanding infielder on the Woodstock High team. Seems that our days of playing baseball in the front yard finally paid off!

Playing basketball, however, is not easy for the kids who live out of town, like me and my best friend, Louise, who sat next to me on the bus the first day of High School and lives in Locke Mills. As freshman and definitely not on the "A" team, we were given the dreaded maroon bloomers to wear. The legs puffed out and it was like sending a message to the world—"these are the pitiful ones." At least that's how we felt at the time.

I had never played basketball in my life. I didn't know the rules. The first time I was put into a basketball game, however, I didn't even wait for the signal to go in. Nope, just wandered right on to the court. The giggles from the "A" team and some in the crowd rang in my ears. Well, I ignored it, stayed in, and played. As Ma knows, I'm a stubborn creature.

After a day of high school, if there are no sports, I wait on the steps at Arthur Vallee's store in Locke Mills for the whistle to blow, the mill to open its doors, and all the workers to spill out and go in different directions. Things have changed since I started high school; no longer can I have the house warm and supper ready for them when they got home from work. Sometimes my mother will come into Vallee's store and pick up a few things for our supper. Mr. Vallee puts them "on the cuff" until payday, which is always Friday.

During sports seasons, my afternoon and evening routines are now much different. Practice is after school and, of course, extends until dusk or sometimes dark, no matter the weather. After every practice, Louise and I start walking up Route 26. Oh, the flat by the ballfield in Bryant Pond is our biggest enemy, with the winter wind hitting us in the face. Both of us bend into the wind, and there are times when we turn and walk backwards until we get near the Mills farm, where trees break the awful, icy sting. Louise was enrolled in a Bethel school before coming to Woodstock High, and the father of one of her friends sometimes drives home from work. What a blessing when Mr. Sumner stops. I hesitated the first time, knowing we should not take a ride with a stranger, but Louise explained, "That's Eleanor's father." So in we hopped.

Finally, Louise and I walk over the tracks and she proceeds up Crazy Knoll to her home. I have the next four miles to walk by myself. I don't mind, and chances are that it's still light enough for me to see the cottages as I walk by. I only had one scare for all the walks I took down that four-mile stretch by the ponds.

One night, I rounded a corner, and there were two men walking ahead of me, but far enough away and almost dark so I don't think they knew I was there...at least there was no indication on their part. They were talking in a language I could not understand, and I figured they had to be some Finnish loggers who were camped in the woods not far from our house. I followed them for about two miles or more—me on my little cat feet and heart in throat. When I was almost home, they did indeed turn and walk up a wood road to their camp.

On the Fifties basketball court, an unwritten rule is that everyone wears white sneakers. At first, I had to wear blue sneakers to go with the maroon bloomers. Oh, it was pitiful, but I was so grateful freshman year to even be on a team I didn't complain.

Fast forward to the third year of high school; I am now on the "A" team and wearing a uniform. And, yes, I finally have white sneakers! Dad brought me a pair of white sneakers from his friend's sister and they fit perfectly...and they are high tops!! Never did a second-hand pair of sneakers feel so good or look so good on my feet. They are just a plain, no-name brand, but they are my pride and joy.

The bus trips away to other schools are pretty tiring, especially when we have to get up for school the next day. Art Farrington, our bus driver for my last three years in school, is so patient. On the way home, he stops the bus at Goodwin's in South Paris, and those who have money go in and bring out French fries and other goodies. Louise and I usually have no money, so we sit, talk, and smell!! If either of us have money, we share. That's how it is.

Sometimes when the away-game bus returns to school, Rex meets me to give me a ride home; other times Ma does, even though she has to rise early in the morning to work in the mill.

These are good years. The old gymnasium with its few bleachers on either side, always full of town people shouting and encouraging. Someone's always standing in the open doorway cheering and watching. There are no photographers on the sidelines taking action shots and no big headlines in the sports section of the newspaper. But oh, do we have fun!

Leaving School Behind

The music starts; "Pomp and Circumstance" echoes through the Woodstock High School gymnasium, and I stand, white gown and cap, shaking in white shoes. I glance to my left, and the boys are lined up, ready to make the march down the aisle, which looks as long as a highway at this point. I catch my brother's eye. Rex is decked out in blue gown and cap, and I wonder if he's thinking of the four years we have just completed. More to the point: Is he as nervous as I am?

There are ten of us graduating, and we have become close over the years. How can I forget our senior class trip to New York City? We held a paper drive to earn money for the trip. My friend, Louise, borrowed her brother-in-law's car and decided we would take the day to knock on doors, asking for old newspapers. Howe Hill was our destination. We drove and knocked, piled the back seat of the car full of papers, and, surprisingly, most people were glad to be rid of them. It never occurred to either of us to worry that, while Louise could drive, she had no license. We were of that age where we believed, no cop would stop us, and, if he did, he would realize the good deed we were doing. At one house, after we collected the old papers, Louise backed the car around and hit a mail box. Well, I won't say the whole thing went to the ground, but it was leaning precariously as we sped off, leaving a cloud of dust behind us. Well, karma stepped in and after all papers were collected, we were told a month later that our work was in vain. Someone at the company who processed the papers had absconded with our funds.

Still, we somehow made it to New York. All of us piled on a subway (none of us had seen one before) for a trip to the Bronx Zoo. Half of us managed to get off at the stop, and the rest kept traveling, arriving at the Zoo an hour later. I never knew how they managed the loop…afraid to ask. Then we were sitting in the balcony at the old Madison Square Garden, watching the trapeze artists from Ringling Brothers swaying in front of us. Oooh, the sideshows downstairs made me sick when I saw a lady with a huge snake. Up into the balcony I dashed in a hurry.

We sat in the balcony of the theater and watched the Tonight Show with

Steve Allen as host and wandered down the street at midnight to our hotel with no fear. The highlight of the trip for me was standing in the rain for two hours to see Perry Como host his fifteen-minute television show. I'm still in shock that I had a front row seat, and he smiled—yes he did—actually smiled at me and asked if I were nervous because he wasn't. What a sweet man! I have a scrapbook full of pictures of him at home!! Oh, those are such good memories.

Hmm, there are a few I would rather forget. I love Mrs. Herrick, our English teacher, Mrs. Crockett, our commercial teacher, and of course Mr. Lago, our principal. We all get along fine, but there was one critical moment in my four years that Mrs. Crockett and I crossed swords. One half of the year we studied Commercial Law; the other half was—eek—math. If there's one subject I hate, it's math and all those figures.

Well, that day there were math problems to solve; is there anything worse? I sighed, chewed my pencil, and dawdled until Mrs. Crockett asked me if I was going to solve it. I told her that I couldn't. She insisted that I could if I put my mind to it. Well, suffice it to say, I lost all patience (sorry again, Ma), slammed my book shut, and within a moment's notice was sitting in the principal's office. (The rumors that I threw it have yet to be substantiated.)

Mr. Lago looked at me. "Did your sense of humor get you in here again?"

Mrs. Crockett immediately laid out the details in fine fashion. Suddenly, I was told that I was no longer permitted in her math class and would not be getting a Commercial diploma, which would have been helpful in getting a secretarial position.

Smarting from being thrown out of class, I retorted that I simply didn't care what kind of diploma I received as long as I had one in hand. Mrs. Crockett was utterly shocked and took a few seconds to recover as she had never seen me in such a state before. I was one of her best pupils in typing and shorthand, she had great hopes for me, and here I was, so dumb I couldn't figure out a math problem. This is not one of my good memories from the past four years. I was wrong and disrespectful and sometimes just didn't know when to keep quiet.

And then there was the time I went to a Sadie Hawkins Dance with Rex's favorite buddy. At first—no way. I didn't want to have to dress up fancy and attend, and I wasn't interested enough in any of the boys to ask them to the dance. Finally, Rex's pleading look got to me when he said his buddy wanted to attend, but would only go with me. Long story short—I asked, we went, on the way to the dance, the buddy forgot to put gas in the car at Phon Brown's filling station, and we ran out just about where the road to Johnny's Bridge is today on Rt. 26. Well, another so-called buddy came along, and off to the nearest gas selling establishment they went, returning with a red five-gallon can of the needed fuel to take us to the dreaded event.

The dance was OK. We might have taken six steps around the floor and talked with everyone else we knew that night. On the way home, we joined everyone gathering at a local hangout by a pond. That's what we did back then—just hung out, talked, joked, some sneaked a beer, and then home we all went. It wasn't so simple this time. For some reason, a guy made a remark in my direction that Rex's "good" buddy didn't like, and he lashed out with his fist. Unfortunately, my date missed the guy completely and drove his hand into a birch tree, bashing up every knuckle on that hand. The ride home was interesting, interspersed with whimpers from behind the wheel.

Another first date was less eventful and so typically Greenwood. Guess where we went... yup, traipsed through a field so he could show me the cellar hole where his grandparents or great grandparents had lived. I can't remember the relatives, but I do remember there was a clump of lilac bushes at the corner. Yes, Dad, your love of history and exploring rubbed off on me—I found the whole cellar hole thing fascinating.

And then there was Career Day. I wanted to be a disc jockey and had contacted one at WCOU in Lewiston about coming down to see how everything worked. He answered that it would be fine. When asked by our principal what careers we were pursuing, I told him flat out, and he replied that NO woman would ever be a disc jockey. If I were to pursue that on career day, he went on to declare, I would get a definite F. Long story short: Louise and I went to Lewiston with Ted Dunham and the mail; she went shopping (I have no idea what her career was going to be), and I sat in with Lou Dennis for four hours on the radio. We met Ted at a pre-determined spot and then rode back home to Bryant Pond. That's a memory I will cherish…I got a definite day off from school and a definite F for my musical career.

And let's not forget when I became Queen of the Carnival Ball during my senior year. When the Winter Carnival was going to take place, I felt I should participate in some way, shape, or manner. I scanned my options and knew deep in my heart that the word FAILURE was stamped on them all. Still, my pride remained.

I decided to enter the snowshoe contest. If I fell it wouldn't be far…how much damage can one do on snowshoes? Dad agreed that I could borrow his snowshoes but to be sure and "bring 'em back." There was one other girl signed up for the event. She appeared with a pair of bear paw snowshoes. COME ON!! My Dad always said they aren't snowshoes unless there are tails on them. What a wuss she was to bring those things. Well, we stood poised at the starting line. Away she went on her little bear paws; I took probably four steps, the tails crossed, and I plunged face first into crust. That stung. It purely stung. I succeeded in getting into a position to take the dreaded LONG TAILED snowshoes off, meanwhile watching a gathering of fellow students studying my face, which apparently resembled a lattice work of little cuts.

Jeannie Mills insisted I come with her to their farm, which was near the event. I cannot remember the treatment she gave me, but it eased the sting and my pride. I probably was the only "Queen" at the Carnival Ball with a beautiful blue gown and a checkerboard face. I returned the snowshoes, intact, to Dad and told him that bear paw snowshoes worked just fine for some people.

It's hard to believe that I'm leaving school, after all these many years. No more waiting for the morning bus at Hank Leach's store at the top of the hill in Locke Mills. On miserably cold winter mornings, the kind shopkeeper would drive up from his home by South Pond and open the door so we could all go in and sit on the wooden plank atop the radiators to get warm. We may have dropped a few pennies for pencils, erasers, or a notebook, but his sales were meager when it came to a bunch of poor high school students. He came in early just to help us.

I'll not be playing High School softball and basketball anymore. I won't be hunting down Rex to get a nickel for a bag of potato chips to go with my tuna fish sandwich at noon. I won't be seeing Mrs. Herrick anymore and having a toga party at her little house down in the village. No more walking to downtown Bryant Pond at noon—one time Louise and I had saved our babysitting money to buy "dog collars" around our ankles at Cole's Hardware. That day, we walked back to school, proudly displaying them just above our saddle shoes!

What am I now to expect out there in the world?

OK, the music is going. I'm the tallest so will be the last girl in the line, and the boys will intermix as we go down the aisle. I'm so happy because my Dad is sitting near the front. Earlier this evening, he came into the kitchen with his best brown suit on, and Ma said, "Where are you going?"

He cocked an eye. "To see Muff and Rex graduate."

Well, Ma almost keeled over, as he never attends such things, but there he is, right here.

We've gone through the whole ceremony, and no one has passed out from fright. I thought I might when giving a long, boring valedictory speech. Even Dad made it through that without leaving.

We've been handed our diplomas, all ten of us, switched our tassels to the other side, and are ready to leave the stage. It's over.

It has been a long but memorable four years. I am going to miss climbing those long steps into our little high school. I wonder where my next steps will lead me.

*

Our class numbers have dwindled over the years, but the fun and companionship live on. Those were good days. How fortunate we were to be students in the Fifties!

139

Woodstock High School

Class
1955

Jackson-White
Portland

L. Farrington
V. PRESIDENT

J. Martin
PRESIDENT

R. Martin

L. Whitman

M. Cushman

W. Mason

L. LaValley

A. Cross

P. Farrington

A SYMPHONY OF SEASONS
The Long, Cold Wait

Chores

Winter is long and harsh in the western mountains of Maine. Snow comes as early as late October, and sometimes a storm will sneak in as late as Easter. Storms can brutally dump a couple feet of snow, which drifts to monumental heights by the ponds. Not even the Town snowplow can get through those drifts.

Dark comes early in winter. Last night, we sat by the table reading schoolbooks by kerosene light. A wick sputtered and flickered, and a look crossed Ma's face. She had hoped the wick would last a while longer.

Our little house is not insulated, and the wood stove struggles to give out enough heat.

This Monday morning, there's frost on the attic roof nails again, and it's time to get up and get going, as Ma calls it. Another school day upon us, but I am so glad we had such a fun weekend. Winnie invited Curt and me to spend Saturday with her on Rowe Hill and sleep over. Dad would come get us on Sunday.

When we arrived, first out came Winnie's glass jar full of chocolate "bits" and an invitation to take a handful. She then took out her View-Master and reels and reels of pictures from faraway countries to look at. One click of the finger and another picture popped in front of my eyes. We took turns and were careful to put the reels back in the right paper container when we were through. Everything looks so real when you hold the View-Master up to your eyes and click, click away! Of course, she made us chicken fricassee, which is one of our favorites, and we hummed our way through that meal! Winnie has the prettiest, plastic window curtains with different colored flowers all through them. This is the first time I've ever seen plastic curtains, and she explained that they are easy to clean and attractive, too.

We watched Wilmer, her brother, go to the barn and return with a pail of milk. What a treat for us! At home, Dad has all the milk because of his ulcers.

Winnie has electricity, which is something we don't have yet. She cranked up the Victrola and played records while we popped corn on the stove. She has one rule: if we start a record, we have to listen to it all the way through. Yes, even if we don't like the song, we have to listen to it. No listening to three words and then replacing it with another record. I think that's the only rule Winnie's ever given us...and a reasonable one at that.

A fun weekend, but today starts another school week, and I hear Ma and Dad already leaving. Roland will be waiting to inspect me and to scrub Curt. We'll go through the usual scrubbing "dance" because Curt always complains the water is either too hot or too cold. Usually by the time I get to the water, I find it just right because the old wood stove takes a while to get a kettle of water hot enough for washing.

You can imagine what Ma goes through when she has to wash clothes. She puts the big boiler, she calls it, on the stove early in the morning and adds a little vinegar. She says it keeps the clothes soft and helps get the stains out. I know it takes her a long while to wash clothes and bend over that scrub board with the brown Fels-Naptha soap. Sometimes her hands are all red from scrubbing. In the summer we hang the clothes on the line outside, but when we try it in the winter, we usually have to bring the clothes in frozen. They look funny so stiff, but hanging clothes in the cold is NOT amusing!

We get on the bus, and Cass looks like he's ready to start the school week, driving us carefully around the ponds, cigar in hand. Sometimes it's lit, and other times I think he holds it just for the company—I'm not sure, but I don't dare ask him. He pulls up in front of the school, and, as the last student jumps out, he backs up the van and heads for his store on the hill.

This day seems like forever. I think everyone is tired from the Christmas holidays and just wants to put their heads down on their desks and sleep. There are already two boys with their heads down—but that's because they were talking, and Mrs. Lurvey warned them twice. After that, down go the heads!! I can tell you, I'm very, very careful to do my work and keep quiet.

I want the day to end, as I am tired. On the other hand, school is nice and warm, and I know what it will be like when we get off the bus at home. We'll wade through snow to a cold house. If Roland's with us, he'll start the wood fire.

Today, I dig the potatoes out of the corner and start peeling. The kitchen's cold, my hands are wet and red, but the potatoes have to be peeled right now, so they will be cooked when Ma and Dad get home from the mill. Rex goes behind the house where there are some skinny trees cut by Dad. They're piled high, snow covered, with limbs sometimes attached as if another idea occurred to Dad in the midst of it all, and he just left the tree where it fell. Rex drags one to the sawhorse and uses Dad's bucksaw to start cutting.

As soon as I get the potatoes peeled, I put on my mittens and overshoes with buckles that Rex outgrew from last year and go outside to help him. I hold on to the end of the tree while he cuts because if the blade goes crooked, it might break and, boy, Dad would be really mad. Almost every week, he balances it in front of the kitchen window and files it sharp.

We have to fill the wood box, so he keeps pulling the trees on to the sawhorse until we figure there might be enough. Then we both start lugging it in. Chunks of snow go down our jacket sleeves—it's cold when they melt against our bare skin. Arms red and cold and hands frozen, we fill up the wood box as the kitchen grows warmer. Our mittens are getting big clumps of snow on them and pieces of sawdust. I think this is the chore we hate the most! Finally done, we sling our mittens on the stove to dry; that smell is awful but necessary. We then lean over the stove to get our arms warm. I throw in some blocks to get the fire going pretty hot, even though they are supposed to be used only for starting the fire. Cold hands call for drastic measures, I say.

I make sure the kettle is full of water so it can heat for Ma and Dad's coffee and get the frying pan down where Ma can put whatever she buys at the store in it. She can't buy ahead of time because there's no way to keep it cold; I think from the feeling, she could toss anything into a snowbank, and it would freeze until we need it!

I check the potatoes to make sure they are done but not too soft to hold together. I think Ma is bringing home fish sticks tonight, as they do not cost as much as other meats. She asked me once to keep an eye on them and handed me a spatula to turn them. Well, you know how graceful I am. I started to turn them, and they all fell apart. Disgusted, Ma complained she wanted fish sticks not mashed potatoes. I felt bad, knowing Ma was tired from working all day in the mill and still had lots of work to do before she could go to bed.

Chores and work. Life sometimes is hard for everyone in the Center, especially in the cold of the winter.

Thaw

I'm so sick of winter. I've been cold since last October—enough already! Yesterday, the sun came out and seemed a bit warmer; Dad said it was slowly getting higher in the sky. Well, I wish it was July high. Icicles are melting off the porch roof, and the heavy snow from last week is falling with thuds from the pine trees by the front yard.

I'd like to go skating on Twitchell Pond but usually wait 'til evening when we can burn the cast-off tires that the neighbors give us. My cheeks always prickle in the cold, so I stay pretty close to the fire. The tires burn really well, but boy do they smell!! Grammy and Uncle Louie sit on their porch and watch us as we skate around the fire. No one in the neighborhood complains that the smell is awful or too much. I think they are glad to be rid of something they don't need and enjoy seeing us having such a good time.

It isn't much fun skating alone, and, mind you, I'm not a good skater. My ankles want to go in one direction and the rest of my body in another. But what the heck—I grab the skates that my brother, Tink, gave me for Christmas and start for the pond. He said they were second-hand skates, but they fit me and are white and look sharp. Makes me look as if I know what I am doing even with flopped-over ankles.

I leave my old boots on the pond shore, and now the skates are firmly planted (I hope). I don't like the sound of the ice…it seems to be making strange noises, and I always think of cars and people crashing through. When Dad was younger, they say, he was snowshoeing across Twitchell Pond, got as far as Elmer's Bog, and fell through the ice. He managed somehow to pull himself out, but I never did get the details. I don't think it was one of his tall tales because I've heard other people talk about it.

Dad stresses to us not to get near the opening of brooks leading into the pond, because of what he calls "air holes." Seems to me that by now everything should be frozen solid. It's the middle of January, and we've been living like Eskimos for months. Nonetheless, those strange noises don't bolster my confidence or enthusiasm.

Oh well. Who might want to skate with me? There are no girls in the neighborhood, so I am thinking Hank Bowers might be at home.

He lives down the road a bit, so if I skate in that direction, he might see me and come out, and at least we can kill some time, tripping over each other as we attempt to stay upright. I start skating, avoiding branches and twigs embedded in the ice, and soon go by Wagner's camp, which looks pretty lonely this time of year, and then round the corner where I sit in the summer, complete with fish pole and thinking cap. I am about to start the straightaway when I hear a noise behind me. It's Keno, our Norwegian husky, trying to keep up with her paws splaying in all directions.

Keno is a wonderful guard dog and will not let anyone near my brothers and me if she senses danger. I wonder if she thinks I am going to go through the ice; whatever the danger, she's not going to leave me. We have had her since she was a puppy, when my Dad surprised Curt with her as a Christmas gift. I slow down and ask her what she thinks she's doing, way out here on the ice with me. Her tail wags, and she snuggles up to my leg as I stop. Giving her a pat, I skate slowly as Hank's house comes into view. I circle around, so Hank can see me if he wants to come out.

The sun is warm and yet no Hank. Knowing boys as I do, he's probably propped up with a comic book or watching television. Keno and I linger awhile and then decide that boys are not worth that much time and start our skate home. So far the noises from the ice have not plummeted us into the cold, briny deep, and we are safe. I don't know why I don't feel as confident on the ice in the daytime as I do at night. Maybe it's because there are more of us, and, if I fell through, someone would try and fish me out.

We are back at the starting point, and I sit on the cold bank and take the skates off. *That was a waste of time,* I think to myself. Keno sits beside me, and I am sure she echoes my thoughts. My legs are tired, so hers must be as well. The sun sure feels good on my face, though, and there's no nasty wind blowing to set the chills going.

We climb the bank to head back to the little house when I hear a voice. "Sandra, have you got a minute?" My Gram Martin has her porch window open a crack and is calling. Slinging the skates over my shoulder, Keno and I walk up the driveway hill to see what she needs.

Ha! Gram doesn't need anything, really. She's been cooking and hands me a fat cookie and a little mug of cocoa...made with real milk, not the

147

evaporated kind! I smell soup on her cook stove, and she has a bone saved for Keno, who waits patiently outside the front door.

January isn't bad when you have a nice thaw to warm the bones, and a Gram who comes to the rescue when she wants nothing but company!! Grams get lonesome, too!

Flight

Today's Saturday, and I don't have to roll out of bed for school. It's too cold here in the attic, however, to lay and read awhile before going down by the wood stove. Sigh.

There's snow on the ground and Twitchell Pond is frozen. Roland built a ski jump on the side hill, but I won't go over it. I would rather take our Speedaway sled and go to the top of Grammy's pasture hill, get a running start, throw myself down on the sled, and zoom all the way to the road. It's especially fun if there's a crust and a bright moon. We love the snow crust. Oh, we can walk everywhere through the pastures and not sink in until the winter sun finally shines. Give us a big piece of cardboard, and we sail down the hills twirling around as we go. The air is very cold, but Ma gives me some cocoa when I come in right before bedtime. She uses canned milk, but I am so cold, I don't notice the taste that I usually hate.

My brothers are in the front yard, unbuckling their skies. I hope they don't make the same mistake they made last year! When any of us are through with the skis, we're supposed to take care of them by leaning them against the house or sticking them in a snow bank.

Well, last year I was up early one morning and had breakfast with Ma and Dad. During winter, of course, it's dark when they leave for work, and Dad always goes out to start the car and warm it up for Ma. Dad had his lunch box in one hand and out over the doorstep he went. Unfortunately, one of my brothers had left the skis right in the shoveled path, and of course he couldn't see. All of a sudden, there was an awful yell. Ma rushed to the door and saw Dad balancing on a ski down the slope in our yard. She said later she thought he was going clear to the pond!

Oh, no! I peeked out the window, couldn't see much, but boy did I hear a lot!! He yelled something fierce, with arms waving in the air and swinging his lunch box. He finally came to a stop and staggered around in the snow a bit. Then he put down his lunch box, took both of the skis, one by one, and threw them as far as he could into the woods. Picking up his lunch box, he crawled into the car—still cursing, I guess.

The strangest thing was that Dad never mentioned the ski flight, afterward. Not a word to anyone. As strange, my brothers never spoke again of the skis or of even wanting to ski. I decided likewise it best that I not say anything either about the skis and had the suspicion that as loud as Dad yelled, my brothers undoubtedly heard every word from their bed in the attic. The rubber bands, cut from old inner tubes to hold the skis on their boots, lay on the stairs the rest of the winter and no one went near them. Neither brother asked where the skis were...not even as weeks passed.

When the snow melted last spring, the skis were found under a pine tree at the edge of the woods. I imagine they will take care of their skis in the proper manner this year. I'm still surprised that Dad didn't sputter. Maybe he figured by keeping still, it would be punishment enough. I'm not sure. Parents are strange that way, sometimes.

It's time for me to go downstairs. I can hear Curt and am sure he is through with his bowl of Puffed Wheat and ready to make a snowman or fort. Sometimes winters are very pretty after a snowfall, but not when the roads around the ponds drift so much the plow can't go through. That's when they come to get Dad and other men to shovel through the drifts.

My favorite place in the winter is sitting in front of the stove with my feet in the oven; the only bad thing about that is the smell of wet mittens drying on the stove shelf. Ma says she can't wait 'til spring comes, and I don't blame her one bit!

Shoveling

Ma is at the kitchen counter and flour's flying all over the place—she's forming her biscuits and they're delicious. I think she does her best thinking when she's busy, because she doesn't say much, but once in a while I hear a "harumph" come out of her throat. She's not pleased about something. Maybe it has to do with gossip, which she dislikes. Ma thinks there's something good in everyone.

It's pretty warm because Ma has stoked the wood stove to bake off her biscuits. Thank goodness, because the snow is piled high against the house, and it's a cold day.

The wooden floor, with all its roughness, looks the worse for wear about this time of year and no one seems to care. One can feel the air around the windows, so Ma takes tiny pieces of cloth and tucks them here and there during the coldest spells.

Dad has gone with a bunch of other men to help clear a storm drift up around South Pond. Up by the old Joe Cummings' place the wind whips across the pond and drifts the snow so high the town plow can't get through. The town then asks for men to take their shovels and just dig through enough so the plow can finish the job and clear the road to Locke Mills.

Ma mutters she wishes he would clear a path to the outhouse at the edge of the woods and a path to the road before he went off to work for the town. Maybe that's why the "harumph" came out of her throat.

Well, it isn't easy getting to the outhouse without a path, and, when Rex and Roland are working, we usually don't have one. Dad owns one shovel, and sometimes it seems he's not keen on finding the end of it—at least that's what Ma said once after she had to wade out there. Ma doesn't rile too easily, but I think that was a bit too much.

We usually have a narrow path shoveled to the road, because Dad hauls bags of blocks home from the mill, puts them on our Speedaway sled (made in South Paris, Maine), and hauls them down the path to the house. At least it keeps the rust off the runners, so when we want to run and do a belly flop at the top of Gram Martin's hill, the old sled really takes off in a hurry.

The wind whips the snow across Twitchell Pond, piling up in good shape in our front yard. Rather than shovel out our driveway completely, Dad leaves the car in a spot by the road. He shovels the spot just the width and length of the car.

In contrast, Uncle Louie shovels out the entire driveway for Gram Martin next door. He slices all of the snow, so that it looks like he's cutting into a wedding cake. Every piece is almost exactly the same, and, when he's finished, there's not a crumb of snow left in Gram's driveway. But then, Uncle Louie is like that. He stacks the firewood in the shed as he cuts it, so it looks picture perfect. Every stick is placed just so, looking like a great creation when he's done. I like to look at it. He does things neatly and perfectly because he's got all the talent for that. Dad just decides to do what's necessary and not a stitch more.

Just let me say I will be glad when the snow melts by the edge of the brook and I can see grass again...and I don't care if it is brown. At least I won't be wading through any more of the white stuff. And Dad won't have to worry about shoveling—at least until this all starts again.

Wishing for Warmer Days

I'm ready for spring. It seems like snow and winter have been here forever.

We've already had our Valentine's Day celebration at school. Mrs. Lurvey brought in pink and red crepe paper. During lunch time, we decorated a box, and she made a big hole in the top for us to drop our valentines in for each other. Some kids have wonderful valentines to give, but Ma usually buys us some that come in a book. The books have about 25 valentines in them, and I think they cost about a dollar or less, so Ma gets those for Rex, Curt, and me. We punch out the valentines and put the names on the back. I gave the funniest one to Kay and on back put "to Kay from Sandra." Sometimes you get a valentine with just your name on it, and you have no idea who gave it to you. That's always a mystery but a fun one! Sometimes I get valentines with a lollipop stuck in it or tabs on the bottom. When I get home and chores are done, I set them up on the kitchen table, all in a row, and just look at them. I love the colors of Valentine's Day and the big hearts. Of course, the valentines are put away when it comes time to set the table for supper.

With that day behind us, there isn't much to look forward to the rest of the winter at school. We hate that we have to sit inside and eat our lunches. The windows are closed, and, if the sun shines in all those windows, we get sleepy after eating lunch. Mrs. Lurvey is very patient when our eyes get heavy, but the learning goes on. I do think I have learned more this year than any other year. She's a very good teacher, and this year I am paying attention!

As the wind howls, and snow falls outside, my thoughts often drift away to warmer days and going for Sunday drives. My mother's friend, Lucy, decided one Sunday that Ma should take us three youngest kids and accompany her on a trip "around the White Mountains." We were some excited, I can tell you.

We started out early in the morning, and her old car chugged up Gorham Hill past the drive-in, as we three kids huddled in the back seat and shared the windows. After what seemed forever, there it loomed. Standing in the ditch, we looked upward, mesmerized by the sight of the Old Man's face on the side of the mountain. It was such a wondrous thing to see. We had heard about it, read about it, seen pictures of it, but there it was—the real Old Man of the Mountains!!! After looking at it a long time, we continued on to another site called "The Flume," where we picnicked. We walked along the falls a short way. Back into the car, on we chugged, night fell, and soon we were lost. Dad was at home waiting, and Ma kept wondering if he was worried. We kids dozed off in the back seat, and I roused when Ma remarked excitedly that there was the Balsams so she knew where we were. We chugged and bucked into the door yard about ten o'clock that night, having been gone thirteen hours. Yet there was no anxious face peering out the window for us—Dad was asleep and snoring loudly when we tiptoed into the kitchen.

That trip was memorable, but it's our usual Sunday drives with Dad that I remember best. Last summer, Dad went to Bethel and bought a 1938 Chevrolet, and it's a wonderful car. He had driven the old 1933 Chevy into the ground; the new one just purrs. Every Sunday afternoon or, at least, most Sunday afternoons when we were not at camp last summer, he wanted to take a drive. He and Ma in the front seat; Curt and I in the back seat, each with a window. Rex was always busy doing something with friends, and Roland was too old for Sunday drives, I guess.

The only thing is—Dad likes to go the same places every Sunday. One day Ma asked him if he thought something had changed in the week since we'd last been there. He just gave her a look and kept on driving. One ride we always make is to Bethel and then on to Newry, where we stop at Screw Auger Falls. At the same point on the road, Dad always pulls the car over and exclaims, "There's old Mt. Speck!" I don't know if that's the right name for it or not, as sometimes my Dad makes up names for different things. I know it's very pretty in the fall when the leaves look like Grammy's patchwork quilt. There are browns, oranges, reds, yellows, and some pine trees stuck in there for green. Screw Auger Falls also is always beautiful. Sometimes Dad stops the car, so we can walk around a bit. Other times he's in a hurry to keep going—he just waves in that direction, and we just rush by!

Right now, the wind is howling, and I am going to stay here in the attic and dream about summertime rides. Outside, the 1938 Chevrolet is parked down by the road with snowdrifts piling high around it.

I can't wait for that snow to melt.

A SYMPHONY OF SEASONS
Finally, Spring

Mud Vacation

Dad and Ma are at work while we enjoy our "mud vacation" from school. This week, there's just so much mud on Rowe Hill that someone said it's like a swamp; once you get into the ruts, you can't get out. When Rowe Hill Road gets too muddy for Cass to get his van up there, we have a week off from school. Everyone hopes that the road will dry up and be dragged by the Town in that one week time, but there are always ruts to dodge even afterwards. This time of year, it's a quagmire up that road and other backroads where kids live. I love this vacation, though. It's starting to feel warm again, and I want to get outside and let the sun kiss my face.

Curt and I are sitting at the kitchen table. He's coloring in one of his books, which he loves to do. I just finished sweeping the floor for Ma. Sometimes the old wooden floor is rough. I guess it looks better than it did before I started.

I can't remember when Curt was not with us, but I do recall when Ma was in the hospital and brought him home. Winnie Hanscom was living on Bird Hill in Locke Mills, and I went to stay with her and her husband, Ray. I was a little upset to be away from home because I was only four years old and used to being with my older brothers. Winnie and Ray gave me a doll that was in the house when they moved there, so I played with that but wasn't happy. Then one day, Winnie told me that we were going to have a big surprise. Tomorrow was Christmas and we were going to Ray's family in Newry! I did not know how we were going to go because they didn't have a car. She said that was the big surprise.

Early the next morning, Winnie, Ray, and I walked to the railroad station near the bridge in Locke Mills. I was a little afraid because I had never seen a train, but sometimes I'd heard one from Greenwood Center. It finally came into sight, big gushes of steam coming out the top, and, oh, the whistle when it came to the crossing!! I put my hands over my ears, and Winnie told me it would be alright. When the train stopped, she helped me up the stairs. I handed my ticket to a nice man, who smiled and asked me if it was my first train ride. Before I knew it, we were chugging up the tracks. I held tight on to Winnie's hand because after a while everything seemed to go by awfully fast. Well, before you could say Jack Robinson, the train stopped and off we got in Bethel. Now, I could tell Ma and Dad I had ridden a train! We had a wonderful day at the Hanscom's house. A very nice man gave us a ride back to Locke Mills, so I never did get the chance to board another train.

After Curt was brought home, I remember Ma holding him. I just wanted to hug him.

"Sandra, you have to stand at his feet," she said. "If you stand up above his head, he can be cross-eyed." Well, I certainly didn't want that. Now he's six years old, and his eyes are just fine, so I guess I stood in the right spot.

Today during mud vacation, I have the front door open to let in some of the spring air. There are patches of snow here and there, but it has melted enough in the woods that Roland has tapped maple trees to make syrup. There's a big rock in Grammy Martin's pasture that's split in two, and in the split is a perfect place for a metal rack and small fire to boil down the sap. We all take turns walking the little snowy path from one maple to another, carrying a little pail and emptying sap into it. We try to guess which tree will give us the most! It's hard work, as Roland, and sometimes Rex, has to use an auger to bore holes by hand and then put in the spiles. I love it when Roland gets the fire going, and the sap bubbles around in the old metal dish pan Grammy gave us. We usually don't get much syrup in the end, but it's a nice treat. It sure tastes good with Ma's warm biscuits! Roland is careful that the fire is out when we are through for the day. Grammy says that's all she asks of us.

I remember one day last year near the end of maple syrup season. We had a little sap we wanted to boil down, and it started to rain. So we brought the sap into the house and boiled it down on the wood stove. What a mistake! When it was boiled down perfect, I touched the cupboard, and it was sticky. Oh, my goodness, everything felt sticky! We quickly grabbed rags, water, and Ma's Fels-Naptha soap and started scrubbing everything within reach. Roland took care of the sap pan while Rex and I scrubbed.

By the time Ma and Dad got home from work, the kitchen looked very clean, and even Ma commented on our cleaning. All during the next week, though, sometimes I would hear her say, "Now that feels sticky. I wonder what that is?"

No one ever said a word.

Spring Cleaning and Smelts

Spring has come at last to Greenwood Center. Twitchell Pond is slowly releasing its grip on ice; each day more water appears at the edges. The first snow to go in our yard is on the bank of the brook; how wonderful it is to feel the crisp, brown grass under my sneakers. Walking as close to the brook as possible, I lean over and break off a bunch of pussy willows. Ma will say this is a sure sign that spring is finally here! I love their velvety touch and always put them in a canning jar for the table. Ma always moves them to the window sill, because our table is so small and there are six of us after all!

Robins make a nest under the eaves of Gram's shed. She pointed it out to me the other day, going on to say she likes to keep track of the little birds as they hatch, grow, and, especially, the day they take their first flight. There's always one little bird that the mother robin has to coax out of the nest.

Another sure sign of spring is the smelting season. Readying his net and bucket, each night Dad takes a flashlight across the road to see if they have started coming up the brook from the pond. He likes to get a head start, so he can get his limit before too many find out they are running.

There's a limit on how many smelts you can dip. Dad has his pail, flashlight, and net and usually can get his limit. As for as he's concerned, the limit is enough for a "good mess" and plenty to eat. Once in a while, a game warden will come along, ask a few questions, and look for someone who has dipped too many. One man once poured some smelts down his waders. Well, the game warden got him in a hurry. No need for waders unless the man thought he was going to chase the smelts back into Twitchell Pond! At least, that's what Dad said the next morning.

It's a crowded and noisy once the word's out. Cars line the side of the road, bumper to bumper, as if there's a grand concert. Everyone, mostly men, try to get the best spot, and they shine their flashlights and jostle others around. A few drink too many beers. I think Roland and Rex might go once in a while, but Ma won't let me near there. She says it's no fit place for a girl, and the language is awful. Well it's loud enough, so I have heard plenty right from my bed. And even from Dad, after a smelter gets too eager or drunk and falls into the brook, spoiling the smelt run for the night. I learned some of my first swear words from one of Dad's ruined smelting experiences. Ma said probably the ground was still soft from the spring weather, and Dad said, no, the man was full of beer. Hushing him, Ma told him to go the next night and get a mess of smelts for us.

Cleaning the smelts can be a slow job, but Dad's showed me how so I help Ma clean them. I love how nice she fries up the smelts all crisp. She gets the grease in the iron frying pan real hot, rolls the smelts in corn meal or flour, and pops them in there, where they snap in the hot grease. Oh, they are so crispy, and they have a little sweet taste to them that other fish do not. I just love them. I could eat them three times a day!

Brook trout are just as good fried up nice and crisp, but, sometimes on opening day, the snowbanks are hard to climb over to find a brook that is running. Dad's usually not much of a one for brook fishing, but when the urge to fish comes over him, and the pond still has ice, he tries it. Dad's not a patient man. I think he expects a brook trout to stay in one place and wait for him to grab it and bring it home. I haven't told him that, though.

Oh, let's not forget the spring cleaning. Gram has been out washing the outside of her windows, her white rag swishing in the sunlight. She says she used to wipe them with newspapers, and they really shone, but now the ink is different, so she uses old rags.

I visited Grammy yesterday. She had her parlor rug out on the line, having just beaten it pretty viciously with some kind of rug-beater. All we have is a wooden floor in our house, so at least we don't have to beat a rug. She looked pretty worn out and told me she was glad that was over with.

Now she has to take down all the curtains and wash the winter soot off them. She says the wood stove really smokes them up, and she can't wait until they are washed, starched, and ironed. It seems like a lot of work, but she told me it made her feel good to see everything sparkling and clean. Soon I see all the curtains out on her clothesline. She really goes at it when it is spring. I think she's beating winter right out of her life when she starts cleaning!

My Grammy is a tiny woman, but, boy, she works hard. She tells me it won't be too long before she'll need me to mow the lawn, given the way the grass is coming along. She has a push mower and her side lawn is actually a hill, so it takes me quite a while to get it all done neatly.

Ma mixes a concoction of vinegar and water and scrubs the windows on her days off from the mill. She's pleased that we can hang the wash out again on the clothesline that reaches from one tree to another at the edge of the woods. They smell so clean once the wind whips through them. I help her hang the washed kitchen curtains on the clothesline. Tink's going to buy linoleum for the kitchen floor to make it easier on her to keep the floor clean. I try to scrub it sometimes when they are working, but the rough wood makes it hard with the old rag mop.

It seems so good to see green again. There are some very cold nights but the days are warm. The mittens and knit hats are put away for another season, and the dreaded long, brown stockings are stashed in my bureau drawer. I hope they get lost over the summer.

The air feels so good on my bare legs. Ma says we can't go barefoot yet, and the ground really is too cold, but the mud has dried up pretty well.

I walk up the path toward my cousins' house to find white trilliums. There are plenty of the wine-colored ones we call Stinkin' Benjamins. They would look pretty in a bouquet if the Benjamins weren't so smelly. If I am lucky, I might also find yellow and pink lady's slippers out by my favorite rock past Wagner's camp. They're so beautiful. Ma has told me to never, ever pick them as they are the prettiest right where they grow. She said if I pick them, they might not grow again. She told me, "Don't pick the lady slippers. If you see a yellow lady slipper, they are very rare. Walk way around it." Ma is part Native American and very strict about nature and flowers. She did show us once what she called Indian Tobacco, a white, stemmy-looking plant. She broke off a piece on top, chewed it, and gave Curt and me a little to chew. It didn't taste bad, but I didn't want it in my mouth very long. Curt just pretended he was spitting chewing tobacco like one of Dad's friends!

Ma was on her knees the other day, scraping aside some old dead leaves and looking for mayflowers in her little patch. She does love mayflowers and says they are her favorite flower. She usually picks just one or two, putting them on the table in a tiny little jar to brighten up the kitchen. They smell beautifully for such a tiny blossom. She leaves most of them outside because, she says, that's where they belong.

Ma gave us our "worm medicine" last night, which she does every spring. She lined us up in front of the kitchen cupboard and said she had pills for us. Tink was first, Rex second, and I was last. She said Curt was too small to swallow the pills. Tink and Rex got theirs and without a sound moved on. It would have been nice if Rex had warned me. Ma had this little white packet and out of it came the biggest pill I had ever seen in my entire life. Bright purple and huge. She said I would not have to take the poplar bark medicine if I would take a pill. I tried but I couldn't swallow it, and I soon had purple all over my mouth and tongue. Finally Ma, just plain desperate, told me to never mind.

This morning, I peeked out the window, and there was Ma, taking bark off a poplar tree or, as pronounced here in Maine, "popple" tree. I wondered why she was doing that because she's told us never to take bark off trees. She came into the house, grabbed a saucepan, and tossed in the bark and a couple cups of water. I didn't say anything because I knew she was in no mood for conversation with her lips set in a fine line, determined to accomplish some mission. About an hour later, I found out her mission—me. I was summoned to the kitchen cupboard again, and there Ma stood, with a spoon in her hand and a bowl in the other.

"Open wide," she commanded. Well, this young lady opened her mouth and got the most foul tasting liquid ever to ingest.

"What's that for, Ma?" I sputtered.

"Remember the purple pill you couldn't swallow?" Short and to the point. Poplar bark tea was a natural medicine to keep worms away. That was her traditional spring tonic.

Ma has other old time ways to heal. If one of us gets a little cut, she sprinkles some sugar on it to stop the bleeding, slaps a bandage on it, and tells us it will be fine. I notice sometimes if she works outside on a really hot day, she comes in and sprinkles some salt on her tongue. I once asked her why, and she said it made her feel better.

Of course, we all eventually have the usual diseases kids will have from one varying degree to another. It took forever for us to break out with the chicken pox, and Ma said we would feel better once we did. Impatient, Dad decided he would go to Dan Cole's, get some "sheep turd," brew up some tea, and that would bring out the spots. No need. The mere thought of it,

163

and we erupted in good shape.

Spring is finally here and soon we will have nothing but green grass, apple tree buds, and Twitchell Pond will once more look as blue as the sky. Life is good.

May

The sun is higher in the sky now, making Twitchell Pond glisten like a layer of diamonds as its rays bounce off blue water. Gram Martin's lilac bush by the road has blossomed and the air is perfumed clear to our yard. We did not touch her lilac bush, because it belonged to Gram and we had never asked permission. That, however, did not stop a summer resident, who left with an armful one late spring day. My Gram sputtered on the porch just about as loud as I had ever heard her!! She thought it was pretty "nervy" to take them; had that person asked, Gram would have probably helped fill her arms full. It was a matter of principle.

Our Greenwood Center ball team goes into full swing in May. The month isn't as showery as April, and we still have patches of mud, but that doesn't keep Curt or Rex from bringing out their baseball bats. Rex always puts some kind of oil in his glove and keeps rubbing it in…I think he says it breaks it in for another year. Maybe they get stiff over the winter.

Another exciting thing to look forward to is May basket hangings. It's so much fun to fill a basket with candy of all sorts, sneak up to a neighbor's house, yell "May basket!" and the person's name, and run until the person catches you. Sometimes at school, we plan the May baskets. Usually we hang them on Friday or Saturday night, as most kids can stay up later. We all pool our money and buy penny candy either at Hank Leach's store or Arthur Vallee's store, squirming with excitement at the fun we'll have.

One year, the tables were turned on me! I was sitting at the kitchen table and suddenly I heard, "May basket, Sandra!" Oh, no! Dark as pitch out, and I did not see car lights come into the yard. I found out later it was parked up the road, and everyone sneaked into the yard. I dashed out the door and could hear shouts and taunts echoing across Grampa's pasture.

How could I ever catch them all in the dark? I think if I nabbed a couple, they might help me get the others. The person close to me was shouting, and I recognized the voice as John Chase. I ran after him, and over the barbed wire fence he jumped. Knowing I could never jump the fence, I decided to squirm under it. I was on my stomach trying to accomplish all this, and he was within a stone's throw still laughing, which, of course, infuriated me.

Suddenly, the seat of my dungarees caught on the fence, and r-i-i-i-p-p-p—what a sound and what a feeling! I yelled out loud, "My pants are ripped!" John laughed even harder, so hard in fact, he tripped over some brush and down he went. He was captive #1.

The chasing went on for what seemed like forever, but at least John helped when he wasn't laughing at the flapping seat of my pants. I think we chased for an hour, and then everyone came out of the hills like worms out of the ground and gathered at the house. We all shared the candy, but there was enough left for at least a week to munch on. The basket was yellow, with pink and light blue crepe paper beautifully wound around with long streamers. I kept the basket long after the candy was gone just to remind me of my friends and what fun we had had.

Fishing is now the topic of the day in May. Dad's just bought a Martin outboard motor to put on Uncle Louie's boats so he can troll for brown trout. Trolling is very peaceful; I sit in the front of the boat and just look at the camps as we pass by—Eichel's, Nick's Point, Wagner's, Jacob's, Cushman's. There are so many, and some I don't even know who owns them. Many people come from Berlin and Gorham, New Hampshire, and Dad says they drive too fast down our road, which is all pot holes and frost heaves.

Sometimes we sell the night crawlers to the fishermen who come to Birch Villa Inn in Bryant Pond. We have a mixture of dry mustard and water that we use at night. I don't know where Tink learned about it, but it works. We find a worm hole in Gram's lawn, put a little mixture down the hole, and out comes the night crawler!! I usually hold the flashlight for this operation. When it rains, we walk the road and find worms, too. This is fisherman heaven, I tell ya!

I love to fish but sometimes too much. One day I was on Mina's wharf, and my line tugged clear to the bottom. I thought there was a whale on there, so I eased the little alder pole slowly here and there and soon...plop!..on the wharf was a big bass. I know bass are not to be caught and kept before June 1st. I had to throw it back. On the other hand, I could see it in my mother's fry pan covered with corn meal and frying up golden and crisp. She would be proud of me to think I caught a fish that big...well it was almost a whole meal! But it's illegal to keep it—game wardens are more to be feared than State Police. I held my breath, dropped the pole, grabbed the bass, and ran for the house. The minute I got to the house, I went to the cleaning rock where Dad had given me lessons in cleaning fish, and, within seconds it seemed, no one could identify that fish as a bass.

Later, I retrieved the alder pole and waited for the folks to come home from work. Dad was the first to see the cleaned fish laying in the cake pan.

"What do we have here?" he asked.

"I caught a fish." That's where I left it.

"Looks to me like a bass."

Well I couldn't lie to him. The man knew his fish, cleaned or otherwise.

"Well, Muff, little early in the season isn't it?"

"Yes," was all I could muster.

"Ethel, get the frying pan hot!" Dad yelled. That was the end of the fish situation.

Peanut, Tink's old tomcat, goes off for weeks and comes back battered, cut up, and usually with one ear hanging down with dried blood and all. Dad says one of these days if he doesn't stop "tomming" he will shoot him. Well, none of us want that. Peanut is a good old cat and does what comes natural to tomcats. He would be much more handsome, though, IF he did stay at home, that's for sure.

Poor Peanut, always fighting. He needs to quit his tomming, take a deep breath, and enjoy with us this beautiful month in Greenwood Center.

Almost Summer

Winter has shed its icy cloak and changed to a dress of green. Grampa Martin's apple tree is full of blossoms, and one can smell the perfume all the way from his pasture.

The dirt is back, the grass is back, and everyone and everything seems to take on new life. My cousins and I crouch in the dirt by the side of the road with our marbles. I'm not sure if we have any special rules, but I love the colors and really want to win the pretty marbles, big or small. I have a tiny bag that I keep the marbles in and draw the string really tight to make sure they stay there until the next time my knees are dirty from the ditch.

We don't worry much about traffic. There are cars, but mostly only when the mill gets out, and people are coming home from work. By that time, we're all back in our front yards and completing chores before our parents arrive.

There are a few kids at school with yo-yos. Now I really, really want one. I know pretty well that I will never be able to "walk the dog" or any of the tricks that some of the boys can do, but it seems like a challenge.

After a little babysitting and saving money, I now have a genuine Duncan Yo-Yo. It's yellow with soft brown streaks through it. I practice upstairs on my side of the attic. Eventually, I make it go up and down quite nicely, but occasionally the string hangs down, and I have to wind the whole thing up again. I'm beginning to think that Yo-Yos are highly overrated, unless someone is really coordinated and skilled.

There's one thing I love to do, but Ma doesn't like it and says it's dangerous. I think she says that because the noise gets on her last nerve. We buy caps in little rolls, lay them out on flat rocks, and then take a rock and hit the little black dot—some make more noise than others. I know they're supposed to go in a cap gun, but we don't have one, so this is the next best thing. Ma says we are never to point a gun at another person, not even a toy gun. It's dangerous. If we point a toy gun, she says, then, someday, when we have a real gun, we'll forget and still point it in the wrong direction.

After Memorial Day, we get brave and decide to test the waters of Twitchell Pond. Curt and I put on our suits and up the road we go, barefoot and all, walking in the ditch. Ouch! Our feet are tender from wearing shoes all winter; by the end of the summer, the bottoms of our feet will be tough like old leather and nothing bothering them. (Well, the hot tar is something we kind of skip and hurry on, but rocks just bounce off our late-summer feet.) When we get to the field that Grammy owns, we scurry across the path to the little beach. We scurry because there are rumors there's a huge milk adder snake in that field, and I am not about to linger one tiny second. Have I told you how much I hate snakes?

It'll be another month at least, before school lets out. Now, let me tell you, I think school should stop the minute the weather starts getting nice. No one can think if the classroom window is open, birds are singing, and a warm breeze drifts in to flutter papers on desks. Some teachers take us outside for a class, and we sit on the grass in the schoolyard. I think the weather has gotten to them as well, and they are tired of smelling oily floors and chalk dust! Now that the ground is dry, we can all take our brown bags out and sit in the schoolyard to eat lunch.

It's so nice to feel warm again after the awful cold of the winter. I run across to Gram Martin's and sit on the porch while she mends, and we visit. She tells me if her hens are laying or not and if we have to collect eggs.

On the weekends, Ma hoes around her delphiniums and Sweet Williams. There isn't much room for a flower garden, but she does love the little plot she has. I have some hens and chickens that Gram gave me. Those are sweet little plants, and Ma has an iris that Uncle Elmer gave her, so we do have a little color at the side of the yard.

My pet rooster was killed over the winter. Last fall, Ma took him to Grampa Libby's to live as we had no place for him to keep warm. Mr. Rooster always rode on my shoulder, and we walked around the yard looking grand. Curt has a fear of birds—domestic birds I guess—and he didn't like Mr. Rooster at all. One day, I was feeling mean and chased Curt, with Mr. Rooster on my shoulder, clear to the main road. I got a real tongue lashing for that. The next day, Mr. Rooster went to Grampa's to live. Ma said it was for the winter, but I knew better.

Anyway, long story short, she announced that a coon came in over the winter and bit his head off. I did not want Mr. Rooster to come to that kind of a death and had hoped he could come back for more shoulder riding this summer. Ma said he was better off dead, as he was of no use to anyone

169

except for scaring kids. I got her meaning without asking questions.

I love spring in Greenwood Center, where it seems like a different world than the months we have just endured. There's one down side to it all—the dreaded black flies. The air is black with them, but you just have to remember to put on some of Dad's "fly dope" and you'll be fine.

Well, almost fine. Sometimes.

Getting up every day to see a beautiful blue pond and smelling apple blossoms and tar warm from the sun…who could ask for anything more?

A SYMPHONY OF SEASONS
Summer Freedom

The Summer People

Our little neighborhood is rather sleepy and quiet until summer arrives, and Twitchell Pond sparkles blue in the sun, again. As soon as school is over in June, the Summer People, as we call them, slowly filter back to their camps. They arrive in automobiles too expensive for us natives on a mill salary, each sporting a differently colored license plate from out of state.

Weeks before, their cottages had been opened, linens aired in the breeze from Twitchell Pond, and lawns raked for the grand arrival. We local residents, though supplementing our income by doing such chores, are never really enthused when the Summer People show up. Ma complains they pick her wild berries in our driveway; Grammy Martin complains they pick her flowers at the mail box. Dad never stops bellyaching about anything and everything pertaining to them. We don't really have much in common with most of the Summer People, so usually Dad hauls us off to the Indian Pond camp when he finds the arrivals too much to deal with.

Mr. Kenyon is usually one of the first people to arrive in his cottage across the road. He has cement sidewalks leading up to his front door and around the side of his cottage. I love skipping on those sidewalks until the day I see the big car with the out-of-state license plate in the Kenyon's driveway and know that my skipping days are done. This year, however, Mr. Kenyon has sold his cottage to Mike and Minna Jacobs. They come from Massachusetts and stay for most the summer, although Mr. Jacobs works for Scott Paper and travels to Philadelphia quite often. The camp across from Grammy Martin's is called the Wagner camp and is owned by Dick Wagner, I think, but Babe and Benny Hoos come stay there most of the time. I think they are all related, somehow.

I am ten years old, so there's not much I can do except take care of Curt while my parents are working. In a couple of years, I think I can find a job babysitting.

Sometimes I wish I had never taken the *Grit* route from Rex when he wanted to give it up, but then I wouldn't have made money and seen so many nice people. On Friday, I put my *Grit* bag on, sporting GRIT in big red letters on the side, and deliver one to Grammy and Grampa Martin across the field. Then I start the walk up the "flat" to deliver to Laura

Seames and past Uncle Elmer's house to Stan and Flossie Seames. As I keep walking, my legs get tired. Everyone is nice to me, so I think they know that it's a long walk. When I get to Dan Cole's white farmhouse, I turn right, start up the Rowe Hill Road, and begin walking the road down behind Twitchell Pond to deliver to Hollis (Hollie) Cushman. I like him very much, and he's always pleased to see me. He makes me sit down and visit a little while, and it does give my legs a rest. He asks me how my folks are; I tell him they are still working at the mill. He always wants me to make sure and let my Dad know to come visit him.

I have had only one mishap on my *Grit* route, when I was spooked by a strange animal. I was on the road behind the pond when suddenly an animal I've never seen before came out of the woods toward me. It was the size of a hedgehog but wasn't one. It wasn't a skunk, or I would certainly have known that! It stopped and stared at me; I stared back, and it didn't move. Slowly, I turned around and walked home. Dad said it had to be a possum, which we usually don't see. Assuring me it was nothing to be scared about, he volunteered to take the *Grit* to Hollie and visit.

Someone has spread the word that the Case family from New Jersey has come for the summer to their cottage above the Seames' homes, and they are throwing the big party for the neighborhood. They do this almost every year. They've built a stage, and we all enjoy music, food, and lots of fun. Ma and Dad don't attend, but they let us go. The Cole family is very talented, so Lillian and Charlotte Cole get on stage and sing in harmony. I like to hear them sing "Winter Time in Maine." It's so pretty, but I'm glad it's NOT winter! Irving gets up and sings, too. There are a lot of people I don't know who get up and sing all evening long. All around are long poles in the ground with lights burning. The food is delicious, but I'm shy, putting only a little bit of salad on my plate. Sitting on a stump in the corner of the yard, I eat with a little, plastic spoon and tap my toe to the music. I think it's so nice that these summer folks want to have us come to their beautiful cottage and have such a good time. The Case family blend into our neighborhood each summer like butter on warm toast. They are not Summer People in our eyes, but neighbors who go away for a few months and return.

Newcomers also have arrived from our own family, but they're here to stay. My Aunt Vi and her husband, Harold, have moved from Connecticut and live with Grammy and Grampa and Louie across the field. I went over one day, and Aunt Vi was on the porch trying to unpack all her boxes. She seemed surprised at first to see me stop by. Smiling, she then said "I bet I have something you would like." She took out a kewpie doll with pink feathers and attached to the end of a long stick. I was so pleased and ran all the way home with it. I have it on my side of the attic, and it makes me happy just looking at it.

Grammy's house doesn't seem the same. It has always been Uncle Louie, Grampa, and Grammy, and we get along very well, thank you. One thing remains constant. We still carry water from Gram's to drink and cook with, so that a few days later I think nothing of carrying the pail across the field and into Gram's kitchen. W-e-l-l. I take one step into GRAM's kitchen, and a godawful screech comes from the other side of the house.

"I just washed and waxed that floor and now you're on it!" Frankly, our own floor at home is made of boards, and we just scrub it. Period. I have heard of wax on cars and skis but on floors? I had no idea. Gram stands behind my aunt, wringing her hands. Now Gram and I have come a long way in my short life, and no one's going to make her wring her hands. I reach down, touch the floor, bring my head up, and say calmly, "Your floor is just fine." Stunned silence. I proceed to fill the pail. When it's full, I strut out of GRAM's house, head held high.

After leaving the water at home, I pass Gram's house to go visit my friend, Grace, and my aunt is still screeching about what kind of a daughter her brother has. I think the word "uncivilized" comes into play—at age nine, a good roll of my eyes suffices as a retort.

Summer is never sleepy here in Greenwood Center. There are lots of happy things going on if you know where to look…and where not to walk!

Another Fourth of July

Strawberry season has passed. Curt and I made several trips to the "flat," filling our white enamel cups with the tiny berries growing near the side of the road. I know there are lots more over in the field, but that land belongs to the Cole family. I know if I asked them, they would not mind, but we get enough for our lunch as it is.

Soon Grammy Martin will have some of her great grandchildren come visit for a week. I love to have someone different to play with, and they always have new games to share. We spend a lot of time on Gram's lawn. My cousins Valerie and Junior Winslow come most summers, and we have fun! They showed me how to play games like "Red Light" and "Simon Says."

Last year, my Aunt Cecile invited me to visit them for a week in Crescent Lake. I didn't know where it was, but it sounded like fun. Ma said it was ok for me to go, so when Valerie and Junior left Grammy's house, I rode home with them. They have a grand house, and Valerie has a room of her own. We played paper dolls for hours. Junior was very good and most of the time he played by himself, but there were some games he joined in on, too. I had never stayed at anyone else's house but Winnie Hanscom's, so I was a bit nervous, but they were so nice to me I hated coming home at the end of the week! There was a dance hall or something almost across from their house, and we sat and listened to the music while watching the cars come and go on Saturday night.

The Fourth of July is coming. Roland ordered fireworks, and they are supposed to come by train. He checks the station each day when he goes to work, and hopefully they will be here by the Fourth.

Let's fast forward a week—this morning I wake up pretty excited, because today is the Fourth, and Roland told us last night the fireworks came in yesterday. Today Ma's going to give us a treat. She's asked Uncle Louie if we can borrow his green rowboat.

Last summer, Uncle Louie's boat got one of us in some real trouble. Oz Palmer's hay wagon from Rowe Hill had stopped in front of my Grandparents' farm, and they were raking the little field by the pond. I remember Roland getting into Uncle Louie's row boat tied to the tree. I was

175

surprised, as we all knew that was a huge no-no. Soon another boy from the haying crew joined him. I don't know what happened, but the boat began rocking and my older brother toppled over the end into the pond. I ran toward our house, screaming that Roland was in the pond. Ma sprinted past me down the field and dove into the pond. She grabbed my brother, who was choking and spitting up water. She took him to the house and we were ordered to follow.

Today, shall we say, there's less drama on the pond. We're going to have a picnic and pick some blueberries! Curt is lagging behind, and finally I tell him if he wants to go on the boat ride, he had better hurry. He wants to bring a truck to play with.

Ma rows Curt, Rex, and me across Twitchell Pond to a little area that we have always called Nick's Point. It's just a little piece of land that juts out into the pond, but it's a source for imaginations to run wild. Who owns it? Did they ever come there? There's no camp, though.

Nearby is Brooks' beach, and towering above our heads is Rowe's Ledge. Curt and I gaze upward, searching for the ledge hawks that circle and shriek. But here, they are silent. We like to think they are sitting in their giant nests, looking down upon us, and wondering who the intruders are and how long their visit will last.

Across the pond, our house is just a speck.

Spreading out an old blanket, Ma takes out the peanut butter and jelly sandwiches. She was going to bring tuna fish but was afraid the sun would be hot and might spoil the mayonnaise in them. We've some puffy pink cookies from Vallee's store and also a couple of white ones with coconut on top. This is really a treat, complete with a big jug of orange Kool-Aid to wash it all down.

After the picnic, Ma hands us each a little pail she has saved from buying peanut butter and sometimes lard. They are perfect for berry picking, and there are fat and plentiful blueberries just waiting for us!

When Curt worriedly asks me if there are any bears here, I calmly answer that they are all busy on the other side of the mountain. He remembers, like we do, that once Dad was picking berries and, knowing bears were in the area, carrying a gun. Well, he leaned the gun against a tree and kept on picking. Soon he looked up and spied a black bear eating berries on the other side of the bank. Dad did not want to shoot him, just scare him, so he yelled and made noise. The bear looked at him, now a bit confused, and then wandered off slowly. Dad said if she had had cubs, he would have been in a lot more danger! So Curt keeps looking around for a bear as much as he is picking berries. Soon, Ma has her pail full, while the rest of us have filled a little over half a pail each. She says all the berries will make a fine pie and muffins.

It's a strange feeling to be out on the pond and seeing the houses from this view. Grammy's house looks so big sitting on the hill. Ours, on the other hand, looks like it was plopped out of a big hand right into a little clearing in the woods.

We head back. Ma doesn't mind rowing, and the pond is nice and calm today. Before we know it, we're reached shore. Rex jumps up with the rope to tie it tight, so we can all climb out.

It is getting dusky now, and we're all eager to see the fireworks Roland bought. He's given each of us some Roman candles but says he'll set them off for us so we'll be safe. We stand on the side of the road to watch while Roland goes to the edge of the pond. The Roman candles are beautiful! Curt and I each have a package of "sparklers" he's also given us, so we run in circles with them, sending off little sparks into the night. Uncle Louie and Grammy are sitting on their porch enjoying the pretty fireworks Roland sets off. He did not buy many with a big boom, and I am glad for that!!

It's been a nice day. We've had a boat ride, picnic, and, tonight, some wonderful fireworks. Maybe next week, Grammy's company will come, and we will have friends to play with again.

Maybe Dad will hold off his Indian Pond trip for another week! Curt and I are sure hoping!

A July Day

Saturday afternoon and I'm sitting in the rocking chair on Gram's porch looking out over Twitchell Pond. The sun has warmed the porch nicely; some might say a bit too warm. Gram Martin sits at her Singer treadle machine, the cloth hanging down in her lap and bunched up on the other side almost to the wall. She's working on a quilt top for another grandchild. The whirring stops long enough for her to adjust the quilt for a new patch, and it begins again. She doesn't talk much when sewing; neither do I. We just kind of sit and breathe in the nice warm air, letting the summer settle in on us.

I can't sew. Ma has a sewing machine and can sew anything. She once made us winter coats from old coats her friends gave her. They were nice and warm and looked like they came from a store. But I can't do it. I'm just not the sewing type, I guess. Ma has tried and tried, but I can't even thread the needle decently. She's finally gave up, saying she knows I would rather play baseball, anyway.

Ma knows her tomboy well. I'm so glad there's a baseball team in Locke Mills. We go up every Sunday afternoon when there's a game. I don't know everyone on the team. I know Chuck Melville is the umpire, Herb Dunham is usually the pitcher, and his brother, Leland (Squeek) Dunham, is the catcher. Well, let me tell you, one Sunday Squeek got so angry at a runner on base that he actually got up behind the plate and chased the guy around the field. He ran pretty fast for having all that catcher's equipment on, too. I just stared because I couldn't believe it!! The umpire and the pitcher grabbed him and got him under control, and the game continued!!

We always wonder if a foul ball might go through the windshield of a parked car, so we try to get there early and choose a safe place. There's no such thing as a completely safe place, but we do try to park behind trees. The wooden benches get a little hard, so we take lawn chairs, sometimes. Diddy Seames Johnson yells at every play, making sure they're playing the game right. She lives right next door to the ballfield there on Howe Hill, so is all rested up and ready to go every time the umpire yells "Play Ball!" It's a fun way to spend Sunday with Ma while Dad is off fishing.

But today is Saturday, and Grampa is sitting on a little ledge next to the steps that lead into the house. His canes, covered with Black Jack Gum, rest next to him as he gazes off down the road toward his potato field.

"Nellie, Nellie!" he yells, and Gram sighs and gets up from her sewing. "Do you think the potato plants are free of bugs, or should the kids be down there picking them off?" he asks, fiddling with the scarf he always wears around his neck.

"Ross, I am thinking the plants will be fine. They were down there in the middle of the week and filled two jars full for you." Gram rolls her eyes when she passes me back to her sewing. That is about as expressive as Gram gets when she runs out of patience. Her little blue sneakers hit the treadle again, and the machine whirrs back to life. She reaches into the box next to her and retrieves another pretty patch to sew.

I look out of the corner of my eye, and Grampa has headed for the barn, using the two thick canes to walk. It must be very hard for him to move around, as he has to balance between them. He's going to check on his pig in the pen at the side of the barn. I imagine it's hard for him to keep busy, because he cannot move around the way he'd like. That's why Dr. Boynton comes to see him on some Saturdays. I think it's arthritis, but no one ever says a word about Grampa and why he is crippled. I think maybe the pain is what makes him seem so cranky at times. I know that now that I am older, but when I was younger, he scared me to pieces when he yelled.

Gram sighs, pushing away from the machine, and I get out of the rocker. It's almost time for supper. I suspect Gram and Grampa will be eating the same as we'll be—beans and hotdogs since it's Saturday night. Once in a while, there's brown bread cooked in a cleaned lard can in the oven and cut with a string. That's so good, even if we only have oleo to spread on. Gram makes real butter, sitting and churning away, and has a pretty little mold with a leaf on it. Her brown bread must really taste good!!

Another summer day is almost gone, and soon the lightning bugs will be out, looking like little flying flashlights. Rex and Roland should be home soon, after working for Winnie's brother, Wilmer, in his field of cucumbers on Rowe Hill, picking them at the right size for the pickling factory in South Paris. A long day for my brothers in the hot sun!

I say good bye to Gram, and she smiles and disappears into her kitchen to check the beans in the oven. I head home, thinking about Sunday's baseball game on Howe Hill and wondering what excitement that will bring.

We've come to the end of another July day in Greenwood Center. Come tomorrow, there'll be ripples on Twitchell Pond, screeching hawks circling Rowe's Ledge, a quiet breeze passing through the trees, and Gram sewing on her porch. Always the same, and always wonderful.

Little Camp in the Woods

It's just a tiny camp with a big front porch, nestled in the trees at the foot of little Indian Pond in Rowe Hill. Just two rooms and an open attic. I delight in the miniscule kitchen, complete with a small black sink tucked in the corner, and the larger living room, where cardboard cutouts of trophy fish hang with the lucky fisherman's name and the date it was caught penciled in. The door bears messages from former fishermen. An old Franklin stove sits in the corner of the living room, and a grand assortment of mismatched chairs are scattered about. A bench has been built into the wall to serve as seats for Curt and me. Our "bedrooms" are the open attic, separated by sheets hung on old clothesline rope.

It's off by itself, as there's only one other camp, usually vacant, on Indian Pond. Our getaway, our piece of paradise, the camp is my father's refuge from the Summer People. He always complains that the out-of-staters ruin the entire span of warm weather with waterskiing and high-powered boats. When the last school bell rings, he immediately summons the family to the kitchen, and we know it's "time to go to Indian."

The bedroll is ready, fastened with a gigantic safety pin, pack basket brimming with necessities. My father barks out orders and reminders in between sips of Maxwell Coffee. "Remember, kids, we're not running back here for anything you might forget! This is going to be your home 'til you go back to school in the fall!"

My father rows the supplies down the pond while my mother walks the shoreline path with my younger brother and me. We top the knoll, and there's the little camp, its porch just waiting for the rocking chairs to be brought forth again.

My younger brother and I look at each other. We're home for the summer! Up the ladder stairs we go to the open attic to make sure our mattresses are still on the floor, and that no family of mice has taken them for their own. Ma is busy cleaning out the two small cupboards in the kitchen.

The next morning, our parents wake early, climb into the boat, and row to the head of the pond to ride to work at the mill. Once again, Curt and I are left to carve out the summer days in any shape we want. We can explore all day. The old dam near the camp is strictly off limits, but still tempting. Rocks upon rocks; whirlpools of foamy water rushing beneath boards aged to the point of breaking with rot. If one could just balance a short distance on one log and jump to the largest rock, there are schools of yellow perch to be caught. Oh, how that dam tries to lure us each summer day. Ma and Dad never know that I sometimes disobey them and fish there—I do always make sure, however, that Curt stays away from the dam.

Ma also delivers a stern lecture each morning on the consequences of wandering too far into the woods. Moose, she warns, are waiting to carry us away on huge racks of antlers like we've never seen before. We do see moose all the time. They break the early morning fog to cross the bog in front of the camp, giant heads disappearing into the water and coming up with a swish and spray as dripping cow lilies hang from their mouths.

Curt and I do our best to stay away from moose. There are rocks to explore, fishing holes to find, and paths to follow. We like the flat fish bed in front of the camp. For hours, we watch as a fish fans the bed, keeping it pure white amongst all the dark muddied water around it. We name it Egbert...male, female, it? No matter. It's our fish and, its name is Egbert.

There's another old rowboat, and, if I am careful, I can take Curt for a row but only around the bog in front of the camp. I cannot, under any circumstances, take him into the main part of the pond. I'm nine years old, he will be five in December, and it's my job to make sure he's safe all day.

During the day, food is not a priority for Curt and me. When stomachs growl, we search the cupboards and satisfy ourselves with bread and butter sprinkled ever slightly with sugar. A mayonnaise jar filled with Kool-Aid and stored in the pond to keep cool rounds out the lunch.

At some point that afternoon, we talk about what will happen on the weekend. Maybe we'll have company, and Dad will jump on a log and start it spinning again. Last year, some big man visited, Dad's feet flew around the log, and he was quickly dumped in the bog. It was the first time he'd ever done it, and he tried to because he read about it in a book. My mother asked him if he read about someone jumping off a cliff would he try that. Dad shrugged and cheerfully said he probably would.

The spring with the sweet cold water is up the path a bit, and we need to make sure there's water for coffee when Ma and Dad come home that night. On the shelf next to the tiny sink is a pail and dipper for the spring water. Around three-thirty, I start a fire in the little wood stove and fill the kettle with coffee water to heat. I peel a few potatoes. We'll have fried fish tonight. After supper, like every late afternoon at camp, Dad will troll around the pond to see if he can catch some white perch for our supper tomorrow night. My mother knows just how to cook the fish, and we're guaranteed they'll be crispy on the outside and pure juicy white inside. The potatoes are always evenly sliced, browned, and a little crunchy. A glass of water from the mountain spring washes down the meal.

We hear the mill whistle blow, and know it won't be long before they're rowing down the pond to end another day. After a fine supper, we'll go to sleep, listening to the night sounds at the little camp on Indian Pond.

The Moose

It's another Sunday at Indian Pond camp. Ma fried eggs and potato for breakfast earlier, and we're now sitting on the porch. The sun's been up just a little while, and the pond sparkles in the early morning light. Curt and I perch on the porch railing and are glad our parents are home today. My father rocks in his chair, coffee cup in hand, making plans to go fishing up in the corner of the pond by "a big brush pile."

Suddenly, there's a thrashing sound in the woods followed by a splash of water around the bend in the cove to the right. My father says he'll bet his last dime it's a moose. Sure enough, a big bull moose comes in sight, his mouth full of pond weeds, hanging and dripping. Dad tells us to be quiet, and Ma says she hopes he stays where he is. Curt and I look at the kitchen door for a quick escape, if need be.

The moose is walking around the edge of the bog right toward the camp. He ends up on the shore, still munching on bog weeds. Dad suddenly decides to see how close he can get to the moose. He's read that it's possible to get a few feet away, if one is careful, and even touch the antlers. Ma reminds him that he will do no such thing, and that his reading is going to get him killed one of these days. I can feel my heart pounding in my throat.

The moose stands and chews as Dad walks very slowly down the two front stone steps. The moose seems to ignore Dad as he takes two more very short steps. Curt and I sit in absolute disbelief. Ma is now on her feet, whispering to him to come back right now and reminding him he has four kids to support. Dad shushes Ma. There's something about the shush that arouses the moose. Up swings the massive head and stares Dad in the eyes. I know I should take my brother and run inside the camp, but neither of us can take our eyes off our father a few feet from this huge animal. Dad takes his hat off; the moose paws the ground and makes a huge snorting sound. Ma asks him if he is crazy. The moose lowers its head and takes one step toward Dad. Dad jumps in the air and, with a very un-Daniel Boone-like yelp, high-tails it up the steps on to the porch. Apparently content that he's established his territory, the moose snorts and lumbers off into the woods.

Wide-eyed, my brother and I just look at each other. Ma tells Dad if he keeps up these shenanigans, she will burn all his books. Dad sits in the rocking chair, grinning and tapping his foot in rhythm. Life at the little camp is never boring.

After the Fire

We're again at our Indian Pond camp this summer, but it's different than in past years. One cold February night, word spread from one neighbor to the other in Greenwood Center that the mill was on fire. We rushed into the yard, coats and hats pulled tight, and could see the red in the sky four miles away. Slowly, we went back into the house. I saw my mother and father's faces as they sat across the table from one another, silently asking, "What now?" As in most of the households, the mill was our lifeline to paying bills. Suddenly it was gone...charred timbers that my brothers and I saw when we went to school in Locke Mills the next morning. Hoses were still stretched out on Main Street across from the school, and the acrid smell of wet burnt timbers permeated our three-room schoolhouse.

My mother searched for work, finally finding a job at another mill. My father knew only logging and working in the woods. The minute the ground was bare enough, he announced one evening over the supper table that he was going to camp and would log timber for another mill owner. As soon as school was out, we would join him. The house seemed very strange without my father, and we couldn't wait for the last school bell to ring.

But now we're here in the peace and quiet Dad wants every summer. There is no one at the other camp on the pond, and evenings are very quiet as we gather on the porch after supper.

This morning my mother left early, walking up the shoreline path to the car and to work again in the mill. My two older brothers, Tink and Rex, are with us for a short time to help in the woods. Because there's no family left in Greenwood Center, our husky, Keno, is also with us. I'm afraid because there are hedgehogs everywhere, and she never learns to stay away.

In the morning, we leave the camp, carrying a sack of sandwiches, a jug of orange drink for Curt and me, and water for my Dad and older brothers. Dad leads us and we all fall in line, crossing the old dam, with the dog bringing up the rear. I keep Curt in front of me to make sure he doesn't lag behind. At last we come to where Dad is cutting timber. As soon as he and my older brothers have the trees on the ground, my job is stripping the bark. I love doing this and seeing how long a strip of bark I can get before it breaks. The sun shines on the wet wood, giving off a wonderful smell.

The husky lays in the shade, and sometimes Curt helps me strip the trees.

The sun is overhead, and Dad announces it's time for a break, so we find a log or a rock to sit on. The sandwiches are peanut butter and jelly; how good the orange drink tastes after working all morning. Keno goes from one to the other, gathering up a pinch of sandwich here and there. Soon, we're back on the job.

In a few hours, Dad announces we have to start the walk back home. He needs to row the boat up the pond to get Ma when she drives home from work. The walk back to camp seems much longer than it was this morning, but soon the old dam is there and camp waiting.

In a few minutes, the fire is going in the little camp stove, and, as always, I start peeling potatoes. We hear the distance sound of a car horn, which means Dad's to go get Ma. By the time she gets to camp, the little table will be set with mismatched dishes, the frying pan out and waiting for her to work her magic on the perch caught last night.

This is a different type of summer at the little camp. But as Dad said today as we worked in the woods, you do what you have to do to get by.

Soon my older brothers will be settled in on the porch, Curt and I on our mattresses, and we'll go to sleep by the night sounds.

Well, perhaps, this summer isn't so different after all.

The Canoe

It's another summer weekend at camp. This morning, after eating fried eggs and potatoes, Ma insists we should ride back to Greenwood and check on the house. I can't imagine why we would want to do that, since my older brothers are there, and Keno, our husky, guards the front door as if it were Fort Knox. But I am ten years old and not about to argue, and Curt secretly wants to get more comic books to read.

The house is, of course, fine, and my brothers are still snoring in bed. I run across the field to see my grandmother and find her churning butter. She has the wooden mold set out with its little maple leaf design and is turning the handle for what seems like forever. Grammy is so tiny, I wonder where she finds the strength. At last the butter is ready, and she offers me a glass of buttermilk. I've never had any before, and oh, how good it tastes on this hot day.

Dad's impatient, so it isn't long before we come back to camp. Curt and I walk the shoreline path. and soon my stomach is talking to me. It's not a good feeling, but I don't want to upset Curt, so we hop over the tree root, jump across puddles in the path, and peek through the bushes to see how far my father has rowed down the pond. Soon the little camp comes in sight, and my stomach says it cannot stay where it is any more. I run behind the camp, and you can imagine what happens! Soon my mother jumps from the boat, hauling it up on shore and tying it down for my Dad to draw in the oars and climb out.

Mothers always know when something is wrong and won't stop prying until you confess. In this case, Curt finally tells her I am sick, and she leaps into the air like a bullfrog out of the bog.

"It was that buttermilk; how many times have I told you that is nasty. I thought you knew better than to drink that stuff!"

Well, I can tell you, I do not answer back. I keep wondering how a person can say no to someone as sweet as my Gram when she offers you something to drink on a hot day and still please your mother. She finally calms down after my father reminds her we are having company this afternoon.

The company arrives by canoe. I like the man and woman but wish they had not brought their dog. He's one of those long, drawn-out, hotdog kind. What type of people have those things for a pet? I keep looking at him and thinking of our husky, Keno. I bet Keno could take one bite and have a meal out of him. Sometimes the hotdog draws his mouth back and hisses through his teeth. Curt puts his hand down to pat him, and the little hot dog nips his hand. I wouldn't have one of those on a bet…never know if they will lick your hand or bite all your fingers off for lunch.

We are all out on the porch, and the man is telling my father all about the canoe he paddled down the pond. My father says how he wouldn't mind having one of those, and my mother snorts that the rowboat is enough trouble now that he has a motor on the back he uses sometimes. The man tells Dad he ought to try it out. I can see a glint in my Dad's eyes, which usually means something is going to happen. I think my mother sees it as well, because she tells my father that it's harder than it looks to keep upright in a canoe.

I bet she's remembering the time he was deep into a novel about old time loggers and decided he should try logrolling on the pond. We stood on shore while he got on a long log and started moving it with his feet. He was quite successful for a while, twirling it around and around until success went to his head, and, apparently, he thought he could throw in a clog or some step and over he went…into the bog.

I guess Dad now has been reading about canoes and rivers or rapids because he is heading for the pond. I can't hear, but the man is bending over and, I guess, telling Dad how to use the paddle. The man gives the canoe a little push, and Dad lets out a whoop and starts to paddle. He paddles a few feet, and we are all impressed. The man hollers that he better turn around and come back. Dad gives a deep paddle, the canoe starts to turn, and I can see the look of victory on his face. I'm not sure what happens next, but Dad lets out a different kind of whoop, the canoe overturns, and all I can see is my Dad's head and one hand with a paddle. The man hollers again, but I can't hear him because my mother is really sputtering to the man's wife, and the hot dog is jumping and barking with a yipping sound. Dad somehow grabs the canoe and swims the few feet to shore, dragging it behind. The man is laughing now, and they right the canoe. My father is dripping wet, and my mother is beside herself in frustration from having a kid sick from drinking buttermilk and a husband who thinks he is a frontiersman. Curt and I stay away from the dog and keep very quiet. Curt pokes me and points at Dad, and we both snicker to see that he still is wearing his hat. We won't mention that to Ma, though.

The Long Walk

The summer days are dwindling down and most mornings it's cool enough so we can see the mist rise from the pond and especially the bog right in front of our camp. Curt and I have picked blueberries the last few days and had them for lunch at noon. We're slowly running out of ideas how to fill our days when Ma and Dad are at the mill. We sit on the porch looking at the mountain that rises beyond the pond. There's a white farm house way up and below that a brown farm. Our friends, Winnie and Ray Hanscom, live in the brown farm. They're upstairs in their own little apartment while her brother, Wilmer, and their mother, Margaret (Maggie), live downstairs.

We have visited with them before during the school year. Winnie graduated in the same class as Ma and sees us as her own kids. We pop corn, dig our hands into her jar of chocolate cooking chips, and she just smiles. Maybe we should go visit her today.

Curt thinks it's a good idea, but it looks to be a long way to walk. I'm thinking what Ma will say when she finds out I've taken Curt on such a long walk. It must be about two miles, but he's six years old now and says he can do it. Besides, we both know once we get there, Winnie will sit us down with milk and cookies to rest up for the walk back before we have to start supper.

I mix some drink powder with spring water, and we have a glass jar of orange drink to help us on our way. Off we start up the trail beside the pond, jumping the tree roots, and, this time, walking around the puddles. After all, we don't want to show up with muddy shoes to track into Winnie's apartment. We agree that when we get to the head of the pond, we'll put our orange drink in the brook to keep it cold and stop to drink it on our way back. We both know if we start drinking it now there'll be none left for the trek homeward.

We are on the last half mile and it's all uphill, but Curt is still holding strong. He asks if there are any moose close by in the woods. I tell him if there are any moose, they're probably busy eating. I have no idea what the moose are doing, but I would rather not think about it, or the hair will come up on the back of my neck. Soon, we arrive at the main dirt road that runs through the hamlet of Rowe Hill. There is Winnie's ice house on the side of the road. Ray carries the ice on a burlap bag on his shoulder to the house and up the stairs. Curt says that would be a good place to cool off right now, and I tell him all that ice was cut last winter off our very own Indian Pond. He looks impressed.

I knock on the door, and there's no answer. Well, Winnie cannot hear us from upstairs, I tell Curt, so we knock on her mother's downstairs door. Her mother comes to the door and tells us that Winnie has gone for the day. Oh, no! We have walked two miles, and there's no Winnie to give us cookies and milk and a rest. I remember to thank her, and we turn to walk back to the camp.

Curt's not happy and tells me I should have known she was not at home. His legs are tired. I ask him if I am a mind reader, and he just trudges ahead of me without a word. I catch up and tell him at least going home is all downhill, and we can rest when we get to the brook. There are no houses on this road except for Miss Hobbs' huge house. It'is at the bottom of the hill, and we scoot by hoping she's not outside. I don't know her, but I have heard she's particular who passes by the house. We were in such a hurry to get to Winnie's, I forgot she might have peeked out her window and saw us pass.

We're now at the brook sitting on rocks. Curt takes a long drink from the glass jar and hands it to me. The orange drink tastes nice and cold from the brook. We pass it back and forth until it's gone and then set out on the pond trail. Before long, the camp comes in sight, and Curt heaves a sigh. I hope he's not going to tell Ma that I tired him out today and took him on a journey that went nowhere.

I light the camp stove and get the potatoes peeled while Curt munches on peanut butter and crackers I've given him. The potatoes are boiling when we hear the boat coming down the pond. Dad's using his motor tonight, so he must be too tired to row.

Ma comes up over the porch and is glad everything is ready. I've put the dishes on the little wooden table, and Curt's already perched on the bench built into the wall. She flips the perch in the frying pan and asks what we have done today. I look at Curt, and he looks at me. Dad is looking at us both. Curt tells Ma we went for a walk and had a jar of orange drink. Is that all, she asks? Pretty much, I answer.

Dad announces we'll probably head for Greenwood on the weekend and close up camp for the summer. School will start in a couple weeks, and Ma says she has to buy us all new pencil boxes.

Digging into the fried perch and potatoes, I nod. My day has just been saved.

Night of the Thrasher

It's been so many years, and yet I remember every nook and cranny of our Indian Pond camp as I knew it as a ten year old. There's the bench my Uncle Glen built...the porch railings where I sat and watched moose slosh in the waters of the cove. The stump on which I sat, waiting to hear the sound of my parents' car horn to let us know they were home from work and soon would be riding the waves in the little motor boat. Time to make sure that the potatoes were boiling on the little wood stove, even in the heat of August! Ma would slap the iron frying pan on the stove and, while the fat was getting hot, roll last night's harvest of fish in corn meal or flour and into the pan they'd go. In a few minutes, we'd all be sitting at the little table with the potatoes and crispy fish ready to be eaten.

As you may have guessed, fish was pretty much the constant food on our table, and we never seemed to tire of it. However, there was one time my father brought a delicacy back to the camp that was met with a wary eye.

*

Horn pouting is a great way to fish, particularly if there's a full moon tickling the ripples in the bog. When we're at home in Greenwood, Dad takes us to Hicks Pond or Mud Pond in Greenwood City, and we fish for horned pout from the shore. At Indian Pond, we go to the murky waters of the bog or the cove.

This particular night, the moon is shining, but not bright enough that we can't see kerosene lamps twinkling from the camp as we row to the cove. It's chilly, so an extra light jacket is necessary. The lines are dropped. In the distance, an owl hoots and bear cubs wail. Nearby tree frogs perform in chorus, with bullfrogs chugging the bass notes. A splash near the shore means a coon has come near for a drink.

It seems as though we've sat on the narrow, hard boat seats forever, no more than three sentences exchanged, when my father gets a tug on his line.

"Ah ha!" he yells. (This is his favorite exclamation when, after a half hour of sitting, he gets a nibble.) Something's thrashing around in the water, and I grab the flashlight per Dad's command. "Shine it here, Muff!" he yells. Oh, yes, I shine it there...just in time for him to bring up this awful looking thing over the side of the boat. It's slithering everywhere and chaos erupts as Dad curses and I start screaming.

"It's a snake!" I leap to the other seat and am now suspended in mid-air, trying to remember to shine the light where Dad wants it. He's moving from one end of the boat to the next seat, chasing the slithering creature. Finally his boot stomps down on it.

"An eel, Muff, it's an eel!" He's so excited. For my part, I try not to retch.

"Well, throw him back!" I yell back.

"No, no, they're fine eating," he replies, getting the hook out of the eel.

We both agree that our horn pouting session has ended. Dad picks up the oars to head back to camp, with the creature still slithering around the bottom of the boat. My feet are still up in the air and I pray it stays on the bottom of the boat. I know nothing about eels, and that's fine with me.

By the time we reach camp and Ma, reading by the lamp, the slithering has stopped. Ma takes one look, rears back as if struck by a hammer, and informs my father that he can take that thing outside. There's no way she's having anything to do with it.

I think, in this moment, she's recalling all the different animals, the many organs of strange animals, that my father has just had to try—and always after reading some dime novels about the old West. The eel is the end of her rope.

Apparently, Dad realizes this as well. The next time I see the creature, Dad's standing by the little wood stove with the eel frying up nicely. I swear it's still moving in the pan. When I question him, he says that "is natural." Well, obviously it's not natural to the rest of us. We take our crispy perch and potato and sit on the porch for that evening meal. Dad remains inside with his eel at the little table.

And that was the last we saw of the thrashing eel. We don't know whether Dad ate it or not that night. We didn't ask him about it. I'd like to believe, in his bravest moment, Dad probably backed down and somehow got that eel out of camp and buried it in the back down by the swamp. Whatever; we're happy enough that it's gone.

Come to think of it, Dad does ask Ma to fry him up some potato before we go to bed that night. The slithering and thrashing probably even got to him. Not that he, the stalwart frontiersman, will ever admit it.

One Last Hurrah

It came as a total surprise last night when Dad butted his cigarette in his gold colored cowboy hat ashtray, tipped his cup to get the last drop of coffee, and then announced we should have one last weekend at camp. Ma protested that she did not have extra food to take except for a few potatoes and such. Dad said it did not matter because he would catch enough fish to keep us going for a day and a half. Ma replied he'd better because she had to be home by Sunday noon to get their clothes ready for work on Monday—if we're going to spend all weekend at camp, when will she get the washing done? Dad didn't answer but started to gather his fishing gear together, so Ma just sighed. I heard her mutter that she would be scrubbing clothes until midnight Sunday. She does have it hard, with nothing but a big tub and a scrub board and always the brown Fels-Naptha soap. Her hands are awful red by the time she gets through.

Here we are though, this Saturday morning, and Ma has the few blankets and odds and ends tucked into a huge blanket held together by what she calls a "horse pin." We'll soon be on our way. Dad has been revving the engine for what seems like forever. Curt and I are excited to go one more time before school; Rex and Roland are working in the woods this weekend.

We turn at Dan Cole's farm, up over Rowe Hill we go, and soon we're past the Colby Ring house and can see Indian Pond from the road. Down past Miss Hobbs' house we go, and Curt swears he sees her peeking out the window.

At last, we've come to the end of the road. Ma is tired, so she's gone in the boat with Dad while Curt and I take to the trail. The little camp is setting there just waiting for us. Dad has brought the boat in while Ma guides him and ties it up. Soon we are inside. The smell of the camp being closed up kind of knocks us back on our heels.

As soon as we get everything stored, Dad is in his boat and off fishing for white perch. He rows the pond, and there's little noise. Occasionally, he drops anchor but prefers the quiet dipping of oars and watching the fish line trailing over the back of the boat.

We know we only have this one day to explore, so Curt and I go down

to the bog behind the camp to see if there are any cranberries yet. Dad told us it would be too early, and he's right. Egbert isn't on his/her bed anymore, so we're not sure what we want to do. Curt tells me there's no way we're walking to Winnie Hanscom's house. I guess he remembers the last time I took him and found her gone. He doesn't forget easily.

There is a deck of cards in the camp, so we perch on the porch railing and play "Go Fish" for quite a while until Ma asks us to carry some wood from the back, so she can start the fire. She says Dad will be back with a mess of fish soon. By the time he's cleaned them, she wants the stove hot to cook them up nice and crisp. We each carry an arm full in, enough for tonight and the morning before we go home.

Dad was lucky and is now cleaning four big white perch on what he calls his "flat cleaning rock" down by the edge of the bog. Ma pops them in the hot greasy frying pan and they snap and crackle as they brown. Curt and I are getting a little hungry, as we had only peanut butter and saltine crackers for lunch. Potatoes are all boiled, and we sit down to a delicious supper. Why does it taste so much better here at camp?

After Ma and I finish cleaning the dishes, she notices that the pail of spring water is way. Wanting to make sure there's enough for breakfast and coffee, she grabs the pail to set off for the spring. Dad offers, but she says no, she likes the walk and will take her time.

Dad, Curt, and I sit on the porch, just listening. When there's a sound in the woods, Dad always tells us what it is. We learn a lot from him, especially at night when we lay on mattresses and there are really weird night sounds. One night we thought we heard a baby crying, and Dad said, no, it was a bear. He's told us about owls, nighthawks, and other animals, and we usually fall asleep while he's still telling us all these things.

Right now we hear thrashing on the other side of the bog. Oh, no! It's a bull moose, and this time my father sits still. He hushes us, saying in a low voice that it's just hungry and has come down for pickerel weeds and water. Curt and I sit very still, but the moose still comes wading across the bog. It enters the woods on the other side of the bog and heads in the direction Ma has gone for water!! OH NO! We look at each other, wondering if Ma will meet it on her way back from the spring. Dad says there's nothing we can do about it now and, if worse comes to worse, Ma can climb a tree. Well, I'll take his word for it, because I've never seen her climb trees, but, on the other hand, maybe she's never met a moose nose to nose. We hear it lumber off and then nothing.

Dad just sits. I wonder how he can be so calm when our mother might be in danger. I guess he knows her better than we do. Finally, he turns and tells us not to say anything to Ma when she returns unless she says something about the moose. We know we should obey Dad, so our lips are sealed.

About fifteen minutes later, Ma comes in sight carrying her bucket of spring water and climbs the stone steps to the porch. Relieving her of the weight, Dad asks how her walk was, and she says it was nice and peaceful; there're still some wildflowers in bloom at the spring. He tells her that's good, and he's glad she had a nice walk.

I figure that's enough adventure for one day and am glad it turned out the way it did. As Grammy always says, what people don't know won't hurt them. I think she's right. Maybe I will tell her about this and swear her to secrecy when we go home, tomorrow.

It has been a good day at camp. We look at the lights from the two farms on the mountain and head up to the mattresses. This is our last night at the foot of Indian Pond. Curt and I will miss it.

The Strawberry Moose

We're back home in Greenwood Center, and it seems like we never left. Curt and I sit at the kitchen table making plans for the day. We missed picking strawberries by the side of the road this year, but we both agree we had a good time at camp with Egbert the flat fish and picking blueberries.

"Maybe we can go see Uncle Roy, and he'll have some strawberries left from the big patch he grows next to his cabin!" Curt proposes.

"I don't think so," I reply, having overheard what Dad told Ma last night. Curt's eager to know what happened, so I tell him the story.

You all remember Uncle Roy—very talented and carves beautiful shapes from wood, toadstools, or most anything. A jackknife slashed into any piece of wood results in an intricate carving.

One day, for reasons never made to clear to me, he just decided to move from his house to a cabin in the woods. I visited him there once and saw something hanging from the ceiling.

"What on earth is that?" I wondered out loud.

He just grinned and said he'd been to the "fair." I didn't ask more questions, since it was obviously a woman's unmentionable hanging there in plain sight! That was my Uncle Roy—he had the very devil in his eyes!!!

Well, the story goes, Uncle Roy decided to have himself a vegetable garden. More than that, he was downright determined to have the largest, best strawberry garden, because he loves them. The lush patch, by the side of his cabin, was watered diligently and weeded meticulously. To ward off birds, Uncle Roy hung around the strawberry patch aluminum pie plates and anything else that would clatter and clang in the wind. Curt laughs when I tell him that Uncle Roy hung so much out there that it sounded like a brass band when the wind blows.

Well, it seems while we were at Indian Pond camp, Uncle Roy had something bigger to contend with than birds. His strawberries were ripe and lush on the vine, almost ready to pick, when one day he heard a ka-thrash, ka-thrash from the doorway.

Uncle has never been known for speed. By the time he made his way across the room to the door, his eyes met those of a bull moose looking in at him. The moose had rammed his head in the open door and couldn't get his head and antlers back out again. Agitated, it started swinging his antlers, knocking miscellaneous articles off shelves hither and yon. Well, Uncle Roy told Dad that made his blood rush, and he yelled "GIT" several times but that just upset the moose even more. He grabbed the antlers and pushed—to no avail. He couldn't shove hard enough, and the moose couldn't maneuver his antlers to get his head free from the door.

Just then, the tip of an antler knocked a can of Old Narragansett beer off the shelf. Enough was enough. Uncle grabbed a rubber mallet and began pounding the moose on the nose. The third mallet pound sent the now stunned moose backward and staggering. He tried to gain a footing, but recent rains had made the ground slippery. And so the moose floundered, going down right into the beloved strawberry patch, and then tried to get back up.

Like climbing out of a mud pie, Dad said Uncle Roy told him. The beast rolled and thrashed. Uncle claims hundreds and probably thousands of his strawberries squashed and stuck to the struggling giant. At last, the moose got to his feet and staggered into the woods.

Somewhere in the Maine woods, my Dad says, there was a moose, hide splattered strawberry red, shaking his head in disbelief. Standing in front of his cabin, surveying a sea of squashed strawberries, Uncle Roy did the same.

The Bat Man

It's been a muggy, hot August night here in the attic where I sleep. My bed is on the right side of the attic with a huge blanket on a clothesline rope hung right down the middle, marking my territory because my two older brothers have claimed the other side. There's a small window by the bed, which I can't raise, but I can see what the weather is like when I wake. Overhead, there's no ceiling, and I can see nails protruding down. It's particularly charming in the winter when frost gathers on the nails, bringing the cold even closer. There's a little blue bureau next to my bed that my great Uncle Elmer gave my mother.

The chimney comes up through the attic a few feet from the bed, and there's space around that chimney as it goes through the roof...which leads me to the reason I didn't sleep well last night. That space is like an entry to heaven for bats. I hate hearing the flutter of wings around my head and throw the blankets over my entire body. I've heard stories of bats roosting in a woman's hair. Not sure if they're true, but I'm not going to do any research. As I fall asleep, there's more flutter of wings around than I care to think about.

The next morning, I'm thinking of presenting this problem to my folks. They're home from work this Saturday, and perhaps Dad can do something about the chimney space. Then again, perhaps not, since he's never been a master carpenter. His best design was our house, which, if you can imagine, is actually shaped like a box. One enters the front door to face the stairs to the attic, which cuts the house in two equal sections. I'm sure my father would rather live back in the days of his western paperbacks and confront outlaws.

The breakfast dishes are washed and wiped, so I gingerly bring up the bat subject to Ma, who tells me to inform Dad of the problem. Curt's playing again with his trucks in the front yard, and I find Dad sitting on a stump in back of the house, filing his bucksaw.

"Dad, I think there are bats in the attic."

"How many?" He's still focused on the bucksaw and continues filing.

"I didn't count them because I didn't have a flashlight," I reply. "I know there must be more than one." In my mind, one is one too many, but I don't want to present too large a problem.

Putting down the bucksaw, he walks inside to tell Ma we have a problem. She shrugs and says there's nothing we can do until dark. Nevertheless, Dad clomps up the stairs and we can hear him rapping here and there. Ma just sighs and rolls her eyes.

Clomp! Clomp! He comes down the stairs, goes to the corner, and grabs his rifle.

"What in the world do you think you're going to do?" Ma asks, now alarmed.

"I've stirred the bats up," Dad declares, "and now I intend to kill them." I know he's been reading his western paperbacks again from the way he's now brandishing his rifle.

"You're going too far and you're not shooting that gun in the house!" Ma exclaims. Dad ignores her and clomps back up the stairs, rifle in hand. I think it's a .22.

Pow! Pow! Pow! Ma sits down in a kitchen chair, shaking her head while her lips move. I think she's praying. Curt comes quickly in from outside. I put my finger to my lips, so he just slides into a chair and waits. We all say nothing.

Clomp! Clomp! Down the stairs he comes and announces that the little—well, a word I can't say—are dead. He puts on gloves, ready to gather them up and dump them in the woods.

Ma's not happy. "What on earth were you thinking of, shooting holes in the roof? Why didn't you just fix the space by the chimney?"

"I could do that," he says, cheerfully, ignoring her tone, "but do you think the bats inside would automatically have formed a line and flown out by themselves?"

Ma's rolling her eyes again.

Propping the gun against the wall, Dad concedes he will fix the chimney space when he repairs the holes he just shot through the roof. Ma mumbles something about that happening when hell freezes over.

I'm just wondering if he will complete the repairs before it rains. Boy, I sure hope so.

Wood Stove and August Heat

The air is almost stagnant this late August morning, even though the nights are beginning to cool a bit, leaving a little dew on the grass out front. The leaves are barely moving, as though they have had enough heat for the summer. Twitchell Pond seems to just lie there, as if it doesn't have energy enough to ripple.

It's Saturday, and my older brothers have gone; one to work in the woods and the other to help a farmer with haying. Curt's already eaten Puffed Wheat for the morning and is out playing with trucks in the dirt. Dad's gone over the field to Gram's in hopes of getting the latest copy of the *Advertiser-Democrat*. It seems he's heard there's an article in there about the Ice Caves he wants to read.

Ma and I have finished cleaning up the dishes in the black iron sink. She declares she has to bake something and had better do it before it gets too hot. "I can't stand this heat," she says, wiping her brow.

"What are you going to make, Ma?" I hope it's something sweet.

"A molasses cake, I guess," she answers, pulling down her brown recipe book and thumbing through it. She hates molasses because that was all she had to eat when she was a kid. But during the war, we were forced to eat a lot of it, and I still like it.

"Your father will eat that, and you know how fussy he can be," she mutters, continuing to flip pages. I also know she's making a molasses cake because she has the ingredients and a molasses cake doesn't need frosting.

"Throw some more wood in the stove," she directs me, and now I know my part in her cooking campaign. "Make sure the stick is poked up tight under the oven handle, or the oven will never get hot enough to bake this off."

Down she reaches into her flour tin and, thank goodness, no mice this time.

"What about the oyster stew Dad wants tonight?" I ask this rather timidly, because sweat beads are already forming on Ma's forehead. She has all her ingredients lined up for the cake in the three feet of counter space. Her metal mixing spoon bangs against the metal bowl as she begins mixing the ingredients. She doesn't answer, so I decide to let the subject drop.

Suddenly, Ma slams down the bowl, puts her hands on hips, and exclaims, "Did you see your father last night? That show he put on?"

I am a little thunderstruck as Dad puts on a lot of shows with or without the aid of his Old Narragansett beer, and last night there was no beer. What's she getting at? Ma wipes the sweat off her brow with an old towel. "He wants oyster stew. That calls for milk. Well, I will just have to see if there's *any* milk left."

Ah ha! Now the picture's getting clear; the fog's lifting. Dad goes to bed early and reads his western paperbacks. Sometimes, his ulcers really kick in and he hurts, so up he gets, wanders to the kitchen, and fixes a bowl of crackers and milk. Sitting there in just his underwear, he spoons it in, saying he feels better, and then back he goes to reading.

Last night, he was in the middle of crackers and milk when headlights appeared in the front yard. Now when you come in our front door, if you turn left, there's the kitchen; turn right and there's the living room and my parents' bedroom. So…if you think about it, Dad's at the table in just his underwear. and the front door is between him and his pants.

Ma snapped, "For heaven sakes, Bob, get in the bedroom, there are lights!" A car door slammed. Dad crouched, but Ma claimed he could be seen through the kitchen window. In the end. Dad crawled past the front door on his hands and knees to the bedroom to retrieve his pants, and Ma greeted the visitors.

So that's the show she's still sputtering about, today. She goes back to her mixing, muttering that she hopes he's learned his lesson and will at least pull on a pair of trousers before going into the kitchen at that time of night. Bad enough the kids have to see him like that.

Well, the mixing is done, and the batter poured into the pan. Ma opens the oven, leans down, tests the heat with her hand and face, I guess, and the cake goes in to bake.

She's through with her recipe book, so I ask if I can copy a cookie recipe from it. She keeps the book in a little drawer at one side of her cupboards and treasures it. Roland has copied some, so I can also, if I want.

Ma puts another stick from the wood box into the old stove and glances at the clock. Pretty soon the smell of molasses cake will fill the kitchen and roll right out the front door.

No time to linger, though. It's Saturday, and the boiler has been on top the wood stove since early, early morning, heating up to do the wash. I put the treasured recipe book back in the drawer and get ready for the next hot late August chore.

A woman's work is never done.

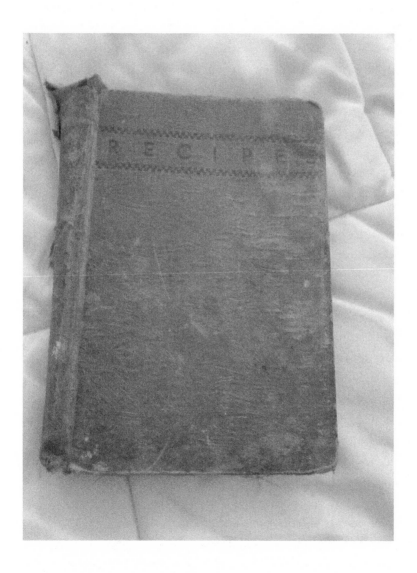

Smell of Success

The nights are feeling a bit chillier now, and I pull the old quilt up a little more to warm my body before finally climbing out of bed. The mornings are cool, but, as the day goes on, the sun warms enough, so we are still going barefoot and having a swim in the afternoon.

A handful of Summer People still remain in their cottages, which means Rex, Curt, and I can continue performing a ritual twice a week. We wait in the hot sun at the end of our driveway on Tuesdays and Thursdays, looking up the "flat" for Ace the milkman to come. I hold the glass bottle from the last visit, all washed and shiny, and we buy a quart of ice-cold milk to drink. Will it be strawberry or chocolate? Both of the boys like chocolate, but my favorite is strawberry, both for the color and flavor. This day is chocolate day, as we take turns.

Ace has no schedule. He might arrive as early as eleven or as late as one. We wait, as the day grows hot, taking turns to run to the house for a cool drink of water. At last, we see him coming and, before he stops his truck, we see him smile. I wonder what he thinks when he sees the three of us, barefooted and this morning's play dirt on us, standing and waiting.

He takes the shiny, empty bottle. "What will it be today?" he asks, still smiling.

"We want chocolate," Rex says, handing him thirty-five cents. Because we give him back the bottle, I think we get it cheaper. I don't know; I just want to start drinking it. We thank him, and, with a friendly wave, he speeds off to the next cottage.

I carry the milk bottle to the house, my hand making an imprint on the frosty glass. We sit at the table, each with a white, enameled cup with blue rim. Dividing up the chocolate milk equally, we drink until it's gone. The bottle needs to be empty, as there's no way to keep it cold. The brook water has become tepid in the summer sun, and one has to look for a hidden nook in order to find enough water to cover a bottle.

Ma is pleased that we spend our work money on milk; sometimes she'll give us a few cents to make up the difference if we are a little short. I think next week is the last week that Ace will be coming, because most of the Summer People will be gone by then.

But today is Saturday and Ma has a visitor. Ma works at the mill, doesn't have time to have many friends, and so is pleased to have one visiting. Winnie Hanscom walked over from Rowe Hill early this morning, and Ma is going to give her a home permanent. It's a Toni, and Ma has the pink curlers and end papers all laid out. The waving stuff does smell awful. Before Winnie arrived, Dad said he was going off for the day, so he wouldn't have to live with that stink. Ma said that suited her just fine. I know she wants to be able to visit, as she says, "woman to woman."

Winnie brought a cake to thank Ma for doing the perm, and we kids are pleased to see that!! On Ma's birthday, Winnie always bakes a cake, and Johnny Howe, our mailman, picks it up at Winnie's and drives it right up to our door while on his mail route. Now isn't that something! Johnny's really good; if I want to send away for something and don't have a stamp, I just put three pennies in the mailbox, and he takes them and puts the stamp on for me.

Winnie is sitting in the kitchen chair and hands Ma an end paper each time she gets some hair ready to be curled. The kitchen is getting kind of smelly, and Ma will be rinsing Winnie's hair and all, so I think it's best if Curt and I just mosey outside and maybe go fishing. Rex has already gone because the smell got to him, as he said.

Curt and I decide to just walk down the road a bit and see what's going on. We go by Grace and Charlie Day's place. They're very nice people and sometimes take us to a show at the Locke Mills town hall. One day, I was walking by and Grace called for me to come and visit. We talked for a while, and she invited me to stay for lunch as Charlie would be coming home at noon. She was cooking something called Welsh Rarebit. I wondered if we were going to have a real rabbit. But no, it was really good, with lots of cheese and stuff mixed together. Oh, they are so good to me. I feel as though I belong there.

Today their car is gone, so Curt and I stop by some rocks, where I cast out my line for perch. Dad says not to keep yellow perch in August as they are wormy. Well, I never catch anything else it seems, but it's fun to see the line tug and ripples around it.

Curt is a little worried, as this will be his second year in school, and he's always a little afraid and nervous. Ma has been to Brown's Variety in Bethel and picked up pencils and some new socks for all of us. She also went to J.J. Newberry's in Norway and got us each a pencil box. Mine is blue and has a little snap on front. When I open it, there are pencils, a pink eraser, a little ruler, and a protractor. I don't know why they stick that silvery thing in there, because I never use one and don't even know how to use it. But there's a little notch for it, so it must be good for something. I like the smell of the inside of the pencil box. Curt does, too, but Rex says we are both crazy.

We have new shoes to last all school year until we can go barefoot next summer. I hope our feet don't grow too fast. The boys have new sneakers, and mine are brown leather or something that looks like leather and lace up. Rex calls them "girl's shoes" and sniffs.

I haven't had a tug on my fish line, so probably I've lost the worm off the hook. Curt's getting hungry, and we've been gone quite a while, so maybe we should start home.

There's Winnie, looking very pretty with her hair all curled up. Ma's looking very satisfied that she has done such a good job. I see a pile of wet towels and know Ma will be scrubbing them on her scrub board tomorrow with Fels-Naptha brown soap and hanging them out on the clothesline.

The smell is mostly gone from the kitchen. Ma hands us the bread, peanut butter, and jelly and tells us to help ourselves. I plaster one together for Curt and one for me, and we head outside to eat on the rocks. That way Ma can still talk "woman to woman" with her friend and enjoy whatever smell is left.

A SYMPHONY OF SEASONS
Autumn Glory

October

I am ten years old and in the sixth grade, this October of 1948. I've always loved October because of the beautiful leaves. I told Grammy Martin that Rowe's Ledge looks like one of her patchwork quilts with all the different colors. In contrast, Twitchell Pond is now fading into gray, looking not quite as beautiful blue as it did in warmer months. Some mornings, a chilly fog slowly rises off the pond, leaving it shivering 'til the sun comes up to take the nip away. Within weeks, there's frost on my attic window when I wake. I know it won't be long before the sun will not be strong enough to melt it during the day.

Grammy asks me to mow her lawn one last time for the year. She always tries to give me a dime, but we don't take money for helping her.

Dad has been cutting pine boughs from trees on Pine Mountain right behind our house (so aptly named, because that's all you seem to see...pines everywhere). He'll use the boughs at the end of the month to bank up the house for winter. Then by Thanksgiving, when we have snow, he'll shovel that up around the base of the house with the help of Roland and Rex. The house seems much warmer, once it's banked. Our only source of heat in the winter is the kitchen wood stove.

I said that we've mostly pine trees around us, but Dad sometimes points out the spruce trees. Today, he takes his jack knife out of his pants pocket and slices something off the side of the spruce. He hands it to me. "Here, try this, Muff, you'll like it."

Well, I usually like most things Dad has me try, but there have been notable exceptions. "Spruce gum, Muff. Chew on it. Good stuff." Hmm, it really isn't too bad. Since we don't get to stores too often, this is pretty good and will do.

Speaking of trying new things, Ma once called Dad and me disgusting because we tried coon meat. I don't know where it came from, but Dad said it couldn't be all that bad. I thought it tasted like chicken, and Dad said the same, but Ma just harrumphed around the stove. Dad shoots rabbits sometimes, which everyone eats except me. All I can think of are the pictures of bunnies in Curt's storybooks. Dad also bags quite a few partridges, which he pronounces as *patridge*; Ma says it takes at least two to feed our family of six.

With the cold mornings, Ma checks last winter's supply of hats and mittens and says she hopes we have enough left to last 'til Grammy knits us more at Christmas. Every kid in school has mismatched mittens at the beginning of cold weather, so no one notices or cares. We usually start wearing them the first of November while waiting for the bus in the morning.

A few days ago I helped Gram slop the pig. She has a big, big place for their pig to wander around on the side of the barn. He's huge and makes a big snorting sound. I don't care much for pigs, and I think Gram knows it because after we carried the "swill," she picked up a handful of pretty leaves and told me how she saves them by ironing them on to waxed paper—but only the good leaves, no holes. After that, we went to her kitchen, where she gave me a gigantic, raisin-filled cookie. I can't describe how good they are. She says she stands over the stove, makes the filling, and lets it cool. Then she makes the dough, plops a bit of filling in the middle, and covers it with more dough.

Sounds like a lot of work to me.

Uncle Louie has pulled his boat out of the pond for another year, and it rests now upside down in the field. Before he launches it next spring, he'll give it a new coat of green paint, getting into every corner until there's not one inch of old paint showing. He's very proud of his boat and keeps it so nice. We borrow it on the Fourth of July, and Ma makes sure we're careful not to leave one scrap of waste or dirt clump in the boat, since he's so good to let us use it.

It's very quiet in October. The Summer People are gone, and their cottages closed for the season. The plumbers have all come, shut their water off, and cleared the pipes for winter. I walk down behind Wagner's camp once more to sit on the rock where I fish before they arrive in the late spring. It's a good thinking rock.

Ma is pondering today whether we should get another charge of her worm medicine, brewed from the poplar bark. We'll try to talk her out of that 'til spring. She checks her can on the shelf in the alcove under the stairs to make sure she has enough lard saved to warm up and put on Rex's chest when he has croup. He always has croup every winter and whoops all night.

Ma has bricks on hand that she warms in the oven for our feet and pieces of flannel saved and stacked near the can of lard for the croup boy.

And she's got cloves ready for my one tooth that always aches. Like other kids, I have made a trip to Dr. Brown in Bethel and have had teeth pulled, but this one tooth will not let me rest. When it's bad, Ma goes to the cupboard, pulls down a can of McCormick's cloves, and tells me to put a dab on my finger, then on the tooth, and it will calm it. It does. I swear I use more cloves in my mouth than she does in her cooking.

I think October is my favorite month because it's so pretty everywhere, and there's a nice smell in the air. The summer heat has been pushed away, and newness washes over our little hamlet. Soon, too soon, the colors will be gone, and skeletal trees will stand against the grayness of the sky.

I won't think of that now. Let's live in the moment, shall we?

Let the Music Begin

Another Saturday morning and I pull myself out of bed and look out the little window in the attic. The leaves are beginning to turn, and many have fallen to the ground. Halloween is behind us. I have to dress warmly, because Dad will be taking me to Grammy Ring's for my piano lesson. Ever since we went to Sunday school at their farm on Rowe Hill, I've wanted to learn to play.

Today is piano lesson day, and maybe both Ma and Dad think a little music will do me good and keep me out of trouble. There's no mistaking that music is a big part of our house. I hear Ma singing "Go to sleep, my little Buckaroo" every night when she puts Curt to bed. She hums when she's washing dishes or standing at the cupboard with flour flying as she rolls out biscuits. When I ask her who her favorite singer is, she always says, "Gene Autry." Then she starts singing "Back in the Saddle Again." I really don't care for that song, but since it's her favorite, I say nothing. Even though Ma works hard in the mill and keeps the house going with all her cooking, cleaning, and washing, I know how much she loves music. Unlike Tink and Rex, she doesn't play any instruments, but I bet she could if she had one and had the time to practice. Can you believe she doesn't like Frank Sinatra? She says that he's just a young kid and Bing Crosby has a much better voice.

I remember what Ma did to me when I was only four years old. I remember it like it was yesterday. She has friends down in the lower end of town and was going to a school play at the Tubbs District School. I guess one of her friends had a child in the play. I don't know; all I can remember is that the teacher asked Ma if I could sing, and she said yes. Before I knew it, I was standing up there singing "I'm a little Teapot, short and stout" and, of course, doing all the hand motions for the spout and all. I cannot believe Ma said I could sing. Had I been older, I probably would have hidden somewhere.

How thrilled I was when one of my brothers showed me how to make music with a blade of grass. It had to be a wide blade, and one held it to the lips with the palm of each hand on the sides of the grass. Oh, the first attempts were pitiful that I blew into the wind, accomplishing nothing but losing my breath and gasping. Finally, with his patience, I learned to squeak out a sound and eventually a short little melody.

Having met the challenge, I was ready to move on to the next step—a short, round whistle with a hole in the top, whittled by a brother. When he held it to his lips, he made a beautiful sound. When I tried it, I finally made a squeak and a squawk and left the melodies to him.

The one instrument I excelled at early on was the wax paper and comb. Wrap the wax paper around the comb and hum the melody. Excellent music, I thought. That music hung around for quite a while until another challenge came along.

How happy I was when Dad said I could lay his guitar across my lap, and then he handed me the round green bar to play. That was it—no instructions. If I wanted to play, then my ear would have to find the right notes. That was after or near the end of World War II, and patriotic songs were still popular. I finally figured out how to play "Iwo Jima Isle" in the key of C and sing along with it. So, I'd sit in a little chair by the wood box, strumming and singing as Ma walked back and forth between the counter and the wood stove, frying donuts to be drained on brown paper in the middle of the kitchen table. I'm not sure if Ma appreciated the serenading or not, but she didn't object.

When Rex and I were in the "little room" with Mrs. McAllister in Locke Mills, we always took part in the little play that was put on at Christmas time. I remember when the second grade got up, and we were to sing "Up on the house top, reindeer paws." I looked out, and there was Ma, sitting in one of the little seats! I was so excited that she took time from her job at the mill across the road and came to hear us sing! She was smiling all the time we were singing, and I was so proud!

Ma says one of her proudest moments was when our school put on a show at the Town Hall, and I sang with my best friend, Kay Dorey. We sang "Mockingbird Hill." The key was too high for me, but we managed to get through it without casualties. Then we sang "It is no Secret," which is a slow pretty song.

So now I'm becoming an even more musical member of our family by taking piano lessons. Here we go again on our drive, up to Dan Cole's farm, hang a right, up Rowe Hill to the top, and down the other side 'til we reach

Grammy Ring's.

Grammy tells Dad to come back in an hour, seats me at the piano, points out my lesson in the beginner's book, and goes to her kitchen, where she's baking.

"I will hear you playing, and if I hear something that's wrong, I'll be right in here." She says the same thing, always. I've mastered this piece of music pretty well. I hate the finger exercises...up and down, up and down...drives me crazy, but I love Grammy Ring, and she's so sweet to teach me.

It is over an hour, and Dad has not returned, so I sit and visit with Grammy. She tells me I have done very well and sees improvement each week. Ah, there's Dad. I pile into the front seat with him. He's grinning as we drive past the Sumner place to the top of the hill.

"Well, what did you play today, Muff?"

" I can play "The Peach Blossom Waltz" from start to finish and no mistakes!" I announce, proudly.

Dad chuckles and says, "Well, you must be doing pretty good." I've never seen him so excited about my music.

Into the yard we drive, and it seems he's driving faster than usual. "Come on, Muff," he says, a bit louder than usual. He opens the door, and what do I see in the corner of the kitchen? A huge old church pump organ sitting in the corner!!!! Look at the pedals to pump and the stops—oh, the sounds that will come out of that.

"Where did you get it, Dad?"

"Never mind, it was five dollars, and I want to hear you play."

Ma is saying nothing but kind of shaking her head. I know she feels that a church organ in the corner of the kitchen is the last thing she needs to walk around.

"Sit down and play, Muff," my Dad urges. I know lots of songs in my head, and there are no pieces of music to read, so I figure I'll just have to listen to the notes and play. Dad likes anything that's harmony, so I play a couple of songs I've heard him play on the guitar. The music is in my head, it comes out my fingers, and this is so much more fun than watching tiny little black notes. Ma finally speaks up, saying that I should only play when I have music and not play "by ear." I tell her it's more fun this way. She sighs, shakes her head again, and goes back to baking.

Suddenly, she turns and asks, "If the organ is there, where are we putting the Christmas tree this year?"

Dad takes a drink of coffee, taps his foot, and says, "Ethel, you worry too much. When Christmas comes, we'll put the organ in the other room."

I can't believe I have my own musical instrument! I don't care if it's an old church organ or not. It has its own bench and I fit on it, perfectly. I don't know where it came from, I don't know how Dad managed to get it in the house, and probably it's better that I don't.

I always figure a house is not a house without music.

Hunting Season

There's no such month as November. From the first day to very last, it's hunting season. This is the only time of year my father rises before dawn, downs a cup of coffee, and is out the front door by first, early light. His .348, or "elephant gun" as he likes to call it, is his pride and joy. He often says it's so powerful the bullet doesn't have to hit the deer but just comes close enough to create a vacuum, so the deer can't breathe and suffocates. He tells several versions of that particular tale. When he does, I promise myself never to look to see if his toe is tapping.

Dad and my brothers are excited for days before the first day of the month. Oh, the planning that goes into each hunt! It's the evening before opening day and there are at least three cars in our driveway. I sit over in the corner by the wood box while the men gather with Dad to plan strategy for getting deer. Chairs are pulled around the kitchen table, heads bent low as Dad pencils a map where each man will go. I hear words like Overset Pond, Furlong Pond, up the Ames Road, and cross over to Spruce Mountain. I have no idea where some of these places are, but it seems that they know the mountains like the back of their hands. Some will "drive," others will be standing here and there. As we kids grow into teenagers, my mother even joins the foray and enjoys every minute of this planning and wandering the mountains. She has a gun and hunts with these men! Unbelievable.

Smoke wafts off cigarettes burning down in ashtrays, so concentrated are the men studying the hand-drawn map that Dad has laid out for them. The kitchen air now's so full of cigarette smoke that it hangs like smog over a city. The smoke is as much a part of the planning as my mother's new glass coffee pot percolating on the woodstove. That glass coffee pot almost causes a casualty—and it has nothing to do with the hunting whatsoever.

Dad has completed a good share of the next morning's hunt and decides he will have a bit more caffeine to brighten his outlook. He does what he describes as a "Canadian Clog," learned in the potato fields of northern Maine, all the way to the stove, grabs the pot, fills his cup, and starts clogging back to the stove. Ma yells to be careful as his feet move faster, his hand holding the glass percolator ahead of him. Fellow hunters watch slack-jawed as he nears the stove. He miscalculates, and there's a huge click as the glass hits the side of the stove. Fate intervenes, and the percolator lands upright and still in one piece. Ma tells him to stop his foolishness and get on with the business at hand. I hear her mutter something about it's a good thing it's Pyrex, or there'd be nothing left of it.

The next morning, the hunters gather and leave at daybreak. I don't know how many deer Dad has shot in his lifetime. He loves the hunt, the chase, but I think he loves being out in nature the most. There's nothing that brings a big smile on his face more than a dusting of tracking snow on a November morning.

When he drives in the yard and the trunk is up, we rush to the front yard to see what he's tagged. One time it was a ten-point buck he'd shot over behind Nick's Point. Another morning, Dad tracked a deer, perhaps shot it, and came ripping back to the house. He needed help tracking a possibly wounded deer. My brothers were still snug in bed, blankets to chins, having had a late night. This was just not done—not in hunting season. Up the stairs Dad bounded, yanked both out of bed, explained in as few words as possible the position he was in, and that they had to get up and at it immediately. Later, one of my brothers mentioned that before he knew it, he was on top of a mountain hunting, glanced down, and realized he was wearing his "dress shoes" from the night before.

My Dad, always full of humor, never jokes about safety during hunting season. He demands it; he drills safety into Tink and Rex, and hates seeing cars with out-of-state license plates located on the road anywhere near where he's hunting for the day. One time, Dad came home from hunting ashen-faced and looking a bit scared. Come to find out, someone had shot in his direction. He hit the ground after just the one shot. When he decided it was safe, he got up and found the bullet hole in the tree next to where he was standing. His one remark was "Damn out-of-stater." Now, it could have been his neighbor, but it's always so much easier to blame someone with a strange license plate.

Hunting is a serious, no-nonsense affair for everyone. Deer meat has to be earned—you get up before dawn, run yourself ragged, eat track soup most of the season, and, if you're lucky, on the last day you get your deer and pose with the tag in the ear. My brother, Rex, sometimes pretends to be

sick after our parents leave for the mill. One year I was so disgusted that when the teacher asked if he was sick, I said, no, he went hunting. The teacher didn't even blink. I guess he had heard that before. The teacher probably wished that he himself was out there tramping in the woods.

After Dad gets a deer, he goes up to Locke Mills, tags it, and then comes home and others help him rope it up in the apple tree by our house. Within a few days, he dresses it and gives meat to all those in the hunting party. He always says whomever shoots a deer must eat a piece of raw liver in the woods. Now, I say that's gross and don't believe that he makes them do it, but knowing my Dad and his wanting to be a frontiersman, maybe he does. I don't know and don't want to know.

After he dresses it out, he drives what we call railroad spikes into the side of the house. He hangs the quarters on the spikes high enough so the neighborhood dogs cannot get to them. We don't have electricity, so the cold air's the only way to keep the deer meat frozen stiff. If it's mid-winter, the meat is hung from a hook in the cold attic where we kids sleep. Often, my first shivering look at a new day reveals the hindquarter of a deer.

When we want meat for supper, Ma gets out the fry pan, and he takes his hunting knife, goes out, cuts off slabs, and brings them in to her.

Dad can always tell by how the deer meat tastes whether it has eaten a lot of acorns or whatever deer eat. One mid-winter hunt resulted in meat that tasted like Dad had sliced pieces of a hemlock tree into the frying pan.

Sometimes he thinks it's a little bitter, but we eat it anyway. Ma made mincemeat once out of the neck and other pieces and it was delicious. There's nothing better than a mince pie made out of real mincemeat; Ma took the meat and ground it for what seemed forever.

Ma's a good shot, they tell me. I guess I'm the last holdout. I don't think I can ever shoot an animal. Curt says he thinks he will when he gets old enough.

"Great," I tell him. "When I'm old and married, you can bring me deer meat."

"Don't count on it," he retorts.

You see? Hunting's practically a religion, here. That's just the way it is. October, Hunting Season, and December—the autumn calendar in the Martin household.

Thanksgiving

It is truly cold this morning, and my blankets are pulled right up to my neck. I heard my brothers go down the stairs some time ago Voices and the smell of coffee come from the kitchen; the slamming of car doors woke me. The hunters have arrived on this Thanksgiving.

Ma hunts as well but today cannot go with the rest as the sun crests over Moose Cove. I know I should be downstairs as soon as possible to help her get the hen ready for dinner. We don't have a turkey, though I've heard some of the kids talk about them. Dad made the trip earlier this morning to the Lester Cole farm and returned with a nice fat hen for us to dress and cook. He doesn't like holidays and tolerates them like he would a rash. He gets through them, but, for him, Thanksgiving is like any other meal, just with more food and a hen.

After I gobble egg and fried potato, Ma asks if I'm ready. She has the stove going nice and hot with a big pot of water boiling. She grabs the hen by its scrawny, ugly feet and dunks it over and over. What an awful smell, but it has to be done. We lay newspapers on the kitchen table, and standing side by side, begin plucking the feathers out of the bird. Thankfully, Ma cleaned out the insides earlier. I helped her do that last year and told her it wasn't one of my favorite things to do. She said she wasn't too keen on it herself!

We finally have all the feathers out, so Ma goes to the wood stove and removes two covers. Time to singe the pin feathers! She grabs its scrawny legs again and thrusts the body down in the stove, turning it around until the pin feathers are all black and scorched. The smell is not getting any better, but I keep quiet as this is the unpleasant part of Thanksgiving Day, and Ma is very busy.

We scrape the pinfeathers and out comes the roasting pan. Kerplunk! The hen's now in the oven. Ma puts the stick up to the oven door to keep it closed real tight and declares it a job well done.

It is time to start on the potatoes, as we always have a big bowl of mashed potatoes. Ma says she hopes this year Dad gets home to eat at a decent time. "If he doesn't," she says, flipping her apron, "we'll go ahead and eat because he knows what time the meal's going to be on. If he wants his cold, well that's the way he'll get it!" Last year Dad and the boys didn't come home until about two hours after the food was ready. That's how my father is when it comes to hunting. He gets on the track of a deer and forgets there's anything else in the world.

Ma is back in the kitchen, looking at the pie she made yesterday to make sure it will pass muster. Biscuits are made, potato's mashed, and the hen has come out of the oven, all nice and brown.

"Well, here they come and on time for once," Ma says, glancing out the window. I put the six plates around the table and water glasses at my brothers' and my plates. Ma has opened a can of peas to go with the potato and hen. The table looks really full of food, with the biscuits and oleo set out now.

Dad and the boys come in and announce there was no luck in getting a deer this morning, but they plan to eat quickly and go right back out somewhere by Overset Pond. We all sit down, and Dad starts to pass the food. He hands the chicken, saying the same thing every year. "Here, have a piece of roadrunner. It's been running around the hen yard for so long, we'll probably break our teeth trying to eat it."

Ma always replies the same way. "Beryl Martin, that's a chicken and it's perfectly good." No matter. All through the meal, Dad will take a piece of chicken and hum..."Hmmm, good roadrunner this year." Ma says he should be grateful we have chicken on the table. He just grins in reply and taps his foot, which he always does when he knows he's made her sputter.

My brothers and I plow our way through mounds of mashed potato with gravy settling into little nooks like potholes during mud time. About the time I decide my stomach can hold no more, I make tracks in the potato, building road upon road, stalling until I can eat one more bite. Ma makes the best biscuits in the Center and perhaps all neighboring towns. How can anything so light be so filing?

Dad decides to have a piece of the pie. Ma sends me to get the red Jello in the glass bowl, which has set in the snow bank overnight. Curt and I especially like Jello and the jiggling it does. We giggle as we chase it on our plate. Once captured, it dissolves like a whisper on the tongue.

We have just finished eating, when Dad abruptly tells the boys it's time to go back out hunting. Before Ma and I can blink an eye, they're out the door and in the car. She looks at me, I look at her, and then we both stare at the huge pile of dishes. She puts the water on to heat.

It was a grand feast while it lasted.

A SYMPHONY OF SEASONS

Christmas Cheer

Christmas Shopping in the Little Village

Winter bounds in on Autumn's heels like one dog chasing another. Suddenly I wake to frosted windows and early morning frigid air that takes my breath way. My three brothers and I divide mittens from the year before and hunt down long-lost knit caps.

Yes, it's gotten cold, but this is going to be an exciting day. I can feel it in my bones. Dad's going to take us to Winnie Hanscom's house on Rowe Hill really early this morning. Roland, Rex, and I are going to visit and then do our Christmas shopping.

We have just passed Dan Cole's farm and are climbing the hill. It sure goes on forever, and I am glad there are no storms today. The sun is shining bright and feels warm for this time of year. The roads have been plowed well, and the old car seems to be chugging along. I always have a fear of getting stuck and being stranded, but Dad has a shovel and tire chains in the trunk just in case something happens.

Winnie is waiting for us and waves from her upstairs apartment window. Dad has errands to do and leaves quickly. We walk up the stairs to the cute little apartment. Her kitchen table is in an alcove at the head of the stairs, and next to it on a stand is a phonograph. I know Roland likes that, as he's wanted one for so long. I don't think we'll have time to play records, today. On the wall is a Mexican face with a big sombrero and ball of twine, so the twine comes out his mouth. She says she loves anything Mexican, and we can see that with the two red plaster peppers on the wall. At least they look like peppers. On her living-room stand is her View-Master, which I love to look through. Oh, I hope we'll have time for that later!

Winnie gives us each milk and a cookie, and we sit and rest before our big outing. We're ready. Roland has money of his own, as he works every minute he can, and Rex and I have a few cents to spend. Winnie digs out her big brown purse and hands us each a dollar bill. I'm rich! I've never had this much to spend at one time. She laughs and says this is her Christmas present to us, and we thank her.

It's about two miles, I guess, to Bryant Pond village. Winnie sets the pace, and we walk along with her. She points out the road that leads to my Grandfather and Grandmother Libby's house. She tells us the big dip in the road is called Velvet Hollow; there are many stories about how it got its name. We then walk up Townline Hill. Before we know it, with all the talking and visiting, we're passing by Birch Villa Inn and are almost into the village. I guess when people are happy visiting, time goes fast, and you don't notice if your legs are tired or not.

The village is quiet today, and we go up the steps into Clarence Cole's Variety Store. Look at the treasures. There are two or three aisles of things laid out flat, so I can see them really well. Winnie tells Mr. Cole that we have come to Christmas shop, and he smiles and tells us to take all the time we need. If we have questions, just ask.

He's a very nice man and patient as we walk, look, pick up, and try to make decisions. I see some pretty hankies Ma will like, and there's a big blue bandana that Dad could carry in his pocket to the mill. It's hard to buy for my brothers when they are walking around me, but I find a box of crayons and coloring book for Curt. When the boys look the other way, I pick up two boxes of pencils for Rex and Roland, who need them. Rex keeps track of his baseball scores and trapping money, and Roland is a wonderful artist. He draws lots of pictures with a pencil, so he will like the gift.

We have been here almost an hour, and Winnie has found a seat in the corner of the store and smiles as she watches us. Mr. Cole has taken my brothers' gifts and totals it all on paper. They both go out on the little landing in front of the store, and that's good. They won't see their gifts when Mr. Cole adds up what I owe. He smiles and even gives me back some change, which I stuff in my coat pocket.

"Don't lose it now," he says, handing me my bag. Winnie asks if we are ready for the walk home. and I guess we are because our hands are full!

The sun has gone a little lower in the sky, so it isn't quite as warm on the walk home. Winnie says we'll keep warm by walking, and she's right. Up the first hill, down Townline Hill, through Velvet Hollow, and soon we know around the bend is her house. We go back upstairs, and the warmth of the house makes our cheeks smart.

Winnie tells us to come into the kitchen and take a handful of chocolate chips from her big jar. Meanwhile, she says she'll make us some hot cocoa to warm us all up. That will taste sooo good, because they have their own cows. This will not be made with the canned milk Ma has to use. It's nice and warm, and we smack our lips. She's put some tiny marshmallows on top, and that's a real treat. Just when I think it cannot be any better, Winnie reaches into her purse and brings out three candy canes she bought at Mr. Cole's when we were not looking.

Dad will be here soon to take us home. What a wonderful day we've had! My legs are awful tired, but I have a bag full of wonderful gifts.

They don't make many people as nice as Winnie.

Celebrating the Early Christmas

Christmas is everywhere. There are little candles in people's windows and brightly lit trees shining in houses, in town, as you drive by at night. That's what my friend, Kay, told me at school. We don't have our Christmas tree in the house yet, but it will be soon.

We celebrated an early Christmas at grammar school at our Friday morning assembly. A teacher pounded the old chipped keys of the school piano, and we sang carols. "O, Come All Ye Faithful" seemed to drag on forever, and the boys sometimes sang Face Full instead of Faithful. I liked the quiet carols like "Away in a Manger" or "Silent Night" because I like pretty melodies, I guess.

Our school tree stood in the corner, decorated just enough to make it look like Christmas. Each year we give our teacher some little present. I have no idea what we gave Mr. Meserve. He seems so stern. Maybe it was another handkerchief he can fold and put into his jacket pocket. (He has it just so…shaped like a sharp point on top…and if it gets jostled during the day, you can bet your last dime he will finger it and get it up righted.)

Every year, we also draw names and buy for that fellow student. I always hope I get the name of someone who does not have much money, because I know they'll be happy with whatever we can afford to buy. Ma does the shopping, and she can make money stretch, that's for sure. If I get a girl's name, I'll buy a bracelet, perhaps, or a pretty pin at Brown's Variety Store in Bethel. I don't want to draw a boy's name, because what do you get a boy? I guess perhaps a book, or something like that. This year I got Kay's name, and she's easy to buy for because I know her so well. She likes pins, so I got her a Santa Claus pin to wear on Christmas Day. She was really pleased. I got three pretty hankies from someone. There wasn't any name, so I figure it was a boy, and he probably was shaking his head and wondering what to buy a girl. Maybe his mother helped him.

Anyway, now we're off for about a week and a half for Christmas vacation. I'm so glad we don't have to get up early and wade out to the road for the bus. I wonder if Mr. Meserve ripped out the Christmas tree and tossed it the minute we left on the last day before vacation.

This is Sunday morning, but in the winter Curt and I don't go to church at Grammy and Grampa Rings on Rowe Hill. I think it would be hard for Reverend Lord to find his way over and back in snowstorms and when the roads are not plowed well.

But today is a special day! This afternoon Reverend Lord has promised to come and get Curt and me. The Sunday School Christmas party—the day we have waited for, for so long! Curt says it's payback for all the Sundays we went to church when we were tired, and Rex stayed home and did what he wanted to do!

Reverend Lord is now following the narrow path into our driveway, and Ma is inspecting us to make sure we are "presentable," as she calls it. Curt has on a nice flannel shirt, and his pants are held up by a pair of brand new suspenders he got last fall when we started school. Ma made me put on a dress, and I hate it because that means I have to wear the long brown cotton stockings to keep my legs warm. But today is the Sunday School Christmas party, and I won't argue. Another early Christmas!

Reverend Lord drives very carefully up the Greenwood Road, and, as we turn on to rutty, unpaved Rowe Hill, he shifts into a lower gear. Although the road is plowed, it still has loose snow and is so narrow. I hope we don't meet another car. Today we're not going to where we attend church but are going to go past the Bryant and Hanscom farm and up a hill to the Palmer farm. I've never been there.

We are making the turn, and the minister says he's glad that the long uphill driveway to the Palmers' house is well plowed. I bet Oz Palmer himself cleaned it up nicely. He's a hardworking man, every summer coming to the Center with his horses and huge wagon to cut hay from Grampa's fields and haul it clear back to his farm here on the Hill. We run next to the wagon as it passes our house, filling our noses with that sweet smell of newly mown hay accentuated with a sneeze or two. Sometimes he lets us hitch a ride on the side of the hay wagon, so odds are that he made the driveway road extra nice, knowing we were coming.

The house is nice and warm! Winnie Hanscom and Elizabeth Palmer Bailey are both waiting for us and other children. We're soon ushered into the first room off the kitchen, and Curt and I take a seat on steps that lead to the upstairs. We're buzzing with excitement because there's a tree in the corner, decorated with little gifts underneath. Reverend Lord stands up in the center of the room and tells us the story of Christmas. We have heard it before, but he tells it in such a way that all the children are quiet and listen. Soon, a lady sits down at the piano in the corner, and we sing "Away in a Manger." That's one song all the children know, and we are very loud. There are some who are singing off-key, but I guess that doesn't matter. At least none of the grownups seem to change expressions. I am sure that our song is echoing right down into the valley, all the way to our little camp on Indian Pond. It's that clear a day, and the sun is sparkling on the snow.

Winnie is handing out the packages. All of us are getting little crosses with a Bible verse in the middle. They are so pretty, and I am sure they are home made. Someone put a lot of work in them. All the girls get a hanky and the boys pencils! Curt is looking over his pencils and the cross. I tell him it's a pretty bookmark, but I don't think he hears me because he's now staring at a basket that Winnie is carrying. There's something in little white cloth bags, and there are a lot of bags. Elizabeth is handing them out. What can they be? Curt takes one and says thank you. Good. He remembered his manners. He waits until one is handed to me, and we open them together. What a wonderful smell. The bag is full of popcorn, and in the popcorn are three pieces of fudge!! Oh, I love salt and sweet, and this is so good. Curt has popcorn in his mouth and is reaching for the fudge when I slow him down, although I know how he feels. I'd like to gobble mine, but we should save some to take home! Reverend Lord tells us that Winnie, Elizabeth, and the other neighborhood ladies—probably Mrs. Sumner and Mrs. Brooks as well—sewed the little bags and then made the fudge and popped the corn as a treat for us. We all say thank you together, and Winnie and Elizabeth smile. I think they're happy to see us so happy.

We've been here two hours, and it seems like we just got here. What a nice time we have had, and we have a gift, candy, and popcorn to carry home. Curt clutches the bag close to his belly as if he knew this is the grand payoff for all the Sundays we crawl out of bed and recite Bible verses in Sunday School. This is our reward—nothing to do with going to Heaven whatsoever. Curt whispers that he bets Rex will be sorry he didn't go to church, and I nod my head and grin at him.

Reverend Lord asks if we are ready for the journey home, so we gather up our coats and thank everyone again. I don't know which I like the best, the story of Christmas, the singing, the tree, the gifts, but I do know I will make the popcorn and fudge last as long as possible.

Celebrating Christmas early is wonderful. And soon the real day will be here!

Bringing in the Christmas Tree

Today is Saturday, and I think Dad will give in and *finally* get the Christmas tree today. He's been putting it off for what seems like forever. Ma asked him last night if he might do it this weekend, and he tapped his foot, took another sip of coffee, and muttered that he would try to find one that would fit in the house. Bah humbug! I've told you that Dad tolerates holidays like a rash. When I asked Ma about it once, she just shrugged her shoulders and said that some people are like that. Well, I'm just hoping he will do it today, so we can decorate this afternoon.

Ma is sweeping and cleaning out the corner, and I don't see Dad anywhere, so I guess he's finally decided he can't put off getting the tree another minute. He hates it, as the only place we have to put it is in the corner of the kitchen, reaching out to grab and startle him every time he walks by. It's the same every time: Dad's snagged by a branch, something goes flying off the tree, and then he mutters!

Ma tells us he put on his snowshoes and grabbed his axe, so he should be home soon with a tree. He seldom gets out of sight of the house before he finds something green and growing upright. If he were hunting a deer, Ma always says, he'd be gone forever, but she gives him ten minutes to find our Christmas tree and haul it home. She quickly clears the corner and moves the chairs, so he can fit the tree there fairly easily.

Curt yells at me to look out the window. Dad's back, dragging a tree behind him! It looks awfully big to me and kind of gangly. Mom's right—I bet he cut the first tree he came to. This looks like no one's first, second, or third choice for their Christmas tree. Curt argues that he thinks it's pretty. I assure him it will be once we can hide it beneath our decorations.

As soon as Dad gets the tree in the yard, he takes off his snowshoes, sticks them in the snowbank, and grabs his bucksaw. He then sticks his head in the door, cases the corner for height and width, and goes back out to saw at least a quarter of the tree off so it can come in the front door. And now, the yearly ritual: Curt and I back into the opposite side of the kitchen as Dad barrel asses the tree into the house with a huge ka-thrash, needles spraying in all directions. Ma yells that he's making a mess. Doesn't sound much like a fun Christmas right now, but we're used to this.

Dad goes back outside and returns with two boards nailed in a big "X" that he attaches to the bottom of the tree and then nails into the floor. Driving a nail into the wall on each window sill, he takes the clothesline Ma is holding and hooks it to one nail, winds it around the middle of the tree, and then hooks the other end to the second nail. This way the tree should stay secure for the few days Dad allows it in the house.

"There, by gar," my Dad says, standing back with a look of satisfaction on his face. "What do you think of that?" he asks us. We nod our heads quickly to show that we think it's the best tree in the whole forest. I still think it might look an awful lot better if we cover it with as many things as soon as we can.

After dinner, Dad announces he's going to visit his brother, my Uncle Roy, for a while. Ma thinks this is a good time to go to the attic and bring down the big box of ornaments. They aren't much to look at, but a few nights ago, Curt and I sat at the kitchen table and colored and cut out strips of paper. Ma made us some paste out of flour and water, and we soon had two, big, long chains of colored paper rings.

Curt digs out a purple, metal cone. Ma says that's Roland's ornament that he got when he was a baby. We find a few more metal ornaments shaped like little bells, cupcakes, stars, and some have glitter. They all look in pretty bad shape, but, tonight, when the Aladdin lamp is lit, they'll sparkle in the light. We pull out one ragged looking red garland and one worse looking green one, which we have had since I can remember. Curt and I string that on, and the tree begins to look better. Well, kind of.

We add the paper chains to make the tree fancy, then dig deep to the bottom of the box and bring out icicles left from last year. There aren't too many, so we drape them one by one on the branches to make it look all even. They will really sparkle in the lamp light tonight!!

Curt reminds me not to hang icicles too close to where we walk by, as usually Dad brushes against a limb and, if he gets any on his sleeve, he has quite a time! Ma says it's hard enough to get through holidays with him without putting icicles in his way. Curt looks at me and snickers, and I give him my evil eye look.

Now the tree stands in the kitchen corner looking pretty decent. It cuts down on our space in the little house, but Christmas comes but once a year, so I guess we can stand it for a week, at least.

Now the gift wrapping is to come. I don't get very excited anymore for Christmas, except I look forward to the orange tucked into the bottom of our stockings. Gram Martin will have knitted us a new hat and pair of mittens. What a treat to wear something new and warm to school!

Our friend, Winnie Hanscom, sent over a box of her homemade candy, which tastes like Needhams but is made from scratch, starting with mashed potatoes and coconut. The top is covered with melted chocolate, and it's ever so good!

Curt starts writing letters to Santa Claus. For about two weeks before Christmas, he sits at the kitchen table, writing a little note to Santa each night by the light of the Aladdin lamp. I help him spell the words, and, when he's done, I fold it up and put it on the sill of the window, which is thick with heavy white frost. He doesn't ask for much, I guess, because it doesn't take him long to print his note.

It's good to see the excitement on his face. Even Dad can't spoil that with his humbugging!

Christmas Day at Last

It's still dark outside. I'm not sure of the time, but I think I heard Curt rustling around downstairs. He's getting his Christmas stocking, I just know it. Last night we hung our stockings. I used one of those ugly brown cotton stockings and thought, at the time, it was the best use for the thing. Curt had a wool stocking with two red stripes around the top. Rex had the same, but his had two green stripes. Roland came in late, so I'm not sure what he hung—maybe he left a shoe, but I think he probably just hung a sock.

After we went to bed last night, I could hear Ma down in the kitchen. She does what little shopping is done, spending Christmas Eve wrapping the gifts on the kitchen table. We know as we can hear the rustling of the paper. Sometimes, I try to imagine getting something very expensive I liked in the Sears Christmas catalog. I know that isn't going to happen, but it's fun to pretend. Dad was already in bed reading his western novel by the light of the kerosene lamp. He doesn't shop—at least not that I know about. Like I said, he wants nothing much to do with holidays. I fell asleep before the rustling of paper stopped, so Ma must have stayed up late. She tries to make a nice Christmas day for us.

I am going to sneak down and get my stocking. Oh, these old stairs creak something awful. There's just enough light coming through the kitchen windows, so I can see presents on the tree. I grab my stocking, and up the stairs I go. There's something big and round in the bottom of my stocking, and I know it's an orange. We get one every year, and I eat mine very slowly to make it last. I think I'll save it until way later in the day.

Sitting on the side of my bed, I dig into the stocking. Of course, the stocking is not full. I didn't expect it to be, but it's the only stocking I had to hang! There are a box of crayons and some little scissors. My tiny flashlight gets dimmer and dimmer as I search. Two pencils, a candy cane, and here's a card with two pink barrettes for my hair. They are little butterflies! And there's the big orange!!!

Wow, what a nice stocking, and now I hear Ma getting the kitchen warm for us. She must have heard Curt get his stocking and decided we would all be up early today.

Breakfast is soon over; dishes are done. Never have cereal, eggs, and potato been eaten so quickly! Rex and Roland sit in the kitchen chairs by the wall, Dad is in his usual place at the end of the table, Ma on the other end, and Curt sits on the floor in front of the cupboard. I have a little cardboard box sitting on top of the wood box and will put my presents in there.

What do we get? Curt is excited about a card game called "Old Maids" and is already asking me if I will play with him later. I have a book of paper dolls. I love paper dolls and sometimes cut clothes out of the Sears catalog that Grammy gives me to fit on the paper dolls. Rex is given a new book to read, and there's a round tin filled with different wooden objects. Tinker Toys! I guess by putting the little wooden sticks into the holes on the round pieces, you can make wheels and all sorts of things. He also has a yo yo! Curt is coloring in his new book already. Roland has a new Hardy Boy book and a new flannel shirt. We all receive new hats and mittens that Grammy Martin knit. Ma has the hankies I bought her, and some pins that my brothers bought. Grammy Martin has also knit her some mittens, which she says will keep her fingers warm going to work in the morning. Dad has leather mittens with liners and two new flannel shirts. We're all pleased, and I can't wait to take my box upstairs to the attic and really look at my new treasures.

As I said, Ma bought the gifts for us. There are two gifts I remember Dad buying once and neither were for me. One Christmas morning, Dad disappeared outside after breakfast and came in with something hidden under his coat. I thought I heard a noise. He said, "This is for you, Curt," and out came the cutest little puppy ever!! Well, that was a surprise not only for us kids but Ma as well. I'm sure she was wondering if there was room in this little house for a puppy who would grow into a dog. Well, that dog was Keno, whom Dad had already named.

Another time, he have a gift to Ma. "I just cannot imagine what this can be," she had said, unwrapping it. We kids stood around her as she took off the wrapping. She was so surprised, she was speechless. I think we all were. Dad had bought Ma a pair of cowgirl boots. Ma kept smiling and gave her thanks while Dad grinned, but I don't think she had visions of riding a horse or moving to the Wild West right away. I never saw them after that morning.

Soon, dinner is almost cooked. Although we don't have a really special meal today, Ma has made her fluffy biscuits, and we also have a small ham, mashed potatoes, and carrots. Hopefully, we'll have a special person enjoy that food with us today.

I can see him coming up the narrow path through the snow. Grampa Libby has walked all the way from his house on Rowe Hill in the snow and cold. He's carrying a grain sack over his shoulder, and, as he gets near the house, I see his beard is white with frost and the cold. He comes in and hands the sack to Ma, who disappears in the bedroom. I take his big black coat and hang it on a hook under the stairs with the other coats. Grampa smiles, and, when he does, his eyes smile, too. I love Grampa very much. His smile crinkles up around his eyes, and the snow melts off his beard as he stands by the wood stove to warm his hands.

Ma comes from the bedroom with four presents wrapped, handing one to each of us kids. I open mine, and there are two beautiful hankies that Grampa has given me. You see, Grampa can't read nor write, as he left school in the third grade to work in the woods and help support his family. Ma puts tags on the gifts he brings. He's one of the nicest people ever. I look at him and say "thank you" very slowly because he's also hard of hearing. He smiles at me, his eyes lighting right up, again.

We all sit down to eat. Dad does not say much to Grampa. I think it's because he doesn't know what to say to him, but we talk to Grampa, and he's enjoying the ham and potatoes. He doesn't get nice meals too often, as my Grammy Libby is sick and cannot do much. After we eat, Dad will drive him back to Rowe Hill, because he doesn't want Grampa having to walk both ways in this cold weather and snow.

Ma and I pick up the dishes and load them into the black iron sink. Grampa says he should get home, because he does not want to leave Grammy too long. We say goodbye, Dad starts up the car, and away they go. I hope spring will come soon, so Ma can drive us over to visit Grampa more often.

Dishes are done, and the house seems very empty. I'm going upstairs and use my new little scissors to cut some of the paper dolls. Curt and Rex are sharing the tinker toys, and Roland is off skiing with a friend on the pasture hill.

We look forward so long to Christmas, and then, like a feather in the breeze, it comes and goes so quickly.

LOOKING BEHIND
Family

The Soulmate

I like to remember the first and last parts of his life. He was my responsibility when the parents went to work each morning at the mill. I was to feed him, see that he came to no danger, and be ready to report when Ma climbed out of the car at the end of the day. She always brought home a bottle of orange soda for him, as if to make up having to leave Curt each day. My little brother always handed me the bottle and told me to "take a sip."

When my parents left for work on summer mornings, it was taken for granted that we took care of ourselves, fed ourselves, and the house would be in order when they returned. There were days when we found nothing in the cupboard to satisfy the knowing and growling of young stomachs. It was those days that Curt and I went on our "red treasure" hunt and returned with strawberries. How many times we sat in the ditch on the "flat," picking strawberries until our enameled cup was full enough to share for lunch. We sat opposite each other at the oilcloth covered kitchen table. The first berry—oh, it was small, but my tongue played with it until it caught between two teeth. Juice sprayed—a little tart mingled with grains of sugar. Closing my eyes, I savored and knew my younger brother was also eating slowly, making them last.

Later in the season, we would pick blueberries. I remember the splash of cold water as Curt and I waded at Grammy's beach on Twitchell Pond during the season of high bush blueberries. They hung over the water, as we gingerly treaded along the shoreline to get our noon meal. The berries were warm from the sun and so sweet that we hummed our way as we went. Barefoot and dirty, we spent the summer days rolling tires up and down the tarred road, knowing it was rare there would be traffic.

Ma sent us to Sunday School at Grampa and Grammy Ring's home on Rowe Hill. It was never suggested that the two older brothers go along; perhaps Ma knew way back then that her two youngest were the kids who would need the most structuring in life. We went, learned our Bible verses, rejoiced at the Christmas feasts of popcorn and fudge in home-made drawstring bags, and never complained.

Life went on. School, high school, marriage for me. I did not see him as

242

much anymore until he started working as a handyman for Miss Hobbs at Indian Pond. Then, each morning, he would stop in to visit at the farmhouse on Rowe Hill and have a snack before going down the hill. Before I knew it, he was in high school and graduated the year I was pregnant with my last child.

He had problems he brought to me. We talked. He got married and had a family. He still dropped in. Once, he brought a kitten he found on the side of the road while working. His humor was the central part of my soulmate, my younger brother, as he grew into a man. One time, I was proud that I had polished my furniture with Pledge, new on the market and smelling like lemon. He came into the house, stopped, sniffed, and exclaimed, "This house smells so good, I could lick the furniture!" And there was the time he offered to give me a jack for my car for free, but its handle would cost me $10.

I think about his loaning me a car, so that I might get to my restaurant job in Bryant Pond. It was designed for a handicapped person and the gears, located on the wheel, were on the left side. He also told me to "gun it up the hills as the fuel pump was on its last legs," and so I did…and also through the stoplight, if possible, in the middle of town.

I don't dwell on the middle part of his life or my own. We both hit bumps that he found insurmountable, while I kind of worked my way around mine. Diagnosed with lupus, his life rather went down the drain, and he only blamed himself—at least to me.

I fast forward to the last few years. There was a soft side that few people saw. He lived in a trailer in the woods and took in an old stray cat and sent pictures. Oh, the pictures! He loved taking photos, sending them to me and asking if I could paint them for him. I painted…poorly…but to him they were Rembrandts. My last visit to the trailer showed them all proudly hung where he could see them. I think they ended up at a dump somewhere…and probably rightfully so.

He loved tulips and flowers and managed to make a garden in the woods to grow. At some point, he dug up some Blood Root plants from the Tracy cellar hole and brought them to me.

On opening day for fishing in April, he always tried to catch brook trout. Sometimes, wading in a snowbank to get to his favorite spot, he was determined to succeed. If he did, that night at precisely 7:30 he'd call and tell me they were in his freezer for my next visit. He always called twice a week at exactly 7:30.

Along with crisply fried trout, he always made a trip to Tom House's for provolone cheese, because he knew I loved it. We sat in his living room, munching on cheese and he'd tell me of plans to improve the trailer. He hoped it would all come together.

We laughed at some of the things that had happened to both of us because we always had. Our humor was identical in that we both saw the funny side of a situation that no one else seemed to grasp. Oh, the Lockhorn cartoons. How we laughed until we gasped for breath at Loretta and LeRoy.

I always bought him a bag of strawberry candies. Oh, how he loved those things.

Curt had his demons, and some overtook him at times. We all have demons; some worse than others. I like to think that for the last few years he was free of them.

God needed someone with a sense of humor to keep the angels happy and He called him April 16, 1998. For years after I expected the phone to ring at 7:30. Sometimes, I would start to pick up a bag of strawberry candies at the local store—and then remember.

But more than anything, I remember his sense of humor. His goodness and laughs filled our lives. Every April, around the anniversary of his death, the Blood Root he gave to me from the Tracy cellar hole presents its pure white blossoms for one precious day.

The Perfect Brother

From the day he drew his first breath, some (add your own number, Rex) years ago, he was the Prince of Greenwood Center, in my mother's eyes. I say this, not as his only sister, but as a well-known fact that he also "took after" her side of the family, with his darker looks. He also had the "look." You know, the "look" that spells innocent in capital letters? It came with him; his own personal birthright. (It didn't take long for me to discover that not only did I not look like my mother's side of the family, with the blonde hair, blue eyes, and don't give a crumb attitude so imbedded in the Martin side, but that I lacked an innocent look. I looked guilty when I was completely innocent...my own personal birthright.)

When Rex and I were very small, we played with trucks in the dirt in front of our house. For some reason, we gave names to ourselves. He was "Hunk," and I was "Toad." Don't ask—I have no clue why we chose those names. The little trucks were loaded with pigweed, which were our "logs" that we hauled to the mills.

As kids, Rex and I argued all the time. I remember one day when we just squabbled all day. Ma kept telling us to "straighten out or else," and we would for a little while and then something else would get us started all over again. Finally we ended up in the front yard throwing our shoes at each other, if you can imagine. I'm a little ashamed, thinking about it. Well, at that point out she came and told us to march into the house and sit in the chairs until she told us we could move. Rex did just that, but I started running for the road. She yelled at me that I had to come home some time, and, when I did, the chair would be waiting. I don't know what got into me. I just walked around the neighborhood and ended up sitting on my favorite fishing rock on the other side of Wagner's camp for about an hour. When I went home, Ma was busy and didn't even look up. She probably figured it was just another day at the Martin house.

Lord, let's also not forget the unscheduled ride Rex and I took in the door yard one summer. Dad's friend, Toivo Lehto, came to visit with his son. Well, he had a mighty fine looking car, and his son wanted to show us the inside, so the three of us jumped in to look it over. We knew better.

You just don't go jumping in other people's cars. I don't know what got into us. Ma was in the house, and Toivo and Dad were walking around the outside, paying no attention. Well, Toivo's son put the car in gear, and we started rolling backwards. I swear I felt my eyes getting bigger and bigger. Toivo and Dad came running as the car slowed to a stop. Toivo grabbed his son by the shoulder and shook him good, and Dad just told us to get out and go in the house. His voice was very low and gravelly, so I figured he was plenty mad.

Rex was involved in moneymaking schemes from an early age. I've already mentioned that he caught frogs and sold them to vacationing fishermen from Birch Villa Inn in Bryant Pond. When he was not at home, it fell to me to fill the orders when a fisherman came. I thought nothing of reaching into the bucket, grabbing as many frogs as the man wanted, and accepting the grand payment at the end of the frog sale.

At one time, my older cousin decided that he, too, would get into the frog business. Rex took exception to someone invading his territory and got into a fistfight by a little bog between our houses. The end result was my cousin landing in the bog with his brand new Sears Roebuck pants on. Rex kept his territorial rights and was not bothered again.

Rex did rescue me a few times from misjudgments on my part. Once I dated a guy and at the end of a very long, miserable evening swore I would never go near him again. One Sunday afternoon, that guy drove into our yard in his very new, low-slung, 1950's wide-finned car and inquired about me. Upon seeing the grill of the car, I ran upstairs to the attic, screaming for Rex to get rid of the guy. I was not an eyewitness to what happened next. (It isn't easy to see when one is hiding under a bed behind two cardboard boxes, with a blanket pulled over one's eyes). However, it was told that Rex wandered casually up to the car, and the guy rolled his window down. Rex then leaned in, put one finger under the guy's nose, and told him to pull a "u-ee" out of the yard and never go near his sister again. The guy blinked and did indeed pull the "u-ee," and I never had to see him again. For that time, I thank my brother.

Then high school graduation came. Rex left and went to Korea. Boy, did I hate to admit missing him. I remember the day he returned, coming through the door at the farm on Rowe Hill. I was married and had a daughter. Seeing Debra Jo, a few months old lying on the couch, Rex crossed the kitchen and said, "Hey, this has to be my niece" For a few seconds, all my cranky feelings of his being Ma's pet went right out the window.

So here's to you, brother. We made it through those bat-sawing, shoe-throwing years, and we're still going strong!

Big Brother

I can't remember when my oldest brother, Roland (Tink), was not looking out for my younger brother, Curt, and me. With both parents working, he was the man of the family, the overseer of the dirty ears and necks each morning, making sure we were neat, clean, and warmly dressed in the winter.

Tink was always quiet growing up; he was not one to make waves or engage in confrontations. I remember him going his own way most of the time. He was content in early years to read Hardy Boy books, which he promptly loaned to me when finished. His Gene Autry guitar hung from a nail on the wall halfway up the stairs to the attic, and one could always hear him strumming on that in his leisure time.

He never pointed out that I was his "little sister," but, as the years went by, he showed awareness of the position he held as big brother. He noted with interest boys who might take me to the movies.

He started high school at Gould Academy but left at age sixteen. I was never sure why, but Ma mentioned that he was ashamed because someone made fun of his clothes. That could or could not have been the reason. I like to believe he wanted to work, so that he could make life easier for our mother. He went to work at Arthur Vallee's store in Locke Mills as a clerk. As soon as electricity was strung through our little hamlet, the first thing he bought was a second-hand refrigerator for Ma. Not long after, he bought Ma a washing machine—a Maytag wringer, which was a joy after years of Fels Naptha soap and a scrub board.

Finally he bought something for himself. I came home from high school one day, and sitting in the corner of the kitchen was a Zenith record player. It was a tall, brown console and probably the most beautiful thing to ever be in our house.

"Sandra, do you want to hear something fantastic?" He was so excited, so unlike him, and he put on a 45 record of Les Paul and Mary Ford singing "How High the Moon." I could not believe the sound. He went into great detail of how it was recorded, track upon track.

When I wanted to ice skate, he bought me used skates so I could join the fun. When I wanted to be a cheerleader in high school, he bought me the white blouse I needed to go with the uniform. One winter he asked me what all the girls were wearing in high school. I said, red corduroy skirts and black cinch belts. On Christmas morning, I opened a package from him. and you can guess what was inside.

When Curt had an ulcerated tooth, he took him to the dentist. He took our dog to the veterinarian when she was sick. That was just the way he was.

He gave me away when I married the first time at age seventeen. I moved to Rowe Hill, my brother Rex joined in the Army, Curt was still at home, and Tink joined the Air Force for four years. He spent a great deal of time in Morocco and wrote to me about life there.

As years passed, he learned to appreciate Chet Atkins and, in time, could listen to his albums and play them exactly the way that Mr. Atkins played. It was a shame more people didn't hear him, but playing in public, he said, made him nervous. His hands would sweat. and he was afraid he would make mistakes.

Tink came home, married, and for years continued to care for our mother and the home she lived in. Like our Uncle Louie, who had so precisely stacked wood and shoveled the driveway, Tink took meticulous pride in the care of his home and lawn. Every blade of grass, I swear, was cut to the same length.

As the oldest brother, Tink was that and so much more. He was my second father. Once, when we were adults, I told him that. I'm so glad I did.

My oldest brother passed away in November, 2010. I miss him.

The Whirlwind

His given name was Beryl and he hated it. The hatred intensified the day he received in the mail an invitation to participate in a beauty shop program. I was about ten years old when I noticed that he was writing "Bob" Martin in the corner of his favorite books to declare ownership. Most of his friends referred to him as Bob. My mother, when she found herself at the end of her rope, called him by his full name—Beryl Aubrey Martin.

If there are two things my Dad gave me, it had to be my love of reading and a sense of humor. Dad was a voracious reader and dwelled in the land of the Old West. His favorite author was Zane Grey and as he read, he would relate stories of Betty Zane and Lew Wetzel to us until they became actual people still living that very day. He had stacks of detective magazines and dime novels.

Dad collected friends like dogs attract fleas. He was known for his story telling, and if you believed everything he said while he tapped his toes, then you were your own fool. One time he was at work. Now the mill sits near a railroad line, and a train was coming through. I don't know what the conversation was, but he was talking to a friend, and the man finally figured out that Dad was giving him a tall tale. He got so frustrated, he bit a piece of Dad's ear off. Not a big piece, but he left a sizable scar there...and a passenger train was going by at the time. Now I wonder what those people thought to see a grown man dancing up and down, holding on to his ear.

My father went to school as far as the eighth grade. Any education after that was through years of reading. He took a test and became one of the first to repair televisions, with all their tubes, when they were introduced. He probably was one of the most educated men I ever knew, but chose to live and be happy in the outdoors. He loved nature, fishing, hunting, and just sitting in his wooden chair at his Indian Pond camp. I remember fishing with him so many times, and he teaching us the night calls of birds and animals as we lay on our mattresses at the little camp.

Unlike my mother, Dad never cared to dance except for the occasional polka, and he wasn't very good at it when he tried. He was not a tall man, but towered over my five-foot tall mother. As she told it, he always grabbed her and SLUNG her across one side of the dance hall, and it was pure hell

when they came to corners as she had no idea where his feet were going or where she would end up. I think the fact that he threw in a few clog steps might have thrown her off as well. Sunday morning conversations afterwards were always a delight. Over the morning coffee would be the usual complaints from my father. The hall was too hot; too much noise.

This, of course, made my mother just cringe having to listen to criticisms of her favorite pastime.

The story goes—and I am not sure this is totally true—that one night at Abner's dance hall there were not enough polkas played, resulting in my father becoming bored. Ma continued dancing, no matter the song, but suddenly heard a strange sound from the orchestra seating. She looked up to find my father had taken a seat at the piano and had decided to become part of the band. He neither knew how to play a piano nor did he care at that point. It's to their credit that the band was very good natured about the sudden appearance of this addition and gracefully brought the tune to a closure, while my mother escorted him from the stage. That whole episode was credited to maybe a few too many "Old Narragansett" beers, if I understood the Sunday morning briefing correctly.

There was also the episode of my father's "disappearance," as we referred to it in later years. Again, mother was so desperate to go dancing, she agreed to have him accompany her if he could "behave himself." At the next morning briefing, we learned that she had heard a polka start and couldn't find him. Thinking it was unusual for him to miss the only dance he would tolerate, she started searching. Nowhere was Dad to be seen inside the hall. Finally, she ventured outside, looked up, and my father was climbing a huge evergreen, being egged on by someone probably just as ill-behaved as he was at the moment. She left him there, went inside, found a polka partner, and claimed for once she rounded a corner with both of her feet still on the floor.

I really liked those Sunday morning briefings.

Dad could be a no nonsense person when it came to his children. Not your Brady Bunch Dad, that's for sure. My father had no patience—that's not a criticism; that's a fact. When he wanted something done, we should be prepared to do it. My two older brothers were the brunt of the Martin wrath when things were not as they should be. Back in those days, most men in that Maine woods area either did not have the time or just did not take the time to show much affection for their kids. Nope, even in my wildest dreams could I imagine him doing what Dads do today—take us to a park, push us in a swing, play catch. Nope. Not my Dad. His idea of "bonding" was not playing toss in the front yard, but slapping an alder in one of his kids' hands and taking him fishing on the shore of Twitchell Pond. Oh, he did once hang a rope and tire from the old apple tree in the corner of our yard. We did a lot of swinging, but Dad never pushed!

His one constant remark was "Come in quiet and don't make a lot of racket." That brings to mind the one occasion I accompanied my oldest brother Roland to Abner's dance hall, when I was probably sixteen years old. After the dance, we rode around as teenagers did back then and ended up sitting and talking with some others. There was no such thing as a clock in our minds.

We drove into the yard and let the car coast to keep as quiet as possible My father was not concerned about my brother as he was, by then, old enough to take care of himself—his daughter was another issue. I tiptoed up to the door, reached out for the knob, and my father was on the other side. He opened the door, looked at me, and, with a grand gesture of his hand straight ahead, remarked, "The sun is coming up over Moose Cove." That was all he said; that was all he had to say. I went up the stairs to my bed in probably three leaps.

Sometimes, in retrospect, I wonder if Dad actually knew he had four kids. It was as though one day my father looked around, noticed his four children and wondered when it all had happened. His worlds where he spent the most time were the outdoors and his books. And yet, he could surprise us. One day we were at Ray Langway's filling station at Locke Mills, and I saw a jacket...oh, it was beautiful maroon and gray, our high school colors. I told him how much I loved it, and he reminded me that it was a man's jacket. I said I didn't care. The matter seemed to be have been dropped.

When he came home the next payday, he had the jacket on his arm.

"This is what you wanted, right?"

I was bowled over, as we were taught not to ask for anything. There was a streak of kindness in the "old man" after all! Sure, the jacket was too big, and the arms bagged a little, but in time I sewed my school letter, a huge "W" I had earned in sports, on the back of it. I loved that jacket and wore it for four years.

A ton of random information about cars that I probably will never use again was given to me by Dad, always when he was the most frustrated with his current automobile. "Whatever you do, Muff, don't buy a Dodge Dart. Those buttons are useless, and wish I had never bought it." (I believe the buttons were gears.) On another occasion: "Don't buy a damn Chevvy. The key broke off in the door and I can't get it out."

As the years went by, he continued to mellow, and a softer, more vulnerable side emerged. One of the few times I saw my father upset about something on the national level was three years before he passed away. I was married and living on the farm in Rowe Hill. I was in the kitchen, and the four kids were all in bed. As soon as I saw his car drive in, I switched on the kettle for his cup of coffee.

He came in, sat in his favorite blue rocker, and balanced the cup of coffee on the nearby windowsill. I pulled out the cherry/ivory plastic covered chair from Sears and sat at the kitchen table. We exchanged a few words on the weather, and how it was getting colder. Suddenly, he sat his coffee cup down, put both hands together, and shook his head. "I don't know what the world is coming to, Muff," he said, softly. "He was the best President I have ever seen in office, and they had to go shoot him. Damn sad."

He loved his grandchildren, especially the little girls, whom he bought purses and hats for to wear at Easter. When my first baby arrived, he sat next to me, took Debra's hands, and said, "Hmm, long fingers. She'll either be a piano player or a thief." That was how his mind worked...and he followed it up with, "You should have named her Francella."

"Why, Dad?"

"Because I saw the name on a gravestone in a cemetery, and it suits her." Never mind that months before, he had suggested I name the baby Debra.

That was my Dad. He had his own language and actually had unique names for people. My younger brother, Curt, was known as Horace Oscar or Oscar Pepper when he was young. I was always "Muffett" and shortened to "Muff" my entire life.

Well, my life until we lost Dad when he was fifty-three-years old in 1966. Sometimes, it seems like yesterday; other times, forever ago. I knew my dad for 28 years, and his sense of humor, impulsiveness, and reputation as a real character never changed.

Thanks, especially, Dad, for your humor—it has helped me more than you will ever know.

Christmas Past

Sometimes it is necessary to rummage through the not-so-good memories to find that special one you've carried through the years. It was a rough patch in my life and my mother, who tolerated me through my teenage years and early marriage, emerged as a total different character in my eyes.

My father had died a few years before, and she lived alone in her little house in Greenwood Center. As life sometimes hands, I was in rather a quagmire of my own. I moved in with my mother that fall of 1973 for the winter. She worked at Ekco in Locke Mills; I was covering stories for three newspapers at the time, so my time was more or less my own and I could plan my day.

We shared the duties. She left for work in the morning and, each week, I tossed the trash in my little VW Bug for the town landfill and the basket of laundry for the laundromat. While the clothes were spinning, I spun the wheels to the dump and back to pick up the clothes. We fell into a routine that I never thought possible. I could cover the stories and still have her supper waiting when she came through the door.

But that's not the memory. Christmas was coming, and neither of us had mentioned that fact much. We kept oil in the barrel to keep us warm and food on the table. Neither of us had money to spare, except for the essentials.

I don't know how the topic of a tree came up in conversation, but Ma thought we should have one. Just a small one, she said, there in the corner where it always used to be when we were kids. I knew there had been no tree in the corner since Dad died, so I figured I'd go along with it. My memory does not allow me to tell you where the tree came from or whether she bought, begged, or stole it. I only know there was a tree on the front porch one night when I came home from working a story.

It was two days before Christmas, so time was tight. Ma had supper on the table and suggested we put the tree up that night. Well, Christmas was not going to mean much for me that year, but why not go along with Ma's plan? After all, she had offered me her house for the winter.

We dragged the tree through the front door, and there it lay on the kitchen floor. The branches were a bit sparse, she acknowledged, but we didn't need anything huge anyway.

"I think we need a cocktail before we begin putting up the tree." The air crackled with silence. Was that my mother suggesting we have a mixed drink? The mother who threatened to disown me if I smelled a bottle of beer in high school?

Before I could answer, the little woman was bent over, reaching under the kitchen sink, and producing a bottle of whiskey. Over to the refrigerator and she whisked out a bottle of ginger ale. Well, this was all coming together rather well, I thought.

"It's cocktail time somewhere, and I'll get the rope for the tree," she declared, heading upstairs and back down in a flash with rope and a small box of old ornaments. And was that a garland of colored ringlets that Curt and I made when we were in grade school? Then out on the porch and back in with a small pail half filled with dirt…she was a whirling dervish.

It was time. We each took a sip of her mixture, and I grabbed the tree. "Hold it up higher so I can get the pail under it and then drop it in the pail."Geesh, she was barking out orders like I had never heard. Up it went. Down in the pail it went. We stood back and admired that it was upright—and took another sip of the mixture. Naturally.

It was then the unbelievable happened. As if in slow motion, the tree started sagging toward us. "Grab it!" Ma shrieked. I grabbed. We took another sip. Back in the pail and Ma got on her knees and pushed some dirt up around the tiny trunk. "That should do it," she gasped, pushing herself back to the kitchen table and another sip.

Refusing to cooperate, the tree began its slo-mo topple again. "The rope!" Ma yelled. It was then I realized that our sipping might have gotten a bit out of hand.

I grabbed the tree. Like old times, Ma slung the rope from one nail in the wall, lassoed the middle of the tree in a circular fashion, and ended with a nail on the opposite wall. "There, you miserable thing, stand there," she snapped. Suddenly, I realized that the Christmas spirit had spiraled into an almost non-existent state. Ma grabbed the ornaments, looked me in the eye, and said, "Let's get these things on before that miserable thing falls over again." We did. The tree stood resplendent in its beauty.

Fast forward to Christmas morning. We sat at the kitchen table, nursing our tea. Ma went in the bedroom and returned with a package. I went in by my bed and also brought out a package. We sat at the table and began unwrapping.

We immediately realized that we both had given the same gift to each other, just in different colors. We had gone separately to Hathaway's store in Locke Mills and bought a turtleneck long sleeve shirt for the other. $1.98—and it is one of my favorite Christmas memories. The year we had so little but so much. The year I discovered a whole new side of Ma.

The Mixing Bowl

It seemed like a good day to make a pie. Just a tinge of cool air that morning and a few red leaves here and there amongst all the green still clinging on for dear life. There's something about the autumn season that makes me want to click on the oven and bake. It's so comforting after the ninety-degree days.

I reached under the cupboard and grabbed the stainless steel mixing bowl. I am way past measuring most of the time, so the flour went in with a swoosh. Out the corner of my eye, I noticed my new set of mixing bowls in three beautiful colors. Why didn't I grab the bigger of the three instead of this old stainless steel bowl?

Because.

Suddenly, I'm back, sitting in Ma's kitchen in Greenwood Center, Maine, enjoying one of the few visits I can make back home because of my work. She sits at the corner of the kitchen table, tea cup at elbow and pencil and pad in front of her.

"Are you writing a novel, Ma?" I tease, as she jots another note to herself.

"I'm trying to decide what to take and what to get rid of," she answers, sighing. "I've accumulated so much trash over the years."

At last it's out in the open...the dreaded conversation of perhaps leaving her home in the Center. For sixty-five years, she has lived in the little house that I once knew so well, but she seems to sense it's time to move on. She's given me a box of pictures and other paper items she thinks I will enjoy—if not, in her words, "toss them."

"Oh, by the way," she says, jumping up from the table, "I wondered if this is anything you can use. God knows I've used it enough, and, if I move, I won't be doing any cooking or baking...well as far as I know." She leans over the little cupboard counter and draws back up, holding a silver-colored mixing bowl. I don't know what to say because, in its simplicity, it's one of her most treasured possessions.

"Are you sure, Ma?" I ask. She retorts that I'm the baker in the family now, and she wants to make sure it's in good hands.

There's a piece of masking tape clinging to the bottom, and on it is a name written neatly so that it would never be lost at a church supper. It's the name of one of her best friends, who did not survive an automobile accident. After the funeral, her friend's daughter told her to take anything of her mother's that she would like as a remembrance.

Her friend's name still stood out on the masking tape through the many washings. I think when Ma used it, she was remembering all the good times they shared.

It was a fall day, a perfect time to make a pie. The flour was all crumbed up with the shortening now; soon I would have that all rolled out for another pie. I held the bowl close and swirled the crumbs for a moment more.

I was holding the memories of the last time I sat in the little kitchen with Ma in Greenwood Center. The masking tape held fast to the bottom of the bowl, faded but not giving up or pulling loose.

Just like my Ma.

The Tower of Strength

She never was very tall. I remember, at 12, looking over my mother's head, but remembering that, in spite of her lack of height, she was the one with the last word—always.

This October day, I try to capture Ma in my memory as I first knew her—and then I realize how little I really knew her. Grandpa Libby built their house in 1905, and my mother was the first child born there in 1915. Her life, as a child, was hard. She accepted that and seldom mentioned it. It was years later I learned that neighbors on Rowe Hill made sure she was warm and well protected from the cold as she walked from her home up the mountain to the little school located above what was to become in later years, the Sumner homestead. Maggie Bryant and Stella Ring (known to me as Grammy) had daughters of their own, Winnie and Norma, and they made sure my mother had mittens, hats, and a coat during the cold winter seasons. She stopped in one house or the other to get warm on those below-zero mornings. In the early fall and late spring, she walked barefoot to school, but they always made sure her feet were well protected come winter.

My grandfather did the best he could, and it was evident all my life that she loved him deeply. She held no malice, even though she had been given the role of housekeeper looking out for her siblings with a sickly mother and doing all correspondence for her illiterate father, who left school at age seven out of necessity to support the family. She ran the household and took care of her brothers and sister as best she could. I only knew of her sister, Addie, and her two brothers, Bill and Pete. It was very late in life that I learned of many siblings who died as infants or at a very young age. My mother kept all of that loss to herself. My Uncle Bill died at an early age in a tuberculosis sanitarium. He wrote beautiful poetry and Ma kept a notebook of his poems. Unfortunately it got lost somewhere in the attic. When she was in her late eighties, I asked, and she couldn't remember the notebook. However, I remember sitting on the edge of my attic bed reading his handwritten poems. I truly believe that's when I first realized how much I loved poetry and then began writing.

263

As I grew older, and we rode together over Rowe Hill and down into Velvet Hollow, she'd tell me tales of how she and her father took the sled in winter and walked to Bryant Pond for bread and molasses. She loved sliding down the hill; the hard part was making sure the molasses stayed on the sled on the way home.

She was determined to graduate high school and did so in 1933 from Woodstock High School. She worked as a maid for summer folk for $1 a week to earn the money for her class ring. That was her prized possession. One time while visiting her in Greenwood, she gave it to me because "she wanted me to have it." It is now one of my cherished treasures.

Ma was a strong woman. She made do with so little, which, as a child, I thought was a normal way to live. No indoor plumbing, electricity, or telephone—Ma never complained about the lack of conveniences if all of us pulled together.

Early memories are of Ma getting ready for work with a "kerchief" tied around her head and wearing a housedress. It was years later that she began wearing slacks to the mill. She was first out of bed in the morning, warming the kitchen for the family, and the last to go to bed at night. Her final chore at night was lining up four paper sacks on the short cupboard counter and making a lunch for her four children to take to school the next morning. The picture I hold in my mind is Ma standing at the kitchen cupboard with four brown bags in a row. To her left is a loaf of bread, to her right, a jar of peanut butter and a jar of jelly. Another rip-p-p-p and the wax paper is binding another sandwich together.

Ma had special friends, but not as many friends as Dad. She "ran" the Popular Club Plan, where her mill friends paid a dollar or two a week, depending on how many "turns" each wanted. When all were paid up, she made out her reward order. She "earned" towels, sheets, and occasionally even a dress for herself. At home, she let Dad do most of the talking while she went about her business.

Ma was probably the one person I knew who could make do with almost nothing. We came home from school one day and Ma motioned us into the little room off the kitchen to "show us something she had done." Because she had no bureau, she had taken two boxes, stacked them, fashioned some drawers with makeshift knobs, and covered it all in

264

wallpaper. It was a work of art and she used that for years. She was as proud as punch to show off her handiwork, and I smile every time I think of it.

There were times when she came down hard on me. Oh, yeah, the woman did not spare the rod. I knew when I skipped my chores, I was "in for it." Many a time, I picked a bunch of "Stinking Benjamins" from the path in the woods and brought them for a peace offering. Silently, she would put them in a jelly jar on the table without a word of reproach. She knew I was suffering inside, wondering what my punishment would be, and that really was punishment enough—knowing I had let her down.

Oh, there were times when I was convinced she was totally unfair. One day I played at my cousins' house way beyond the time to prepare for the parents coming home from work. They came home to absolutely no chores being done. Before I knew it, I was running toward home on the path through the woods with a very upset mother behind, wielding her "switch stick."

As I grew older and in high school, I appreciated my mother more. She gave us the fifty cents we needed to take to high school for the Reader's Digest subscription. She worked all day in the mill but did not hesitate to load me in the car and drive me to the Woodstock High School gym so I could play a basketball game. She said if I wanted to play softball and basketball bad enough to walk from Bryant Pond to Locke Mills and then the four miles down the Greenwood Road to home after dark, then the least she could do was drive me to the games. Being a typical teenager, I did not appreciate how very tired she must have been as she sat on the wooden bleacher and cheered as loud as the next person.

Sunday afternoon, we took in a few summer baseball games between towns played here and there, or, if Doris Day musical was playing at the Bethel Theater, we didn't miss it!

It's strange the memories that are stored. As I have already remembered, she loved Gene Autry and his singing "Back In the Saddle Again." I remember my sputtering once, "Oh, Ma, puhleeze," and she defended her choice. "Hey, he knows how to sing." When she returned from a rare visit to Boston, she handed me a paper bag. Inside was a 78 rpm record of Tony Bennett's "Stranger in Paradise." Yes, I remember squealing and the look of

delight that came over her face.

Ma loved dancing more than anything, even after working long days in the mill all week. At the time dance halls were "the thing!" Saturday night was the night for her to "kick up her heels" and head over to Benny's or the Bluebird Pavilion down on Route 26, Abner's in Albany, or sometimes the Top Hat Pavilion over Hanover way to hear Lord's Orchestra. Fine with my father as long as he did not have to participate. There were times, though, when he gave up his western dime novels, changed his mill "dickies" for his "good dress" pants, and off they went. She taught me how to dance the polka around our kitchen floor. "Remember to move those feet fast in two beats and shift to the other foot," she'd say, and away we'd go.

She probably was the best seamstress I have ever known. We wore coats she fashioned out of old adult coats given her. The treadle machine stood in the corner of the kitchen, and, without a pattern, she eye-balled my brother and me and away the machine would whirr. Later on, she made all her blouses to wear to work...no pattern, just the old eyeball.

Oh, we had our ups and downs as most teenage daughters and mothers. She sometimes had little patience with her only daughter who would rather play baseball then learn to sew. But the day came when I became a mother, and slowly all her sacrifices seeped into my mind. I understood her moments of impatience; her frustration at not providing what she thought her children should have.

Ma became a widow when she was 50. There were a few weak moments shortly after my Dad's death, but I never saw her cry—never in my entire life. She kept working at the mill and still went dancing when the mood hit her. Ma loved performing and did skits with her sister-in-law, Norma, at the mill picnics. She teamed up with Willie Hathaway and was a howling success at many shows in the local town hall. My mother's sense of humor shone for the whole world to see. She loved every minute of it.

After Dad died, Ma also took an active part in her local union and traveled to many union conventions. At that point in life, I was out and about, interviewing and writing for several newspapers. She knew I had nice clothes to wear for interviews. I came home one night to find her in the bedroom, raiding my clothes for her next convention trip. I called her "the

267

thief" for many years after that.

The funny memories creep in, and I smile. I HAVE to smile. I was riding shotgun the day she took the wrong turn, and we ended up going the wrong way on the Jacques Cartier Bridge. I yelled while she put the car in reverse. I fell in love with Canadian truck drivers that day; they actually blinked their lights and slowed as we backed off the bridge. Phew!

And then there was the time we went camping in Rangeley at a lake I want to say was named Cupsuptic...beautiful country. Ma was indignant to think our fireplace was almost non-existent. She waited 'til dark and took one rock from each fireplace in the camping area. The next morning, we had the best looking fireplace in the area. "Don't even ask," she said, as I raised my eyebrows. I called her shameful while she laughed and drank her coffee.

The last adventure in Maine was in 1976 when she, noticing my yearning for the Maine coast, reserved a cabin for two nights. We wove our way through Augusta, right down the middle line until she could decide which way she wanted to turn. The cabin turned out to be fly infested, the breeze from the ocean so hot we sat with beads of sweat on our brows. Not to be defeated, we jumped in the car and found an air conditioned restaurant. It was inevitable, however, that we returned to the cabin, where we spent a sleepless night, whacking at huge house flies. We packed for home at 5 a.m. and didn't bother to ask for a refund.

Later on, after I left Maine, Ma came to visit. We spent weekends visiting garage sales and returning home with treasures. Once we happened upon a nice sale with a handsome vacuum cleaner. I had needed one for some time and, yes, I was assured it worked beautifully. Home we came. I proudly sat it in the middle of the floor, and we both agreed it was handsome indeed! It was self-propelled, the directions proclaimed, which would make it easier on my back.

Ma said we should give it a whirl. She plugged it in, and that cleaner came alive. It actually started chasing me. Ma started yelling to stop it, and I yelled back I didn't know how. I jumped on the sofa, the vacuum hit the sofa, did a swirl, and headed in Ma's direction. She ran and got behind a kitchen chair. The cleaner went right up to the chair and spun its wheels. In that one lucid moment, we both remembered how to stop it. She reached

over and pulled the plug. We looked at each other and collapsed on the sofa laughing. For years after, she would ask if I had bought any more good vacuum cleaners. In the last conversation I had with Ma, I reminded her of that great adventure, and, in spite of her illness, she laughed and laughed.

Sometimes when she visited I knew, in her heart, she still saw me as her little girl. As we shopped, she'd reach into her purse, draw out a bill and tuck it in my pocket. The first few times I protested violently until one day she said, "It's the only thing I can do for you now." I realized that even though I didn't need the money, how much it meant for her to give it to me.

It was during her last two or three years that I noticed, out of the blue, she suddenly would look at me and say, "I told God I wanted a little girl with blonde hair and blue eyes, and my prayers were answered." She realized that I had mastered the bumps in my road, and she knew I understood, at last, some of the decisions she had to make and the hardships she endured. Gone was the impatience at having a tomboy for a daughter.

Last spring, I went out to water my one tomato plant on the deck. It was early in the day. "Water them in the morning," Ma always said. "You burn their feet if you wait 'til noon." OK, Ma, that one stuck with me, and I even passed it on to a friend the other day.

So, Ma, here's to your donuts draining on the kitchen table, the Thanksgiving hen we singed in the woodstove, the red Jello cooling in the snowbank, your pumpkin pies, and fluffy biscuits. Here's to the edge of the porch you backed into with the car, the snake you killed with the shovel in the shed, and here's to your four feet, ten inches of just plain guts and courage. You taught us manners, respect, and the dignity in hard work. You always said no matter what one does for a living, if it's honest work then be proud. Thank you for taking me in when I needed you; thank you for rejoicing when I finally found happiness.

You left us eight years ago today, October 16, 2007. Here's a Mayflower to tuck in your hair. Thanks for the memories. I love you.

270

Spending the Morning with Gram

It was a long time ago…over sixty years ago, in fact, when I married (the first time). It feels as though it was in another lifetime, but occasionally there is something…a memento that takes me back in time to the little villages in Maine and the lovely people. One of my most cherished gifts was a recipe box filled with wonderful recipes for everything imaginable. They were all hand written and signed by the ladies of Locke Mills.

Over the years and sometimes bumpy road that's been my life, the recipe box has moved with me. Now and then, I'd pull out a recipe, see the name, and sigh because that lady was no longer with us. Her contribution, however, lives on.

And so it was this morning when the urge and, yes, need arose for me to bake. I have so many cookbooks that I am ashamed to admit I could have a library of those alone. There are stacks of printed recipes from the internet. Yet, I dragged out the little box and started going through them. That's when I spotted my Gram's handwriting. A blueberry cake! Hmm. Very neatly on the back was written in beautiful script "Nellie Martin."

And suddenly, I was back there, then. Gram reaching as far as she could to get the last berry from the high wild blueberry bushes. On her kitchen counter, a big bowl of blueberries my Uncle Louie had brought home from his week of logging on Overset Mountain. She would gather all the ingredients on her kitchen table and begin. Four cups of flour she would sift with cream of tartar and baking soda.

This morning, I looked at the "four cups of flour" and thought *boy, that's a lot of flour*. It was then I noticed on the back at the bottom of the recipe a warning: "This makes a very big cake." Gram was still instructing me, after all these years.

Gram would then go to the shed and bring in an armful of wood to stoke up the fire, her little blue sneakers just a humming over the kitchen floor. When the stove would begin to heat, she'd push her tiny black rimmed glasses up on her nose and say, "Now stay there."

So today I labored on, recipe propped high. The four cups of flour, the cup of "sweet" milk, the cup of sugar (sugar must have been very dear as that did not seem like a lot of sugar in proportion to the other ingredients). Take the pint of blueberries and roll them around in the flour and dry goods. Well, Gram, all I had was a bag of frozen blueberries, so forgive me. If the cake looks horrid, no one will know but you and I, and the squirrels will love it. Maybe.

Everything mixed together and was looking good. A lot of dough, and as my Kitchen Aide whirled it around, I wondered aloud how Grammie ever mixed that by hand. I found the biggest cake pan in the house, pushed the dough in, and leveled it off.

Whoa! Wait! There is no oven temperature or time in the recipe. Hmm. What to do?

I remembered the gauge on Gram's wood stove. When the needle pointed straight up, she always plopped her cookies or cakes in. That needle might have meant about 350 degrees. As for the time, that would be any one's guess…at least I had a window to peek in my oven.

I peeked and then peeked some more. Thirty-five minutes later, out came the cake…slightly brown. I drove a toothpick down the middle of this massive project. Came out slick as a whistle.

That cake is a masterpiece, Gram. It's on the kitchen counter, and, yes, I sneaked a corner piece before it cooled. It was some good. Not as good as yours, however, because you were smiling and filling it with lots of love before you chucked it in the oven.

It was great spending the morning with you, Gram.

LOOKING BEHIND

Farewell

The Return

The memories remain. Rowe Hill, now paved, rides like an interstate in comparison to the dodging of mud ruts that threatened to wipe the bottom of the car into oblivion those years I drove that mountain road. How we loved it as children because it meant "mud season" vacation from school; how we hated it as adults trying to maneuver between the ruts and praying we met no one until we approached the one "turn-out"!

How narrow the Greenwood Road has become since I moved. I wonder if I dare drive it, when for years, I geared down my little VW Bug and ripped around the corners without a thought in the world. I am sure someone has come in the night and made the road smaller!

Oh, we stop in front of the little house where I grew up, and it looks lonesome. The porch sags and I am sure if I went closer, I could hear my father cursing the bats in the attic or my mother putting the coffee on to perk in the wee hours of the morning. I decline the invitation to go closer than the main road. Memories sometimes go astray when one ventures too close...but, then again, I wonder if Ma's delphiniums have come through the ground and are ready to bud.

Grampa and Gram Martin's farm still stands upon the hill, but lacks the splendor I knew as a child when running across the pasture path to get another of my Gram's raisin-filled cookies she kept in the clear gallon jar on her kitchen cupboard. I don't know who lives there now, but the path has worn into oblivion after all these years. Behind the farm stands the rock, split in two, which held our maple syrup production, year after year. Roland, Rex, and I gathered the sap with the help of our husky, Keno, and Roland built the fire. We made a pitiful, but tasteful bit of maple syrup.

Down the road is the home of my brother, Tink, and his wife, Martha. How many years I walked that field when it was a potato patch and gathered bugs off the plants for my Grampa Martin. Many times he dug in his pocket from his perch on the porch railing to give me a nickel or a dime for my efforts. Tink left us in 2010, but the home on the knoll is a testimonial to how much he loved the spot, and Martha has kept it the same since.

There's the home of Charlie and Grace Day, who many times took in this dirty little urchin, scrubbed her hands and arms, and sat her at their lunch table to share their noon meal. I can almost smell the Welsh Rarebit and how I loved it…and them.

My Uncle Dwight and Tessie are gone now, but their beautiful home graces the country side.

One thing remains the same; Twitchell Pond is at its most beautiful this fine spring day. Rowe's Ledge stands out in the sun, and I remember Dad and I climbing to Pie Rock, and how small it was as I stood there looking down at the pond and houses.

You can go back to memories, and perhaps that's good. Those memories are in little boxes on the shelves of my mind, and I like to open a box now and again to see what I can find. My Uncle Roy fighting off moose in his strawberry patch; the sound of Fred Davis and his banjo from my Grandparents porch on a Sunday afternoon; turning the grindstone for my Uncle Louis and watching as he stacked firewood with such pride.

You can't actually go back in time. But in my mind are my four little ones, with perhaps a friend or two, coming up the road after school, perhaps stopping to pick a lilac or even a dandelion.

It is good that I can go back in my mind whenever I want to open the door.

You Will Find It

Strength is a hard word to define. Picture me as a young girl, with boundless energy. I was a dreamer. I know that now, but knew no word to describe it at that age. I loved everything in nature from the fish circling over her bed, tail fanning in sunlight, to feeling the bark on a tree. How smooth the white birch, compared to the darker, rough trees. One must never peel the white birch bark from the tree. How lucky we felt to find a piece on the ground on which to write or sketch!

But this Sunday morning, I'm going to write about strength. What is it to a young girl? I thought and walked miles back in the caverns of my mind, barely coming out with anything that matched that word. Strength was not screaming when my mother forced boiled poplar bark down my throat to ward off "worms."

Fast forward—married at seventeen; new mother at nineteen. Was it strength that had me walking in snow to my hips from Johnny's Crossing to the farm at the top of Rowe Hill? I worked at Penley's in West Paris during the day and, should there be a storm, as Dad said, "You gotta use *Shank's Mare* to get home." I can't tell you how many wading sessions I had, but didn't consider it strength; it was necessity. I didn't relish spending the night in a snowbank.

Eighteen years later; another upheaval in my life. The little girl from Greenwood Center had long gone, and a much more mature women had taken her place. Oh, there were times when that little girl wanted to go into a corner and wrap herself into a blanket and not come out for a few days, but it was okay. A divorce was necessary; that in her mind was not strength, but survival. (Let me add a sentence of advice, which I try never to do and don't think I have. From pure experience, never judge a situation unless you have every fact you can possibly have and then, even, it is better to let someone higher than you do the judging.)

We'll take a big leap now. The little girl from Greenwood has been married again, this time for forty-one years. She's worked and loved every job she has had. Her four children are scattered like leaves on a windy October day. Her husband, not feeling well for some time, sees a doctor and, after months, the news is not good. There will be no recovery. Her youngest son will share the duties of caregiver, and they will make him as comfortable as possible. Her mind argues with itself every night; how can she do this? She cannot watch him waste away; this man with whom she has shared so much. Is there a choice? The doctors say no.

Every day, climb out of bed, take a deep breath and reach as far back into your body and soul as you can…she kept telling herself, knowing her son was doing the same. They shared the twenty-four hour duty, day in and day out.

It was becoming harder. She kept reaching and sometimes would walk into an empty room, shed a few tears, turn around, and get back to business. That is what her mother and father would do, she kept telling herself.

And then one day late August it happened. Her youngest son finished a nine mile run, smiled, waved, and fell flat on his back with a massive heart attack. The husband, unable to do anything but watch, was distraught. The young girl screamed his name and, with no response, called his friend next door and then 911. What a beautiful sound…those sirens were like angels' harps on the winds. The girl's son died three times and was brought back three times as he was rushed to the hospital.

The girl sat down in a chair next to her husband. She had no one. Her daughter (who came within two days) was in another state, and her other two sons had lives of their own. This was so far away from the hot roads of summer in Greenwood Center with her Gram, her aunts, and her family. For the first time in her life, she had no one…absolutely no one. It's a feeling so empty and raw you feel as though you are floating and having no idea where you are going. She spent the next twenty-four hours getting word from the hospital and taking care of her husband's needs. Neighbors came in with food and anything else she might need; she thanked them and hoped it was adequate. Two men volunteered to sit with her husband so she can get a few hours sleep. She's not alone; yet the feeling is there.

I can look back now. My husband is gone. He left us on October 25th. My son is recovering nicely. I have no idea where I got the strength to keep going all those many months. I like to believe we all have a reserve of strength and, when it is needed, we have our own special Angel to turn the tap, and God regulates the flow. I don't know. It was there when I needed it.

Now there is another hurdle, but I am ready. As I lay having an echocardiogram last week, my mind went to Rowe's Ledge, the hawks screeching, the blue waves with white diamonds bouncing from them. I felt the tar under my August feet as we raced up and down the road. So my heart has a few problems...hmm...it's operating at about half what it should, but I have an excellent cardiologist who is working wonders. I know there is more strength in that reservoir.

There will always come the time when each of us is tested...early in life; late in life. Remember, you, too, have a reservoir. Time for my angel to turn the tap! Let's go!

Epilogue

Home, Once More

Another day working for Miss Hobbs, and I'm on my way home. One thing about walking home every night, it sure gives me time to think. Sometimes I get thinking so hard, I find I've walked to the top of the mountain and am going down the other side. When I realize that, it makes me pretty darn happy, as my feet and legs are tired.

Today, Miss Hobbs thought we should have a cleaning day in the two bedrooms upstairs. I dusted her bedroom first, and I really enjoy that as I can look out the window facing Indian Pond, and it's so pretty. I wish I were down at the foot of the pond with my brother, Curt, looking at our flatfish and fishing off a rock. Anyway, Miss Hobbs has an old, old bureau, and I make sure everything is shining when I am through. She has a lovely set…I think it's plastic…but it's baby blue and has designs on the round one and the square one. I think she keeps her pins in there and maybe some jewelry. I don't look in them! I make sure they are clean and dusted well. I always enjoy cleaning them, as they are very delicate and my favorite color.

Miss Hobbs stayed with me today during the cleaning and dusted the other bedroom. Then we had to do her "trunk." It sits at the head of the stairs in the hallway…and so big I swear it used to hold pirate's booty. She uses the key and opens the trunk, and that's when the mothball smell hits my nostrils. I can't stand the smell of mothballs and am allergic to them, but I also want to work and get my ten dollars on Friday! The trunk is full of blankets, and we take each one out, give it a good shake, fold it again, and put it back into the trunk. I haven't figured out just what that does for the blankets unless they need fresh air. Miss Hobbs says some day we will hang them on the clothesline. I hope we have someone mighty strong to help us!!

With all this daydreaming and thinking, I've now reached Dan Cole's farm and a mile to home. Greenwood Center has changed. There are more camps on the pond now…really pretty cottages and many of them are owned by people from Berlin and Gorham, New Hampshire. I remember when I rode in the boat with Dad fishing, he pointed out Johnny Howe's camp, Cushman's, Eichel's and a few others. Now it seems there are so many on the backside of the pond. I walk by Stan and Flossie Seames's house—how I wish I lived where they do, up on the little knoll. They are nice people. Someone has bought the house where Uncle Elmer lived, and Tina Morgan has moved now. It makes my head spin to see the changes.

My cousins moved away a few years ago and I miss them. The path in the woods isn't used much, only when I want to walk up it to find flowers or to sit on the ledge and think. Sometimes I take a tablet and pencil and write while I'm sitting on the ledge. This summer I haven't had time!! Maynard and Mary Hazelton have moved into their house. They have five children, and Curt has someone his own age to play with. He and Butch are good friends. Sometimes I babysit for them in the evening, if there is an emergency.

Henry and Janet Bowers have built a beautiful log home almost at the foot of Twitchell Pond where once there was only woods. I always hate to see trees cut down, but their home is really nice.

I am on the "flat" now, and, when I go by Howe Brook, I'm going to look in and see if any brown trout are coming up from the pond. Usually there are none, but I like to look and then can tell Dad.

Home at last! Dad is sitting on the front steps, hat cocked on the side of his head as always. I swear if he didn't wear a hat, his head would fall off! His dickies still have sawdust from the mill, and he has a jar of what looks like sand in his hands. He holds it up and asks, "Have you ever seen anything like this, Muff?"

Well, to me, it looks like sand, but I simply say no.

"Well, this is some dirt I gathered off a grave up near Upton." He's labeling them as he collects. I don't think Dad collects anything else in this world except important (to him) grave dirt. Maybe it makes his head rest after working in the mill.

He moves to one side, and I go in to find Ma having a cup of tea at the kitchen table. I bet she would like to hear about the pretty blue containers I dusted today. I grab a piece of bread, plop a hotdog in it, grab a glass of water, and sit down to tell her all about it.

Feels good to be home.